A PATH TO WISDOM

How to live a **balanced**, **healthy**
and **peaceful** life

This book is dedicated to:

My loving parents Lutvije and Shaqir, my grandparents Akik and Sinan, Linda and her family, my sisters Feleknaz, Hanumsha, Selime, Drita, my brother Selim, their families, children and grandchildren for their unconditional love. To you wise souls who love to expand and choose a path to wisdom that integrates your spiritual and material wealth through love, acceptance and gratitude. Lastly, to my own spirit, who volunteered for this assignment and continues to guide me to its ongoing unfolding and fruition.

A PATH TO WISDOM

How to live a **balanced**, **healthy** and **peaceful** life

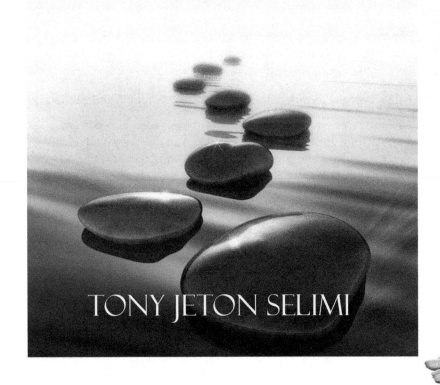

TONY JETON SELIMI

A Path to Wisdom
How to live a balanced, healthy and peaceful life

First published in 2014 by

Panoma Press Ltd
48 St Vincent Drive, St Albans, Herts, AL1 5SJ, UK
info@panomapress.com
www.panomapress.com

Book layout by Michael Inns
Artwork by Karen Gladwell
Photography:
Stephen Morallee
Ed Miles
Daniel Deveny, Pierre Lemond

Printed on acid-free paper from managed forests.

ISBN 978-1-909623-57-6

The right of Tony Jeton Selimi to be identified as the author of this work has been asserted in accordance with sections 77 and 78 of the Copyright Designs and Patents Act 1988.

A CIP catalogue record for this book is available from the British Library.

This book is available online and in bookstores.

Contents

Acknowledgements

It would have been impossible to write this book without the 43 years of contribution by thousands of people who have been part of my life since the day I was born.

A special thanks to my mum and my dad, without your support, care, nurture, protection and unconditional love I would not be here today and be the man I am. I love you with every beat of my heart. I would like to thank my sisters and their husbands, my brother and his wife, and all of their children for their support, love, and for all the joy that their presence brought into my life. I also would like to thank my grandparents, my mum's and dad's family, uncles, cousins, and all of the people that live in the neighborhood that I grew up in.

To the many people who have been part of my journey, all the teachers, healers, coaches, professors, work colleagues, friends, spiritual teachers, spirit guides, and the many clients I have worked with for all their support, knowledge, and for letting me be part of their life.

I have been blessed to love and be loved by extraordinary people, your unconditional love has been the light that helped me in my journey to acceptance of self and freed me from my own inner prison.

A special thank you to Stuart Hall, Marcello Gregorovic, Daniel Meekins, Christine Pavlov, Nathanael Degryse, Lova Rajao, Daniel Browne, Sabine Popp, Will Pike, Nick Frank, Stephen Jones, Paul Kurton, Stephen Morallee, Tina Fotherby, Alan Burrows, Mouna Salih, Paul Miller, Nora Rodriguez, Ben Morley, Jenny Dainton, Mary Naish, Philip Carvil, Ian Dodds, Daniel Reimer, Martha Friedlander, Denko Godec, Sepi Honarmand, Dan Lyons, Richard Bennet, Susana Da Conceicao, Steven Chaby, Sophie Clark Thorp, Balz Bless, Sento Marco, Hera Hassan, Jotham Annan and the many of my friends that I hold dear to my heart for your unconditional love, for being the mirror from which I can reflect, learn and grow.

Thank you to all the amazing authors whose books I have read, scientists, and you the reader for all the gifts you bring into this world. To my reviewers Dick Van Der Meer, Michael Bell, Anna Orchard, John Breedon, Viv Grant and Avni Trivedi.

To my client and personal friend Farhan Rehman for patiently sitting for hours to read, process and clean up the grammar. For being a light that has kept my path shining bright, for being caring and for being thoughtful. I love you and thank you.

Big thank you to Nick Bolton and Paul Kensett from the Animas Institute of Coaching for their support, teachings and creating a superb coaching community to share experiences and wisdom.

To Daniel and Andrew Priestley, the KPI team, and everyone in the KPI community for their wisdom, support, and helping me develop some great partnerships.

Finally, to my publisher Mindy Gibbins-Klein and all of her team for their continued expertise and support in taking my manuscript and turning it into a book that is distributed in many languages and countries throughout the world.

I love you and thank you for your guidance, keeping me focused, and sharing your wisdom that helped me create the mind maps needed to bring this book to fruition. Without your talents, love and support this book would not have made it to the form it is today.

Foreword

Having known Tony personally, and worked with him as a client of his, I knew that his book would be something special.

I just didn't appreciate or realize just how powerfully Tony would capture the body's internal workings, and introduce it in such a succinct and sophisticated manner as to leave the reader fully empowered to take the reins of their life, and start taking back control of the direction their life is taking them.

Tony's many years of deep personal study, his depth of spiritual perception, as well as his background as a technologist have meant he's been able to weave the science, spirituality and psychology of what makes us human into a manual that helps us unpackage and make sense of our inner ALARMs.

The subtle nuances and inner workings of our bodies, our minds, and our spirits have been laid out in careful detail, to leave no question unanswered, and to empower each of us to take full control and responsibility for the results we've created in our lives.

If like me, you have spent a lifetime of deep spiritual study, studied NLP, behavioral psychology, and have a deep yearning to understand yourself

better, than you will find reading Tony's book a most enriching and rewarding experience.

If you're completely new to it all, don't worry, Tony's gentle approach and subtle style weaves the most complex topics, and the most cutting edge science into really easy to understand bite-sized chunks that anyone will be able to understand easily, be they a personal development novice, or a seasoned veteran of introspection and self-reflection.

Give yourself the best gift you could possibly wish for, and read this book cover to cover, to unlock your inner wisdom, and access the latent knowledge that already exists in your inner ALARM.

Having read and studied for many years the domains of personal development, spiritual development, as well as through personal journeys, I've never come across a book that so powerfully synthesizes the wisdom contained within our body, mind and spirit.

Read this book with a childlike curiosity and your life will be deeply enriched, as mine has already been. Be prepared to go deep within, and get to the root causes, and tackle the true source of your challenges, and you will feel uplifted, inspired, and empowered when you finish, with a set of practical tools and solutions to help you get started on uncovering the Path to your Wisdom within.

To creating order out of the chaos in your inner world.

Farhan Rehman
Entrepreneur and Social Media Expert

Introduction

It is a privilege to be in a role to service humanity, to teach you how to start the revolution inside of you. To help you uncover the intelligence that is within you that you can use to create and live a purposeful life that is pro-evolutionary.

The book you are holding in your hands and the TJS Evolutionary Method you are about to learn was born out of the path I walked since I was born. Each path I took created its own lessons, each situation presented to me on this path had its own challenges, and each person I met on this path was my teacher that taught me something different about me. Thank you and I love you.

During all of this time I invested a lot of time, energy and money into my spiritual, personal and professional development. In the process I healed many physical and emotional symptoms, I learned how to do this with others, and in 2009 having faced redundancy I started my entrepreneurial journey.

I set up my own integrated healing-coaching company with a mission:

"I Tony Jeton Selimi declare before myself, others and God that my primary mission in life is to be a master healer, life coach, and teacher through continuously learning and absorbing the knowledge from western psychology and the eastern methodologies of natural healing of the body so that I can serve people in the most efficient and effective way in the shortest period of time. I have in return the opportunity to receive incredible financial and social compensation. In my pursuit of the universal laws of healing and teaching others I am enabled to travel the world, explore ancient healing places, and create healing centers, products and services that are cosmo ethical and pro-evolutionary. I am also learning and meeting the most extraordinary professional healers, coaches and well-being professionals known to mankind."

With this mission in mind I went ahead and integrated and synthesized the essence of all that I have learned so far into the TJS Evolutionary Method you are about to read and may choose to learn.

No matter who you are – a young adult, a professional coach, therapist, lawyer, banker, CEO, millionaire, billionaire, or simply curious and young at heart and are seeking greater significance and purpose in your life – you have come to the right place to learn, grow, and empower yourself to be the creator of your life.

Let's face it, life has its ups and downs; what I am about to share with you are the five major breakdowns in my life that created the biggest breakthroughs.

1. Health

In 1980 at the age of 10 I was hospitalized due to severe pneumonia, irregular heartbeat, and a whole range of other illnesses. I spent two years in hospital, for six months of which I was unconscious, heavily medicated, and gained a lot of weight.

One day, my mother was told that I would not make it. It was time for her to take me home, and prepare for the worst. She was informed that the doctors tried all they could and there was no way I would make it. The truth is, the moment she was given the piece of paper that said I only had a few weeks to live, she ripped it up and told them there was no way her son would die. She called my dad and told him to come home immediately as my situation had worsened. The next day when my dad arrived they took me to the state hospital in the capital city Skopje.

They sought the best doctors that could help bring me back to life. They also turned to various healers for help as they already had great results in helping my brother overcome and fully cure his epilepsy, a condition the doctors could not cure. My mum believed I would make it despite what she was told. She slept on a chair by my hospital bed for months, and often fell asleep praying.

She also went to seek help from a lot of healers and priests, and prayed at sacred tombs. Deep in her heart she knew I would be well again. She continued to pray every day.

Two years down the line I got better, my life started to get back to normal, and I was able to get back to school. For years I had to take special medication as my heart, lungs and immune system were too weak. Having spent so much time being with ill people, observing the many hospitals I was being taken to, as well as the many other gifted people who helped me heal, I became curious. What is it that makes us ill? Why is it that some people get ill and others don't?

Why is it that a doctor told my mother I would die, and a simple old man who never went to school knew how to harness the power of nature and energy to heal me?

It simply did not make sense. I started to ask a lot of questions and developed a hunger for a lot of knowledge and answers.

At the point of this realization, a quantum awakening happened and everything I started to experience made complete sense with an utter clarity that changed me forever. This experience lead to my first breakthrough in life: to learn and know without a question of a doubt that everything is possible in life when you pray to God and believe in the infinite wisdom of love. So I would like to take this moment and thank my mum for always believing in me. I love you!

2. Civil War

The next big event that happened to me was back in 1989. You may remember that this was the beginning of the civil war in the former Yugoslav Republic. Having been robbed of my freedom and conscripted by the state to serve in the army, I soon realized that the people's army that I grew up to believe in was not what I started to experience as the civil war broke out.

I was forced to do things that were not aligned to the values I grew up with. I spent 14 months in survival mode, constantly being threatened, and not knowing if I would live to see another day. During my 14 months of service I developed a very close relationship with a senior officer and his wife.

He was the captain I reported to, had no kids, and I used to spend a lot of time with him and his wife. Over time I became the son they never had. As the civil war continued to spread in Croatia, he knew it was only a matter of time before it spread into Bosnia and the rest of the country.

He called me into his office one morning and told me: "Tony, you completed your duty a long time ago. The army I once believed in is disintegrating. It is not a safe place for any of you now, and it's time for you and your unit to go home to your families." He issued a discharge order on the same day that the war started to spread from Croatia into Bosnia. Many of our comrades had already lost their lives in the conflict in Vucovar and other parts of Croatia.

He helped us cross the border into Macedonia and advised us to get out of there as it would be the next place where the war would spread. Just as he predicted, the conflict reached there as well.

The war continued to spread, Macedonia became unsafe too, so once again my mum intervened and saved my life. She borrowed some money and the next morning my cousin and my mum drove me to the airport, got me a ticket and I was told I was going to London until things calmed down and that I would be safe there.

We cried. In each other's eyes we could see the fear. We questioned if we would ever see each other again. She hugged me, kissed me and blessed me as I was passing passport control. She waved and told me not to look back. Her last words I could hear in the distance were: "You are a survivor, do not worry, you will be in a safe place once you get there, I love you."

It was the most heartbreaking experience to once again be separated from my family, not knowing if I would ever see them again. I kissed the land as I boarded the airplane and did not stop crying until the moment when the captain announced that we would be landing in London shortly and that we should fasten our seat belts.

Four hours passed very quickly. Throughout the flight all I could think of was the many friends, family members and all the people I was leaving behind. I felt helpless, emotionally broken and I could not stop thinking: Will I ever see my family again?

I landed at Heathrow airport. Deep inside I was fearful. I had no place to go, no friends, not much money, and I could hardly speak any English. When the immigration officer checked my passport he asked me what I was going to do in the UK. Instantly I became brave and told him I was going to study engineering and that I wanted to make a difference by helping people around the world.

He smiled, told me that I had a great ambition and a big job ahead of me. He put a stamp on my passport and with his nice English accent welcomed me to the UK.

I lived on the streets for a while, with no money, home, job, family or friends I could turn to for help. I knew nothing about any social support or benefit system. Once again, I felt I was left at the mercy of God and my mum's belief that I am a survivor and that I would be okay.

At the age of 20 I lost my sense of belonging and identity. The country I once knew was being destroyed by the hour, and the passport I had became invalid as Yugoslavia ceased to exist as a country. Back at home the situation worsened, the war spread, and there was no end in sight.

I made the trip to the Home Office in Croydon and applied for refugee status. I had no home to go to, no identity, no contact with my family, and did not know if I would ever see them again. I felt emotionally destroyed and spent many nights crying as I hit rock bottom.

I could not see a way out from what then seemed an impossible mission. I prayed each day. Deep down I believed I would be okay, and I knew the worst had passed and from now on things would just get better.

And so they did. Eventually my path led me to meet my first friend Enisa. She offered me a place to stay in her Earls Court flat for a few days until I found myself a job and accommodation. She wrote down the addresses of a few employment agencies where I could go and register to seek work. Within two days I found myself a job in an Italian restaurant, and a small bedsit to live in.

I remember that day so clearly. I felt so happy, grateful, joyful and full of hope. Once again I knew my mum's prayers and belief that things would turn out okay helped me meet the right person, get a job and put a roof over my head. So, a big thank you to my friend Enisa who was one of the first people to help me get my life back on track. I love you.

The breakthrough: I freed myself of attachments, material possessions, and learned how to survive with nothing while remaining congruent with the values that my parents taught me. I gained trust, confidence, and an understanding of myself as to how I could function in the most effective way.

3. Career

From what you have read so far, you can imagine how thrilled I was. I had a safe roof over my head, a job, and I was alive. I worked an average of 18 hours a day working three to four jobs to pay for my education, support my family back in the war zone, and get my life back on track.

I knew if I wanted to accomplish what I had said to the immigration officer when I entered the country, I needed to save enough money to pay for all the education I needed to reach my goals. Firstly, I enrolled myself on an evening course to learn English for Business.

Three years went by fast. I met some amazing people, made new friends, and my awareness of what is possible by living in a city such as London expanded exponentially.

Once I completed this course, my next step was to look for ways to further my education. I wanted to continue studying engineering which I had started in Zagreb and which was interrupted due to the civil war. I enrolled on a two-year course at City of Westminster Adult Education Centre in Paddington and completed my Higher National Certificate in Electrical and Electronic Engineering with Mathematics with the highest grades possible (straight As).

The next two years passed even faster. I got an award from the Mayor of Westminster for achieving distinctions in all my subjects and for being an exemplary student at the Westminster City College.

My tutors saw my talents, recognized my abilities and encouraged me to apply to the top four universities: Imperial College London, University College of London (UCL), Cambridge and Oxford.

Months later I received a letter telling me I was accepted by three of them. I chose UCL and enrolled for BEng. in Electrical and Electronic Engineering with Management Studies and Organizational Behavior. Three years down the line in 1998 five blessings came to me:

1. *I received a £500 scholarship from the Engineering Council which helped toward paying my tuition fees as an international student.*

2. *I achieved my childhood dream and got myself a degree. I graduated with honors from one of the top four universities in the UK.*

3. *The situation back home improved. After eight years I reconnected with my parents. I had saved enough money and was able to fly them to London to be with me at my graduation ceremony.*

4. *I got my first IT graduate job at Traffic Directors for London which became part of TfL (Transport for London).*

5. *The final blessing was receiving my British citizenship. Once again I had an identity, a place to call home, and was able to travel.*

Thank you to everyone who helped me in this journey, some of you I know are reading this book.

INTRODUCTION

Once again I was counting my blessings and felt the luckiest man on earth. I continued to work three jobs, and in 2000, exactly 10 years since arriving in the UK, I had saved enough money for a deposit on a mortgage to buy my studio flat in Pimlico from where this book is written.

For the first time since I left my family, I felt the warmth, the joy, and the happiness of having my own home. I had a roof over my head. I was safe. I had income, friends, an identity to relate to and London became my new home.

I then spent the next 11 years building my IT career working with a range of individuals and businesses, from entrepreneurial start-ups and family-owned companies to big corporations in the city of London, Europe and USA. I became successful, determined, and continued with my professional and personal development.

During this time, many breakthroughs happened; the one that changed the course of my life forever happened in 2009.

Having been made redundant from a secure job that I held for more than nine years, I was forced to reflect and re-evaluate my entire life again. As I sent out thousands of applications, and didn't receive any interviews, once again the foundations of my life were shattered.

Eventually I realized I did not belong in the corporate world. There was more I was meant to do with my life, and deep down this voice became stronger and stronger as time went on.

It was like an inbuilt ALARM that kept repeatedly ringing inside awakening me to my life's true calling, telling me I needed to do something different. At the time I did not have the clarity or certainty of what that should be, I just knew I had to make a change and take a different course of action.

Something I knew for sure: I wanted to be an entrepreneur. One who makes a difference by serving a conscious community.

I also knew from everyone around me that I was great with people. I inspired them and helped them feel good about themselves by just talking with them. I also knew many healing techniques and gathered a lot of knowledge throughout this time. I was already used to coaching, healing, and inspiring people from all walks of life to find acceptance and true love in themselves.

The breakthrough: I let go of the fear that kept me stuck in the rat race and stopped living a life dictated by pay check. I took action. I learned to listen to the true voice that knows. The voice that when silent triggers the ALARM to guide you to do what you love and awaken you to your greatness. During this process I got the clarity that I needed to align my life with my true purpose.

4. Identity Crisis

There were many identity crises I faced. The one that caused me the most distress was my sexual identity. Fear, guilt and shame was the coat that I wore for many years. I got married hoping I could fight the feeling, change my identity, and fulfill my own and my family's expectation of self.

I was torn apart between two identities that existed in me. I knew I had to do something about it. I had to overcome the fears, the threats, and the homophobic abuse that first and foremost came from the deepest part of me. It also came from the culture I was born into, the environment I was living in, and to top it all off, my family – the very same people I was loved by and whom I loved the most.

It took me years of inner work to gain the confidence that I now have. Coming to terms with my sexuality and creating the acceptance of myself and others. All of the emotional turmoil, conflict of beliefs and values stifled my own sense of belonging, and I knew it had a major impact on my well-being and my spiritual life. It affected and destabilized all areas of my life, from my career, to my relationships with my family, friends and partners.

Despite the many threats, fears and judgments, I knew I was not living my values. I was not congruent, and was not being true to myself. This had to stop. If it meant I would never see the people who told me they loved me the most and yet could not accept me for who I am, I said so be it.

The breakthrough: I honored my truth, my own feelings and what felt right. I took the decision to come out to my family, to accept myself for the magnificent person I am, and I walked away from a traditional heterosexual marriage in which two great people suffered in silence. I learned to be authentic, to listen to my inner voice that came from the depth of my heart, and to love and accept myself and others unconditionally.

5. Healing

I met Lova during the university days when I started working at Harvey Nichols as a sales assistant for Mulberry. Instantly we became friends, I knew I could trust her; she was a guardian angel in disguise who had come to help me in my journey to accept and overcome my fears of being myself.

She introduced me back into the world of healers and helped me embrace my destiny of being a great healer. She would always give me spiritual books to read that shaped, changed, and helped me reconnect with being a healer.

I read all the volumes of The Celestine Prophecy, Conversations with God, The Sedona Method, and learned about the principles that The Secret and the Law of Attraction talked about.

I was fascinated and curious to learn more on how and why the human mind works the way it does. The more I was learning, the more I started to reconnect to the childhood conversations I had with God about how nice it would be to have an instruction manual that I could use to help mankind heal.

Self-help subjects, books and courses were my hobby outside of my professional career in IT. I studied Neuro Linguistic Programing, Cognitive Behavior Therapy, and Life Coaching to help me understand myself and how to be the best manager I could be.

My appetite for wisdom grew stronger. I felt empowered and I created the belief that I could naturally heal all of the residues of my childhood illnesses. I turned east for answers. What helped me to understand in a scientific way the eastern methodologies of natural healing of the body was Barbara Brennan's work and book *Hands of Light*.

Being a scientist myself, her scientific explanation resonated with everything I had learned so far. It opened me up to a whole new way of thinking. The voices and the visions that I saw when I was in a coma started to make sense. I knew the time had come to heal every single illness since childhood and then as I accomplished that, to teach others to do the same.

Everything I was learning started to remind me of what I learned in my early childhood about the mysticism of the Sufi religion. A big shift started to happen as I understood more the spiritual teachings of the Bektashi Sufi order (tariqat) that my parents and grandfather instilled in me since a very young age. I saw clearly how the mysticism I was taught in my childhood related to every discipline I had studied so far.

Everything started to make perfect sense, as if the pieces of this big life puzzle started to slot into the right places. Bektashis hold that the Quran has two levels of meaning: an outer (zahir) and an inner (batin).

They hold the latter to be superior and eternal and this is reflected in their understanding of both the universe and humanity. The very same view can also be found in other religions including Christianity, Buddhism and Judaism.

This helped me establish the foundation I needed to continue to explore the purpose of life and our human potential. I continued to learn more and trained in many healing disciplines including Reiki to master teacher level.

The next shift that happened was when I met my friend Sabine at a party of mutual friends in Munich. We instantly hit it off, we danced all night, and we knew our paths had met before. Years down the line she moved to London and she was the one who introduced me to Martin Brofman's Body Mirror System of healing.

When I met Martin, I suffered from a lot of chronic back pain, tennis elbow, and had a poor immune system. My first healing session with him changed many perceptions I had about healing. I closed my eyes and trusted this great healer to heal my back, and he did. I felt his hand going into my spine, removing my damaged discs and putting in a new one. I opened my eyes and was asked how I felt, I said "great."

I walked, twisted, bended and there was no pain. As if by magic the pain had simply disappeared. I attended many of Martin's workshops and learned about his method which instilled the belief that "anything can be healed."

Thank you Martin for being my teacher. For your help in helping me expand my conscious awareness to the extent that I was able to see the great healer in me, and for helping me find my way back to acceptance. A big thank you to my friends Sabine and Lova for being wonderful friends in my life. I love you guys!

Despite all the evidence around me, I continued to invest time and money to understand the science behind energy healing. I was not alone in this mission. The scientists around the world study the universe and the world that exists within us in search of proof, answers and a greater understanding of the inner world.

This quest also had a knock-on effect: it kept me in the "skeptical" mindset. In a place where you continue to search for answers before you adopt the truth, despite the knowing and the certainty that comes from within that I am going to talk about throughout this entire book.

This idea that you are unworthy, powerless and separate from one another is a misinformation. What you do to yourself is what you do to another person. You know that we are all energy beings. Your energy is with you everywhere you go. All of your thoughts, experiences and emotions travel and are present in your energy field – your aura.

If you are familiar with Dr. Emoto's book *The Hidden Messages in Water* or have watched the documentary-style film *What the Bleep Do We Know*, you will know about the energy of thoughts and its effect on you, other people, and your environment.

The central premise put forward is that human beings can affect the shape and molecular structure of water through conscious intention. Emoto demonstrates this in two ways:

Firstly by showing images of water molecules from the Fujiwara Dam, before and after they have been blessed by a monk.

Secondly he shows the impact of labeling bottles of distilled water with thoughts. Some bottles feature positive thoughts, while others feature negative ones. He then freezes contents from each bottle and photographs them at sub-zero temperatures using a high-powered microscopic camera.

The resulting shape, color and structure of the water crystals shows marked variation. Water from bottles that were labeled with positive messages has intricate structures and shiny, diamond-like reflective qualities. Water from bottles that were labeled with negative thoughts has deformed collapsed structures with black holes and yellow-tinged edges.

If you look for answers and evidence, you will find that there is a lot of scientific evidence on how each one of us is interconnected and how you really affect other people with the power of thought.

It is not the outer world that created the changes I am talking about here, it is the journey I took to look within that created the transformation I was seeking.

After seeing so many healers, coaches, therapists and having so many different experiences that my rational mind could not explain, I reached an inner place of acceptance, I concluded that the rational mind cannot justify the irrational experiences I was having.

All the above helped me in my journey to heal many physical and emotional issues, to find my true self, life purpose, and lead me toward leaving the corporate world and starting my own healing and coaching business.

The breakthrough: I healed the physical issues I had since childhood, and restored myself to perfect health. I gained mastery of my emotions. Through my work as a coach and healer I started to share my knowledge and wisdom and used my insights to heal others. I became the change I wanted to see in the world, and continue to learn and grow.

In summary, the five breakthroughs you've just read helped me grow into a successful Elite Life Coach, healer, speaker, mentor and entrepreneur. I put everything I learned into practice and started to work with thousands of individuals from all walks of life who felt their life lacked clarity, direction and purpose.

Throughout *A Path to Wisdom* there are powerful exercises to help you break through your fears, your body's current conditioning, and overcome obstacles that prevent you from living a balanced, healthy, and purposeful life.

I recommend that you take your time and complete these exercises as you go. And finally, congratulations on following your intuition, reasoning and your heart's true voice by picking up *A Path to Wisdom* – and choosing to pursue a life of greatness.

Know Thyself

"He who knows others is learned;
He who knows himself is wise."

Lao-tzu, Tao Te Ching

Spiritual awakening starts by questioning our life's purpose. Who am I? Where did I come from? Why am I here? Where am I going once I go through the experience of what is commonly referred to as "death"?

Surely there has to be more to our being, our experience, our existence. It is the quest that you, I and humanity have had since its existence. What is this all about? Why am I being pulled into this search for myself?

Whether you acknowledge it or not, you know that inside of you a spiritual alarm clock is going off that no matter how many times you put it on snooze it keeps ringing to tell you that you can no longer ignore the voice that comes from the depth of your being.

The problem is that at some point in your life you made a decision (consciously/ subconsciously) to ignore it, you stopped hearing it, believing in it, trusting it, and listening to it – your soul's true voice.

So, how do you go about shutting down the noise that stops you from listening to your true voice that knows?

You can no longer use your outer world as an excuse for not doing, for not loving, and for not trying to find solutions to the problems in life that force you to live your life on snooze.

They say that there is no better moment than the present moment. Whoever said it is absolutely right. It is the present moment that creates both your past and your future. It is truly time for you to make that decision right now before you go any further. May this book be your path to acquiring the wisdom that comes from looking within and from knowing yourself at a deeper level.

As you start looking within, you start to be more aware of your body and what is happening in your physical, emotional, mental, astral, etheric, Buddhic (Nirvanic), and Casual pure consciousness body. The more you tune in and listen to what is happening inside of you, the more you become aware of who you are as a consciousness with infinite innate abilities to create, protect, adapt, learn, change, heal, and love.

The moment you decide to recognize and accept that you have been given this God-given gift since birth is the moment you allow this gift to unleash the power you have to change your circumstances, habits, choices, actions, and ultimately your life. This is the very moment you start being the change you want to see in the world.

As you do so, you raise your vibration. You start loving yourself for the dual nature you are, and you see love in the eyes of everyone you meet. You inspire others by becoming more aware of your own values as well as those of others. Your understanding of life changes, and you improve through the feedback your body is giving you about yourself.

As you uncover your many layers, you discover a lot about who you are. You get to know your faults, limits, and the many parts of your personality that you have disowned. Fear not, you also learn everything you love about you. As you let go of the illusion that you are only one side of the coin, you create acceptance of self and others around you. You start to experience inner joy, love and an inner peace from which you can truly listen to the voice that knows.

I am often asked how I got to this place. To the place of knowing, trusting, and believing. I can tell you for sure, it was not easy. I can also tell you with absolute certainty it is the path I am taking you on as you read this book.

As you read in the introduction, I had many predicaments throughout my life. Each of them taught me about the good and the bad that co-existed in me. The ego and the love. Let me share with you in more detail my personal story. It starts at the age of five.

I knew then that I was different from everyone else around me. I did not know how, but I knew I was. I was a happy curious kid who wanted to know who I am and where I came from.

Until the age of eight, each time I asked my mum the question I was told that a white stork brought me to my parents from very far away. You might have been told similar stories and now laugh about it. Believe me, as you are about to discover, there are so many hidden lies in you. Lies that you learned since childhood that you have not questioned and remain subconsciously true to you.

The truth is, even as a young child you know when something does not feel true to you. Although I was being told a lie, something inside of me told me to reject this information, this belief that a bird brought me into this world. So how did I know this?

At that point in time as a child I didn't process information through logic. As children we develop that part of the brain from the age of seven onwards. Younger children learn about the outer world by listening to their feelings and what they experience within. I did not know this information then, but what I did know was through observing the white storks for eight years and never seeing a single one carrying a baby, I knew that my parents were lying to me and that adults cannot be trusted.

My question was answered years down the line when I started school and studied the anatomy of the human body. It was a eureka moment. I remember I was so happy, I knew where I came from. I ran home, told my parents, and guess what? I was now told that was true, but this time they taught me not to talk about it as it was shameful and disrespectful.

So now I started to think that although my parents taught me not to lie, they were not walking the talk. My appetite to question my existence grew stronger.

Each night I would go to bed thinking I wanted to know who I am. There was something inside of me that was telling me there must be more to life. I knew I was a rebel, a warrior and I had a voice inside of me that was always telling me to learn more, to question the unquestionable, and to go and travel the world to find it.

I grew up on a small farm in the small town of Gostivar in Macedonia. During the hot summer nights I would go outside and stare at the stars. The strange thing was that the more I was doing it, the more connected I was feeling.

I knew each time I saw them shining, I felt happy that I too came from the place where the stars lived at night, the place where God lives. At that point in time I did not know about science, had not seen any *Star Trek* movies, nor learned about geography, history, or quantum physics.

So the question I asked throughout my life is: How did a five-year-old me know about my connection to the universe? How did I know I was part of something bigger than the environment I was living in?

I was certain that each time I would look up, I would know that's where home is, that is where I come from and one day that is where we all go back to.

This is the time I started to have transparent conversations with God. Having learned that my parents would occasionally tell me little lies, I knew he was the only one who does not lie.

I would ask God: Why did you put me here? Why is it that you abandoned me? Why are you not sending someone to bring me back home?

Each day I would experience something different. Each night I would have another conversation with God about the things I would learn during the day and was not clear about.

This continued until the summer of 1978. This is when my dad bought us a Grundig color TV. It was the first one in my entire town. Everyone would come and watch. There were long conversations about the achievements of science.

There were four channels, and there was so much I was learning. It came with an instruction manual in a few different languages. I was given the task to unpack it, set it up, and use the little box (the remote) that came with it to switch it on.

We were all thrilled! It was such an exhilarating experience for everyone. I learned about all the different settings. Within a day I knew how it operated and how to troubleshoot it if anything went wrong.

That evening I took a pillow and a blanket and went up to the terrace. I lay there once again looking up into the sky watching the stars. I remember having another dialogue with God and asking him: Where is my instruction manual?

Everything my parents purchased had operating manuals. Surely since everyone is telling me how powerful you are then why is it that I was born without one?

Just the way that there were manuals to help me fix TVs, radios and the many other electronic devices, why didn't you create an instruction manual for people? A manual I could use to help people who are sick, need replacing body parts, help disabled children, sick people in hospital, and heal the dying.

I kept having this conversation with God each time I needed to question something that adults were too busy to teach me. As life took over I continued to remain curious. Why is it that we don't have a manual that tells us how to fix ourselves?

I remember each time I asked something that grown-ups could not give me an answer to, they would say to me: "Only God knows, and you do not question God's will." Although I had huge respect for God, I knew after the many conversations we had together that he was happy for me to learn, question and be curious, despite adults telling me that it was not a good thing to question my Creator.

When my uncle taught me about beekeeping, I was fascinated to know how they found their way back home. Back to the same beehive they lived in. How did they know where to go and how to gather the pollen? How then did they produce the honey? The honey that each morning my mum would spread with homemade butter on to freshly baked bread for me to eat on the way to school.

I would have another conversation with God. How do bees know this? Where is their instruction manual? The roads they travel on, who created them? Where are the directions? I concluded God built it into their tiny little heads.

As I am writing this and recalling this moment in time, I can still taste the honey they produced. At an early age in my life I learned to be grateful, respectful and kind to nature and everything that lived in it. Ever since then, knowing about myself and the world I live in became my way of living, and it still is.

So, can you see your own moment when you started to question everything there is to question about yourself?

Right this moment, you know that not much has really changed since that moment in time. You still truly don't even know who you are. But what you do know for sure is that your past mistakes became the lessons of the future.

You also know that when you are young you are not inhibited with other people's values; you are simply living, being curious, experiencing life with freedom that as an adult you forget you had.

You are here to learn and in some cases unlearn. To question everything you do, everything you are and everything you want to have answers for. To know thyself is an old wisdom of the Delphic Oracle, of many religious teachings, and the teachings of science.

At some point in my journey I came to the conclusion that I am okay with not knowing it all. I let go of the illusion of the expectation that I needed to know everything. I started to trust that whatever I needed to know about me and the world I live in would come my way. That the right experiences to teach me what I needed to learn in that moment in time would manifest.

All the experiences I had, the good and the bad, helped me see the bigger vision I now have and share with you. I took meditation as a daily practice. I learned more and more about me. I now live my life with a greater understanding, appreciation, and from a place where my spirit dwells: my heart.

I believe that if you remain open in life, you come to your own conclusion of who you are. At some point in your life, you may experience a moment of truth, a moment of knowing, a moment of trust in which you know without a shadow of a doubt that you are an immortal spirit living and experiencing life in a metaphysical form.

This is the moment that you truly start living. The moment where you see life as the most precious gift you have. It is the moment you free yourself from the cocoon you have kept yourself in. You may have done many things in life, experienced success, love, death, failure, fear, etc. but have you given yourself the permission to experience being free from the cocoon you may be living in?

It is your desire to learn and do more that takes you to new ways of thinking, doing, experiencing. If you had another life and were lucid about this life, would you make the same life choices you have done so far, go for the same relationships that failed and left you feeling broken, sad and alone? Would you pursue an education and career that is not aligned to your soul purpose that you already have awareness of?

What I am talking about is that state of awareness in which you consciously choose the reality you create. That state of awareness that you know without a question of a doubt that each path you take has its own wisdom. Each experience that you create leads you to fulfill your soul's existential program.

Right now you might be on your own soul journey, how much do you truly know about who you are? What is the level of lucidity you have about your inner world? Your soul's voice and your heart's desires? How aware are you of the inner communications that are invisible to the human eye yet you know that they are happening?

You may have heard the phrase "your inner world determines the way you experience your outer world." Why is it that some people know this, and some have doubts? The reason for the latter is that some choose to use the experience as an excuse to needing proof to believe in things.

If you belong in the second category, then know this. As a child, your brain patterns tend to be unique. In the first six years of your life, the patterns of your brain waves are so slow that you function and learn from your subconscious mind. Everything you are told up to the age of six or seven you accept as true, as you have no analytical facilities to be able to process what you are being told.

All of your awareness is on your internal environment and you notice changes and how you feel inside of you. When you feel differently inside of you it perks your brain up and you pay attention to whatever or whoever caused it. This event in itself creates a memory and the repetition of exposures over time creates a habit, behavior or belief.

Knowing about how you function helps you take control of your life, and creates your inspired destiny. Would you go and drive a car without knowing how to drive, knowing it is simply not safe for you or others around you? No, you would not.

Instead you first decide you want to drive, find a driving school, sign up and learn the theory. Then you take a set number of lessons with a driving instructor who will teach you how to drive safely, first in a test field, then on the roads, and at some point you take a test and get assessed. Once you pass your test you are given a driving license that confirms you have the skills, knowledge, and practical experience to drive safely on public roads.

Now ask yourself the question: Why would I not invest in a coach, therapist, or other professional to help me with taking control of my life?

At some point in your life you may have heard about Einstein and the general theory of relativity – one of the two pillars of modern physics. He concluded that "Energy cannot be created or destroyed, it can only be changed from one form to another."

You too are energy, a being full of billions of atoms, and you too change from one form to another.

Everything about you – your emotions, your thoughts, your organs, your brain – it is all energy. You are just like a TV signal that carries a lot of information. You are both a transmitter and a receiver, and so is everyone around you. Accept your ability to change at the same speed as the way you flick from one channel to another until you find a program that you love seeing and spending your time on.

Life is exactly the same as that TV channel. Hence, the more you know thyself, the way you think, do, and feel about things, the more you learn about how to switch to another personal life program that you love to watch.

Practice makes perfect. The more you start to open up to love, empathy, and acceptance of the uniqueness that you and each person of this planet has, the more it becomes your default way of being.

As you start to get to know you at a much deeper level, you will instantly start using the infinite wisdom available to you. A wisdom that when acknowledged opens infinite possibilities and ways of living your life.

As you learn to let go of ideas, illusions and fantasies, you start seeing that life is perfect in any given moment in time. You engage all of your senses equally so that you can gain a different perspective from each sense.

You start discovering how you're built, how you have learned to hide, cope, and safeguard yourself from you and the world outside of you. You start identifying everything you have engineered: the coping mechanisms, your attitudes, and the way you give reasons to yourself to keep you in your own self-made prison.

As you continue to discover things about you that you never knew, or that you may have forgotten, you learn more of who you are, and the more you see the wisdom that you are. The greater knowledge you get of your inner world, the greater control of your emotions, thoughts and feelings you develop. You start to reconnect to your own spirit.

This inside revolution then creates the outer evolution you seek, as you tap into your greatness and remain authentic to who you are. You become an inspiration. A person that you and the world can trust. A captain who can safely navigate from a place of isolation to one that instills trust, confidence, balance, success, joy or whatever that person might need. You accept that giving and receiving a service throughout your life is one of your life's purposes.

On my recent trip to Croatia I was talking to Deni, a senior manager for Croatian Telecom, on what it meant to him to "know thyself." To him it was about knowing how to feel, react and what to do in certain situations. As we discussed this further, I asked some of the questions you have been reading about.

A PATH to WISDOM

He took some time to think and said:

"I don't really know much about myself. Trying to answer these questions made me think that even what I know now is only a glimpse of what is possible. I see now that it is a constant process that one goes through each and every day."

As we continued our conversation he recalled a time when, to his surprise, he reacted badly to a certain situation in a way that he never thought he could. The lesson he learned was that at the end of the day what's important to know is what you truly want from your own life, have the clarity, and make the choices that lead you toward what you truly desire.

Sometimes in certain life situations it becomes a question of whether you really want to know yourself. You fear the idea of questioning yourself as you might uncover things you are ashamed of, things you want to forget about, or discover something that could conflict with all the conditioning you may have had.

In one of our conversations we discussed the importance of subconscious communications. Like me he is also an engineer, but unlike me he is not a great believer in the healing work – though when challenged he could recall times and situations where he knew subconsciously he was sending, receiving and perceiving information about self and others.

Deni doesn't consciously go about getting to know himself, although when he gets faced with a situation or someone else's situation in which he might be present, he would subconsciously do the self-analysis, reflect on what was said or done, and learn from each situation.

You too have the same ability to "know thyself." This can happen through many levels, which include conscious and subconscious behaviors, communications, and signals you give.

Just like Deni's example above, you may start thinking about your behavior, thoughts and feelings when it's often too late. When something happens to you, when you are having a go at someone, or when you think someone has wronged you.

If this is the case, you live in a cause and effect world. You get involved in the ego talk as you might end up defending a belief, a way of thinking or you also subconsciously defend your higher values.

To "know thyself" is really a lifelong journey. One that takes you on a path to oneness. The path where "I am..." becomes "We are...." A path worth taking as it helps you open your heart to compassion, empathy and you feel at peace with yourself and the environment around you.

It really is like the house you live in. You keep it clean, you look after it and repair it when something is broken. It's where you welcome and entertain guests.

Some of you may go to your doctor's surgery once a year for a full health check-up. If nothing is wrong with you, they will only do specific tests for the most common conditions. They will not do a thorough check-up unless you have a serious illness.

You behave the same with your life: you only tend to pick up and work on areas in your life that you may think need the most frequent check-ups. This way of thinking and treating your life can leave you in danger of not detecting deeper issues that prevent you from living an inspired life.

Jenny, a single mother of two young daughters and a PR and marketing professional, came to see me for healing to help her with her frequent anxiety and panic attacks. After taking many medications she decided to stop and seek alternative methods to help her overcome her illness.

In our first session I took her on an inner journey of self-reflection. We did this through a deep analysis of the eight key areas of life and looked at which situations would cause the symptoms to appear in each part of her life. At the end of the session, she had the clarity of where it all started. She was simply overwhelmed with the number of things she had to do on a daily basis at the expense of her well-being.

Her time was spent looking after her mum, her two kids, and having a demanding job that consumed her. She had no time for herself. She would feel that she was being a bad mother if she said no to all of the demands of her two teenage daughters.

After three months of a combination of healing and coaching work, she learned to pay attention to the various warning signs – the **ALARMs** that her body, feelings and gut instinct were telling her.

The moment she put herself in situations that were at the root cause of her illness, which at times she consciously or subconsciously chose to ignore, the panic attack and anxiety would manifest. This was the reason she feared to leave her house.

From every session, she took the actions that were needed to take ownership of her life. As she continued to learn about herself, she built the confidence required to stop saying and start doing what she always wanted to do, though felt could not find time or the strength to do.

After a year of coaching, her entire life changed. She left the job she was not enjoying, walked away from a controlling relationship, and started to listen to her inner voice. Her relationship with her daughters improved, and she started to give herself permission to love herself.

To "know thyself" is definitely a lifelong process. It is not something that anyone can teach you. It is something that each individual needs to experience. As you grow older you tend to become more comfortable with yourself. Your awareness of what's possible increases, and you embrace your authentic journey.

Once I was referred to work with a lady who had just become a mother and from her fear she was unable to nurture her own baby. When I asked her when this fear started, she said from the very first moment that she saw her baby.

The fear of the unknown took over her life. As the baby was given to her, she realized she knew much about how to make money, run a business, and engage with adults, but she knew little about being a mother.

Her inner alarms started to ring. Negative self- talk took over, and in time her self-confidence decreased. She gained weight and employed a nanny to help her cope. This also had an impact on her relationship with her partner.

The interesting thing was, as I made her write down all of her fears, by the time she listed them all she smiled and said: "Don't tell me, I know some of them look stupid and there is no way I would do that."

I took her through TJS Evolutionary Method and she learned everything she needed to learn about her fears, her perceptions and expectations of being a parent. A lot of hidden myths, illusions and traumas were uncovered during this process. One of her deep beliefs was that no matter what she did, she would never be a good mother.

The process of writing all of this down not only uncovered her beliefs, but it also gave her some peace of mind after learning that 99% of her fears had no real evidence attached, nor were there any known statistics that could support her fears.

As she started to allow herself to learn about herself, she started to gain clarity on the skills she needed to develop in order for her to feel that she was a great mum.

She allowed herself to make decisions that supported her new life without feeling guilty or feeling that she was being judged by her employer. She signed up to a course that helped busy city professionals overcome the challenges of parenting. Her personal relationship improved, her confidence increased, and so did her quality of life.

Throughout life you will have different challenges. The coping mechanisms you develop become greater and invisible to you. Your built-in ability to protect yourself creates even more intelligent ways to help you keep yourself in your survival mode. This results in creating a world in which you are a prisoner of your own prison – is this truly what you want?

One of my significant hidden blessings came to me when I started to notice, acknowledge and trust that experiences I had created (good or bad) throughout my life served a higher purpose.

Normally when you experience something good, you are happy, you feel good about yourselves, you thank God, you tell your friends, family, and feel overwhelmed with positive feelings.

Now, what about those moments in life when the experience is negative? When you feel the situation is totally outside of your control, and when deep down you feel helpless, unworthy and see no light at the end of the tunnel? What do you tell yourself? What is your attitude and what does your inner self tell you about you?

The thoughts, the feelings, the attitudes, the actions, the resistance, the choices you make in any given situation are a great feedback mechanism that you create to help you dig deeper inside of yourself. You can use them to unlearn the different coping strategies that you have built over the years, and unpeel the layers that prevent you from seeing the magnificent you.

Your spirit has been through this process many times. If you are like me and have done a lot of self-development work, you know that you know, you have an inner wisdom that has always been there with you.

The problem is that over the years you have become so good in creating many coping strategies, learned to self-sabotage, distrust yourself, and not listen to your inner guidance. You create an environment in which the seeds of distrust of your true power have been planted.

The truth is the more you go within, the more you can discover the seeds that prevent you from seeing your infinite potential. The potential you have in you to heal your body, your mind, and take control of your own destiny.

You are your own best feedback on how much you know and accept the infinite nature of your being. In this journey of "knowing thyself" you also realize that it is not only the most difficult thing to know oneself, but the most inconvenient one too.

No matter where you are right now in this process of "knowing thyself", you know that you know there is so much you can learn. You can go deeper within and search parts of yourself that lie deep in your subconscious mind.

When I first completed my diving certificate and started to do open water dives, I discovered a whole new world that I was not aware of. As I became more experienced I started to dive to deeper depths, and learned certain life forms were living at different depths.

The depth in which you know yourself determines the width of the life you can experience. This process of "knowing thyself" helps you align your vision, as well as your personal and professional life in fulfilling your existential program.

You may have heard before the aphorism mentioned above, though you cannot acknowledge that unless you know yourself first, you really can't achieve much in life. If you choose to "know thyself" you need to overcome the barriers that prevent you from knowing yourself. You start to realize you have the immense potential to create amazing things and find lasting happiness.

Yet most people don't even scratch the surface of knowing who they really are, let alone figuring out what they have the potential to become. You are so confused that you keep oscillating between overconfidence and low self-esteem. One minute you are filled with a definite purpose for life and the next you are completely desolate. It becomes an impossible task to find lasting happiness in this state.

In my quest for clarity, purpose and self-growth, I realized that asking the right questions is sometimes in itself the answer. As I became better at asking better questions, I came to realize the quality of life I was experiencing was directly proportional to the quality of questions I was asking.

Each path you take in life has its own obstacles, lessons, and the learnings that you go through. Asking the right questions, and learning about the immortal nature of your spirit will help you release the potential that is trapped within and consequently help you find clarity, inner balance and peace.

Years ago I was a very different person, doing a very different job and having relationships that were based on fulfilling a need. I spent years studying many disciplines; I worked with inspired teachers, personal coaches and various healers to help me understand myself at deeper level. Now I do the same. I pass on the knowledge I learned to members of my family, friends, and clients I work with, and through this book to you, the reader.

When you stop searching outwardly for answers to the problems you are experiencing, and start looking inwardly for answers about any obstacles you may face, you start receiving many blessings. Adopt a new way of being, a new way of thinking, and allow yourself to always remain open to learning.

You can ask yourself a simple question or try to understand something that is important in your life and come up with a convenient answer. By asking why, you find a much deeper purpose and meaning.

Exercise for you

Take a day and revisit this chapter to answer questions that you may have always wanted to ask yourself but did not dare to. Remember, each question is just another way of learning about who you are. You may feel more comfortable to work on your own, or you may want to work with someone.

The important thing here is to commit yourself to starting your inner journey to "knowing thyself" through answering some simple yet powerful questions. Make a decision that you are open to start this journey without prejudice, judgment, and fear. Question from the place of being curious about life and about you as you did when you were a kid. Look at each question as a way to make you a better driver of your life.

1. *Where am I in my journey to knowing myself right now?*
2. *Is the way I think about life outward focused, inward focused or a combination of both?*
3. *How can I use the resources I have in my life right now to evolve, to be pro-evolutionary, and to start living a purposeful life?*
4. *What is holding me back, and what options do I have to overcome my challenges?*

1. KNOW THYSELF

5. *Am I fully aware of my "self" and if not why?*
   Which part do I need to work on?

6. *If I were to observe my behavior outside of me,*
   what do I see?

7. *Am I someone who concentrates on the weeds?*
   Or am I someone who concentrates on the flowers?

8. *Identify your key values, and write down the five key*
   elements that make up your foundation.

9. *What makes you choose what you do in life?*

10. *Why is it important to you?*

Allow yourself to go through this process to discover more about who you are. As you do so, you go deeper within yourself, uncovering the layers that prevent you from seeing your inner light, your inner love, and your true potential.

This deeper exploration of you takes you to a whole new world, and a more profound level of awareness of self that you never thought existed.

Start Your Journey

"A spark may ignite the passion, but now let's light the candle and start walking A Path to Wisdom."

Tony J Selimi

Why do you live the way you do?

Take a moment and write down your answers and let's continue the journey you started in the previous chapter.

This time try and go beyond the why. Asking further questions of yourself takes you to a whole new level of awareness. It stretches your mind, it opens up new possibilities, and helps you build further trust in your ability to grow, learn, and adapt.

Now that you have gone through the process of establishing a foundation of why you live the way you do, let's look at helping you build a frame by asking the next series of questions to help you establish the path you are going to walk on.

There is some level of order to the following words; however, put them in the sequence that helps you most.

Now ask yourself:

HOW? – Once I have established why, I need the next logical step to understand how I can start my journey of "knowing thyself." The interesting thing about how is that I need to bring this word back many times throughout my journey because it is the light that shines my path. It brings other questions forward like who, what, where, and when.

WHAT? – Now that I have a better idea, what is it that I don't know about my inner world? What am I destined to do? What do I need to do to learn about me, my body, or to heal an illness? Where do I need to go? What will make me happy?

WHO? – Who do I need to collect and bring with me on my journey? Who do I need to talk to so I get more insight? Who knows someone in the area that I am interested in and can share their knowledge and insight?

WHERE? – Where can I find information and resources? Where will this take me? Where should I be looking?

WHEN? – Is this something I can do now or do I need more training? When will I know the time is right? When will I know that I have arrived?

I am asking much of you at this point because these are very deep questions which you must continually be asking yourself. You must find the champions and enablers who are there to guide you along the way. This is not a solo journey, despite what you might think.

The reason why the last two exercises are so important is that you guide your path. You need to take control of your life and drive in the direction you want to go. If you don't, people and the environment you live in will dictate your direction.

It is in your hands to ask the questions. It is in your hands to search for the answers. It is in your hands to start the journey. It is in your hands to appreciate the journey. Answering these questions will help light the darkness around you and the path that you are on.

Be Authentic

Now take a moment to ask yourself what being authentic means to you based on your life experiences and the lessons you've learned so far.

Once you answer that question, write down your answers to the following two questions:

1. *Who am I and what is authentic about me?*
2. *What is the one thing that makes me special and unique?*

> You can download a guided meditation from
> **http://www.apathtowisdom.com/resources**
> to help you answer the questions above.

There is no other person on this planet quite exactly like you. For just a moment, quit focusing on what you are not, what you wish to be, or what others expect from you and find out what is the one thing you already have that makes you special. Identify your "special-ness." Acknowledge it. Respect it and make it central to how you carry yourself.

Phil, a personal trainer and a scientist, came to see me about his low self-esteem. He had confidence issues, and wanted help with finding the right job and making more money. He needed to discover his authentic self.

After a few sessions I learned that he was one of approximately 200 space physiology scientists in the world. Pretty fascinating, wouldn't you agree?

Interestingly, I knew the problem was in him not valuing himself. So I smiled and asked him: "Do you know how many coaches there are in the world?" He instantly replied: "Thousands." In that moment he self-actualized his own authentic self.

Since that point he started his journey of aligning his life with his authentic self. I coached him to create a vision of what his business would look and feel like. Months down the line, not only did he make great progress in creating this vision, but his confidence grew. He became clear in what he wanted, and stopped going for jobs that did not bring fulfillment. His focus improved, he aligned his life to what he loved the most, and each time I see him, he is happy, clear, and trusts his journey.

I so look forward to my first trip in space and being trained by the very same man I coached to create the business that will support me in achieving my childhood dream – to travel to space.

Be Seen for Who You Are

Do people see you for the special person that you are?

Do they appreciate your unique abilities?

If not, what is the reason?

How can you change it?

Maybe a quote by Henry Longfellow has the answer?

> *"We judge ourselves by what we feel capable*
> *of doing, while others judge us by what*
> *we have already done."*

How can you bridge the gap between what you are uniquely capable of being and the person that you currently are?

Money Trap

If money was not a constraint, what would you be doing with your time? Writing a book? Becoming a singer? Growing a beautiful garden? Spending more time with your family?

Take your time. Feel free to daydream. Once you have the vision in your mind, think of what is the one thing you can do now to move just one step closer to that vision. When you have a vision and start taking action, the universe will conspire to make it a reality.

Hera came to see me at a point in her life when she was not happy with the way her life was going. She knew that she needed to do something about it. In one of our sessions when we went through this exercise, what she truly wanted for herself was to be an entrepreneur. She wanted to create a TV show to empower, educate, and inspire Asian and Middle Eastern women.

Know what you want to do

Each time you meet someone, you are asked what you do for a living; there is nothing deep about this question. It really is as simple as it sounds.

If your answer matches (or will lead you toward) what you answered to the previous question, you are on the right track. If you answered "Writing a book" above and you answer "I am an engineer" to this one, you need to figure out how to bridge the two. Maybe you can start a tech blog, or write a book about the adventurous engineer who went on to become the world's best seller. Whatever it is, figure it out.

Count your blessings

Each day when you go to bed count your blessings and answer the following question: What are you grateful for?

How long did you have to think to answer that question? If your answer was not immediate, if the images of your family and friends, your health, your ability to see, hear, walk and talk did not come to your mind instantly, you should start looking into developing an attitude of gratitude. Remember the quote: *"I cried because I had no shoes until I met a man who had no feet."*

Imagine your death

If you die tomorrow, will you be happy with the life you've lived?

If you die today, who will miss you the most?

What will they say in your eulogy?

Who are the people that have you on their list of most cherished people?

You don't have to have led a life that warrants a national holiday when you die, but are you leaving behind a legacy that a handful of people will cherish?

Why will these people miss you when you are gone?

Will they read out your eulogy out of rote and move on with their lives? Will they choke up unable to continue, or will they smile all the way through because you showed them life is to be celebrated?

Remember, there are no right or wrong answers – this is just an exercise to get you to know yourself better.

Create Your Movie

If someone made a movie out of your life, what would it be like? There are several billions of authentic people on our planet, everybody has a story – what is yours?

Would the story of your life be filled with melodrama, self-pity, hatred, anger or frustration? Or would it be a story about inner peace, happiness, love, growth, joy and transcendence? If you are happy with your answer, keep doing what you are doing. If not, you know that nobody can go back and start a new beginning, but each one of us can start today and make a new ending.

Always improve

Are you a better person today than you were last year? The source of a lot of misery in our lives is we keep comparing our worst moments with the best of those around us. The only way to break out of this is to change your reference for comparison. Are you on a path of growth? Are you moving forward, standing still or slipping backwards?

Be Kind

What was your last random act of kindness? When was the last time you helped someone carry groceries to their car, or just smiled at a stranger who looked like he could use one? When did you last give something knowing that it would never be paid back? What goes around comes around – what will come back to you?

Manage your time wisely

How many hours in a day do you spend on unproductive activities like texting, surfing the net, watching TV, snooping around on others' Facebook profiles, dating websites, negative self-talk etc.?

Now, multiply that number by 2.5, and that is the number of years of your life you are wasting away, assuming you live to be 80 and discounting the first 20 years of your life. (X hours/day * 365 days/year * 60 years) / (24 hours/day * 365 days/year).

Agreed, we all need some time to unwind – but are you okay with the number you came up with, or does it boggle your mind? (On the flip side, if you have kids, how many hours a day do you actually spend with your kids without distractions like TV, phone etc.? Multiply that by 0.75 and that is the number of years you actually spend with your child assuming that they live under your roof for 18 years.

If your answer bothers you, come stop by
http://www.apathtowisdom.com/resources
and we'll figure out a way to fix it.

Take control

Who is making most of the decisions in your life: you, those around you, or your circumstances? Know that you are the master of your life. Some find it easier to give up that power and make circumstances – or worse, the people around them – the masters of their lives.

Do you ever find yourself saying "I'm not happy because..."? It does not matter what comes after because...; that "because" is the way you hand over your power. Watch your thoughts, watch your words and reclaim your power over your life.

Before we move on I want to ask you a bonus question. You may be reading incredibly powerful articles, books, you might have a coach, you might regularly watch YouTube – but what do you do after doing all of this?

Do you just go on with your life, treating it as drudgery, whining and arguing your way around the people closest to you? Or do you live each day as if it were a treasure, enjoying the little moments with those dearest to you as opportunities to make lasting memories?

It really is a choice – what do you choose?

When I was growing up, I was very deeply influenced by a quote from Mahatma Gandhi:

"Whenever you are in doubt, or when the self becomes too much with you, apply the following test. Recall the face of the poorest and the weakest man/woman whom you may have seen, and ask yourself, if the step you contemplate is going to be of any use to him/her, will he/she gain anything by it? Will it restore him/her to a control over his/her own life and destiny? In other words, will it lead to swaraj (freedom) for the hungry and spiritually starving millions? Then you will find your doubts and yourself melt away."

I'll admit this doesn't apply to many decisions you'd take regularly these days, but it's important to keep it in mind knowing the realities you live in, and the fact you're part of the very few insulated from the harsher things in life.

Exercise

From Buddhists to elementary school teachers, at some point in their lives everyone asks some simple, yet powerful questions that can reveal various things about themselves. Now it's your turn to answer the following questions for yourself:

1. *What kind of questions do I ask myself every day?*

2. *What are some important decisions about myself that I didn't make myself?*

3. *What is the most important thing I could be doing, and when will I do it?*

4. *Who do I love, and have I told and/or showed that person(s) lately?*

5. *Where do I most want to go, and when will I go there?*

6. *Who do I most want to meet, and how will I meet her or him?*

7. *What action(s) can I take that will make me happier?*

8. *What do I most want to learn next?*

9. *What can I do to make the lives of others better?*

10. *Will I be happier in 10 years on my current path or happier if I change course?*

11. *Is thinking for myself important, if so how?*

12. *What one action can I do every day to help me achieve my goals?*

Asking these questions helps you get at your likely unspoken beliefs about who you are. By changing how you see yourself in various situations you can actually change your actions and who you are. You can go deeper in yourself and continue to shed the layers that prevent you from living an inspired life.

I believe there is only one important question for you to answer:

What do I want to do now?

2 START YOUR JOURNEY

Spring Clean Your Mind

"The way you look at life determines your experience of it, what you become is what you think you are."

Tony J Selimi

I started to become aware of my thinking process in my teenage years. I was intrigued, inspired, and curious to learn more about life. In my twenties I came across James Redfield's book The Celestine Prophecy. It inspired me to know more, to look for synchronicities and remain open about life. On average I was reading two books a week, each book I was reading had another perspective, another point of view.

In my thirties I went on a journey of new possibilities. I discovered a new way of thinking, started meditating, fasting, exploring the mind, and the universe. Although at the time my career was in IT, my interest in spirituality, self-growth, and personal development increased.

I became even more aware of synchronous events. I started to meet people who were on the same path, shared great insights, read similar books, and loved to grow.

By this time I knew about The Secret, Tony Robbins, Dr John Demartini and Abraham Hicks' teaching of the Law of Attraction, though I didn't really understand them until I started to put the time in to learn the universal laws that were behind these great teachings.

They were only a doorway to infinite wisdom that was just sitting there for centuries waiting to be explored by hungry souls that were on a quest to knowing more about who they are, where they came from, and where they are going.

I continued to study further and through my personal experience I realized that as my mind became clearer, I could see an infinite number of possibilities, and I felt connected with the entire universe. It was as if the entire universe was living in the center of my chest – my heart.

The more I learned to shut down the noise, the more present I became and the more I could listen to my heart's true wisdom. The more I explored the universe, the more humbled I was to this magnificent order that is sitting there.

Even though you may think you have chaos, there is hidden order to it all. The more I became aware of it, the more grateful I was, the more present I was, the more loving I thought it was, the more accepting I became.

I truly became aware of the power of my mind, my thoughts, of my vision, how I talk to myself, and how I feel about myself. I knew then that if I changed the way I looked at things, the things I looked at changed. Such a simple insight presents you with an opportunity to make momentous changes in your life. It's your thoughts, your vision, and the way you talk to yourself that determines your experience of life.

The truth is you operate most of the time from an unconscious mind and you don't pay much attention to your thoughts. As a result of your thoughts, you influence what you see in the world, how you act in your world, and what decisions you make.

Your thoughts actually emerge because of your value system and they influence the direction in which you think and act.

Fundamentally the Law of Attraction boils down to whatever you consciously concentrate your thoughts on you increase the probability of seeing in your environment. Things that can support it (i.e. what you want to create) and taking action in your environment that are assisted.

You start to become synchronous with those, and start to bring into your life what you think about.

By taking conscious effort to focus on what you really love, you become present to all the opportunities around you that you don't normally see.

What tends to happen is that you start to see all the things that can help you fulfill that which you really love and you take action on those things.

If you don't think about it, you just live your life in the react-response way. You are reacting to a situation instead of taking command of your awareness and your actions. The question I have for you is why do you choose what you choose in life? You know that the only limits are the ones you create for yourself!

Unlike your ancestors, you live in a very fast-paced world. A world where you are bombarded with billions of pieces of information every day. A world in which information is freely accessible.

In this world you can ask a new kind of question; not simply inquiring into "what is" but inquiring into what you want and what grasp of the universe would nurture and support a choice to be balanced, more loving, more peaceful and more secure.

Move away from the contemporary cauldron of pessimism so that you find a more useful and inspiring point of view. Rather than wait for a pie-in-the-sky apocalyptic event, you can take charge of your own evolution by changing your world view right now.

Current events, as illustrated by the media, bombard your consciousness with one catastrophe after another, reinforcing a "victim" mentality. Next time you take the subway, pay attention to how each passenger is feeling, especially the ones reading the newspaper. See how many people are laughing, and how many are feeling negative.

I rarely see happy commuters in London. Imagine how commuters would feel if what they were reading empowered them, made them laugh, and inspired them on the way to work. You would definitely make more friends, you would be surrounded by happy and positive commuters.

The media endlessly parades for your literary or visual consumption: the bodies of those killed, hurt or noticeably diminished by war; disease; violent crime; economic recession; poor parenting; drug or alcohol addiction; sexual abuse; food poisoning; train wrecks, air crashes, vehicle collisions; tornadoes, hurricanes, floods and more.

Although you remain attentive, you numb yourselves, trying to put some distance between you and the brutality of those onslaughts. In the evening, you wonder how you made it through the day in one piece or, worse still, how you will survive the unseen catastrophes of tomorrow.

At the end of the day you could decide, flat out, to stop watching and listening to the news – and to stop reading it, too. You can read about something that enriches your life. Let's say you work in retail. If you used your commuting time consistently for two years to learn about how to become a top expert in this field, at the end of two years you are the expert.

The new kind of addiction that I see more and more is the one of the constant need to be kept "informed." As if knowledge of disasters could somehow contribute to your sense of well-being and serenity.

Your life will never be enriched by the gloomy pronouncements of unhappy people, fearing and judging all that they see. They follow fire engines racing toward billowing black clouds of smoke and ignore the smiling youngster helping an elderly woman carry her grocery bags.

One dramatic traffic accident on a major London road sends reporters scurrying, while the stories of hundreds of thousands of other vehicles that made it home safely go unnoticed. Newscasters replay over and over again a fatal incident but rarely depict the tenderness of a mother nurturing her newborn infant.

Simple acts of love, safe arrivals, peaceful exchanges between neighboring countries and people helping each other are noteworthy events. The media bias toward sensationalism and violence presents a selective, distorted and essentially inaccurate portrait of the state of affairs on this planet. No balance here.

We feed our minds such bleak imagery and then feel lost, stressed, depressed and impotent without ever acknowledging fully the devastating impact these presentations have on our world view and our state of mind.

Why not inspire ourselves rather than scare ourselves? You choose your focus of attention from the vast menu of life's experiences. Wanting to be happy and more loving on a sustained basis directs you to seek peaceful roads less traveled.

Though you might not determine all the events around you, you are omnipotent in determining your reaction to them. Some people live on the earth's crust thinking the world is a hostile place and focus their attention on the world's horror, while others will lift the stones and see beauty beneath. Your embrace of life will be determined not by what is "out there" but by how you ingest what is "out there." Your view becomes almighty.

What you have been taught about yourself and the universe around you conspires to have you believe that living requires awesome energy and great struggle. I was told many times by my parents: "No pain, no gain."

So many people around me think:

"Life is a constant struggle; there is not enough out there."

"You have to take the bad with the good."

"You never really get what you want."

"You're unlovable."

"Something is wrong with you."

"There is no justice."

"No one cares." etc.

These become communal mantras, shared with others and elevated to the status of treasured folklore. They color your vision and send you searching for the experience (rejection, attack, control, loneliness, indifference) that you anticipate.

Usually you find it! Your vision blossoms into a self-fulfilling prophecy, which each new experience tends to verify and reinforce.

I never met a man who lived forever, a man who was always happy, and a man that never slept. I also never met a man who believed he could live forever. You become your beliefs. You get stuck in your head by the limiting beliefs that you hold.

Suppose you set aside the rigid concepts you might have learned about how the universe works. If you can now begin to entertain the possibility of many world pictures, then you might want to experiment by putting aside a logical, linear view of existence with fixed points and "hard facts" and consider a metaphor which reveals the ever-changing nature of the known universe.

You swim in a river of life. You can never put your foot into the river in the same place twice. In every millisecond, the water beneath you changes.

Likewise, in every moment, the foot that you place into the river fills with new blood. Instead of celebrating the motion, you try to hold on to the roots and stumps at the bottom of the river as if letting go and flowing with it would be dangerous. In effect, you try to freeze-frame life into photographs. But the river is not fixed like the photograph and neither are you.

Did you know that 98% of the atoms of our bodies are replaced in the course of a year? Our skeleton, which appears so fundamentally stable and solid, undergoes an almost complete transition every three months. Our skin regenerates within four weeks, our stomach lining within four days and the portion of our stomach lining which interfaces with food reconstructs itself every four or five minutes.

Thousands, even millions of neurons in our brain can fire in a second; each firing creates original and distinct chemistry as well as the possibility for new and different configurations of interconnecting signals. As billions of cells in our bodies keep changing, billions of stars and galaxies keep shifting in an ever-expanding universe. Even the mountains and rocks under our feet shift in a never-ending dance through time. Life celebrates itself through motion and change.

Although you can certainly see continuity, seasons come and go. Trees grow taller and people get older. You can acknowledge that each unfolding moment, nevertheless, presents a world different from that of the last moment. You could say that you and the world are born anew in every second and your description would be accurate scientifically.

Therein lies an amazing opportunity for change. You can stop acting as if your opinions and perspectives have been carved in granite and begin to become more fluid, more open and more changeable, even inconsistent. You are in the river. You are the river!

Every stroke you make, every thought or action you produce, helps create the experience of this moment and the next. And the beliefs you fabricate along the way shape your thoughts and actions. Sounds rather arbitrary, some might say. It is!

Quite simply, you try to move toward what you believe will be good for you and value, and away from what you believe will be bad for you, operating always within the context of your values and beliefs. Even your hierarchies of greater "goods" and greater "bads" consist only of more values and beliefs.

You hold your beliefs sincerely and defend your positions with standards of ethics or "cold, hard facts." You treat much of what you know and believe as irrefutable. You tend to talk in absolutes.

Once your beliefs are in place, you then use all kinds of evidence to support them, quite unaware that you have created the evidence for the sole purpose of supporting whatever position you favor. In essence, you have become very skilled at "making it up."

Many years ago, I used to suffer from a heart murmur, and had chest and lower back pain. Despite many trips to various doctors, physiotherapists, chiropractors and other specialists, my pain kept coming back.

I was used to taking medication to numb the pain and was told by many specialists that I would have to live with the symptoms for the rest of my life. When I was introduced to Martin Brofman's Body Mirror System of Healing by my friend Sabine, as I mentioned in my introduction, I was extremely skeptical about Martin's philosophy that "your body is a mirror of your consciousness."

At the first workshop that Martin held in London I experienced what I can only describe as a "miracle." This sent me on a whole new path and I started to learn new eastern disciplines on the power of the natural healing capabilities of the body.

Months later, I went back to more healing workshops, I continued to learn about the chakras and The Body Mirror System of Healing. Martin's teachings inspired me to go deeper into the consciousness and understand the relationship that exists between the body, the mind, and the spirit.

As I continued my healing journey, I started to shift my thoughts, took responsibility of my life, and changed the way I was thinking about myself. As the years went by, I healed the many issues I had experienced since childhood. My hay fever disappeared, and I had no more headaches. I was able to deal with stress effectively without causing me any issues, and my exploration of the belief-making game became even more mesmerising as I pursued it further.

What did I want to believe? In this case, my intention was to be healthy. Although keenly aware that my upbringing and Martin's teachings held different "truths" about the same data, I still wanted to find a meaningful way for me to select beliefs and behavior which would support my health.

I resolved the dilemma by choosing to consult what I call my "nonverbal/nonconceptual resource within." I would make a decision about my health based on what felt good to me physiologically.

I decided now I would make decisions, think thoughts and do actions that felt good and gave me positive energy. I would gather new evidence to support my new criteria or new belief. Within weeks, I felt the difference.

Now, just because you think you need to clean your house, it does not mean you will do it. In the same way, you may have been inspired so far to spring clean your mind, however that does not mean you have done it. So it's time for you to take some action!

Exercise for you

1. *Start a daily journal of your thoughts; this will help you know what you think about on a daily basis.*

2. *Once you have a week's diary, check and see what proportion of your time you use thinking positive and empowering thoughts, and what proportion of your time you spend on negative self-talk. Continue keeping that diary and reflecting regularly.*

3. *If your mind was your house, write down how you would like it to be. Is it busy with lots of things lying around collecting dust, or is it clean and clutter free?*

4. *Be curious and observe the way you think throughout the day. If something does not feel right, explore it, and go deeper.*

5. *Recycle anything that does not support you. Free room for new thoughts, beliefs, and metaprograms.*

Your Choices =
Direction Your Life is Going

The way in which I live my life today is different from the way I used to live my life. I've made a lot of decisions that led me down the path I'm on now. There are all sorts of things in my world that could be better, but I'm extremely grateful for the position I'm in. Everything falls into place the way it's supposed to and it's just amazing. I have a lot of faith that I'm exactly where I'm supposed to be and because of that, I wouldn't change it for anything.

Years ago I saw a great movie that beautifully captures decision making and the life outcomes that each decision can create. Every time I make a decision in this life, small or big, I think about the movie *Sliding Doors* with Gwyneth Paltrow. I think about whether I should step in or wait and let the doors slide shut without stepping in.

The choices we make have such a big impact on everything around us. In regards to the multiple universe theory, which I believe in, I think the best we can do is to make the best choices we can, given the current information we have to hand. Always think about how your world would change if you made a different choice, and then make your decision accordingly.

For those that have never heard of it, the plot of the movie centers around the two possible lives a woman may have had depending on whether she made it into a subway carriage or not on one fateful night. How many sliding doors do you take or miss every day in your life?

According to some physicists, every decision you make is a sliding door in the making. Every decision creates two or more possible outcomes, with every possible outcome potentially occurring in separate universes. Some of those sliding doors lead to minor, almost undetectable changes in your life; others can have dramatic effects. It's enough to paralyze one's decision-making ability, which I'm sure is one of the sliding doors.

It makes you wonder what your life would be like had you taken a slightly different path earlier in life – in my case a psychology degree instead of engineering. A skiing trip instead of the beach or going home for Christmas break; taking the subway instead of the bus to work. Would you still be you?

The truth is, many of you go through life not really thinking about the sliding doors you may or may not be going through. You don't think about what doors may be closing for good on you as you walk past them.

Are you making an effort to ensure that you do everything you can to maintain your health and your ability to remain open to learning new things each and every day? For me, I am actively looking for the sliding doors that I think will make me a better, stronger and inspired coach, healer and teacher of inner wisdom. I am looking for things that will enrich my life and help me be a healthy old man.

It's still a guessing game. You never know for sure which sliding doors lead to where, but you can make educated proactive guesses and do what you know is right for you. Sitting on the couch with a tub of ice cream after dinner or going for a walk? On any given day, either choice will probably not have any ripple effects, but making the same bad choices on a daily basis certainly will.

Lisa, a senior HR director of a very reputable retail company, came to see me for some coaching as she was experiencing a lot of stress at work. She felt she was doing four people's jobs and had no choice in the matter.

As time went by she became unhappy with herself. She stopped enjoying the work she once loved and became withdrawn, ill and overweight. Deep down she was afraid of being judged.

She felt powerless. As we continued our coaching each week we started to discuss her options, the outcomes she wanted to have, and we looked at the choices she had for all the things that were causing her stress.

At first she resisted the idea that she was the cause of it all and that she had any choice in the matter. We continued exploring further each issue she was having. We looked deeper into her beliefs and values, and she started to identify those that were at the root cause of her problems.

She learned of the subconscious choices she was making that made her feel the way she was feeling. As she got clarity of thought, she started to manage her subconscious behaviors better, and as a result she made better choices and decisions.

Old patterns that held her in the space she was in became things of the past. We created affirmations that were more empowering and were supporting her with her daily challenges. The one that she fully embraced that helped her the most was: "I am wise and I apply my wisdom so that I make choices and decisions that serve my highest purpose."

She remained open to taking ownership of her thoughts, decisions and the outcomes of the choices she was making on a daily basis. As the year went by, her stress levels reduced, her happiness and confidence increased, and she started loving her job and life again.

Let's now look at what I mean by "choice." Is a choice the same as a decision? Many people make a distinction between them. Some decisions are "big", such as: "Shall we buy that new house in the better school district?" "Shall I take that new job?" etc. The word "decision" sounds so final, as though there is no going back once the decision has been made.

Other choices often seem so much simpler, like "Shall I have dessert?" or "What hotel shall I use for my next coaching session?" These types of choices appear to have less effect on your life. They may be more open-ended and you know you can always choose again.

Nevertheless, choices and decisions involve the same process. You weigh alternatives (sometimes not for very long) and then you take an action. Choices still affect the outcomes of your life. We often forget that decisions can still be changed by making another one. In order to highlight this similarity and to eliminate some of the anxiety associated with "decisions", I will use the word "choices" for all of the selections that we make in our lives.

How do you learn to make choices that enhance your soul's existential program and get the outcomes you want? First, focus on outcomes – the results of the choice. Identify what the outcomes will be from each of the alternatives (at minimum three and preferably more).

Determine what you will see, hear, and feel with each choice. From this sensory experience, choose which anticipated outcome you want most. Immediately, take some action toward that choice. Do something. As you continue to act toward your preferred outcome, relate what you see, hear, and feel with what you want. If you like what you are getting, continue doing it. If you don't like what you are getting, do something else!

Consider the outcomes from each choice. As you do so you will feel your own sense of satisfaction at your accomplishment.

Working on many projects with many clients, one common thread that prevents people from making the right choice is self-esteem. Firstly, low self-esteem affects the accuracy of your perceptions and predictions. When you are loving and feeling respectful of yourself, your projected outcomes are independent of your ego – of any need to do things only to please others.

Secondly, self-esteem affects your connection with your feelings and your connection with others. There is more to effective choices than the material side of what you see and hear. You allow the childlike sense of wonder and having fun to influence your choices.

Additionally, when you are in touch with your feelings, you know when you are not getting precisely the outcome you want and you take actions to change.

Thirdly, your self-esteem affects your willingness to consider new alternatives, new ways of doing things, and not just continuing with more of the same.

Making conscious choices helps build your self-esteem. Choosing for yourself increases your feelings of self-respect, your self-love. You realize your capability and responsibility for building your own life and your own self-esteem, choice by choice and outcome by outcome.

Sometimes we think that the big choices, life's "decisions", are the most important. In fact it's the little things we do every day that make the difference over the long term – things as simple as choosing what to work on today or how we will treat ourselves and others.

Throughout this I have taken the perspective that you know you are extensions of nonphysical energy, taking thought beyond where it has been before, and through contrast, you will come to conclusions or decision.

And once you align with your desire, the energy that creates worlds will flow through you, that is enthusiasm, passion and triumph. That is your destiny.

To make appropriate choices on an ongoing basis, you need to know what is truly important to you. What the overall outcome is for your life. You need to know your values. When your values are clear, choices are easy. This is your self-esteem, it lets you discover and live your values.

Exercise for you

1. *Make a list of your core values. Once you have them the next step is to see how making choices consciously can change your life.*

2. *Next, take a moment and think about the choices you make each day, do you make them consciously, or are most of your choices automatic?*

3. *Finally write down the choices you are currently making, and the choices you would love to make instead. Then answer the following questions:*

1. How do your choices impact your life?

2. How can you make better conscious choices?

3. What choice can you make to best utilize and enhance your existential program and life purpose?

4. When will you take action on one of these new choices?

Don't Second Guess

A recent study in the journal *Personality and Individual Differences* reveals that second-guessing your decisions may lead to unhappiness. For people who seek to always find the "right-choice", life can be more difficult. Fighting against second-guessing isn't impossible, so here I will highlight a few tricks to curb your regret.

The research is based on a type of person psychologists term "maximizers." These are the people who tend to obsess over their every decision through the day. Since maximizers tend to research and weigh up every decision they make, they don't ever fully commit to one even after they make it. So they don't get the psychological benefits of making a good choice.

Basically, they're never happy or content that they've made the right choice, regardless of how much they're enjoying the decision. This causes a bit of grief and self-judgment. While it's thought that real maximizers may not be able to curb their self-doubt, many people can by asking a few questions.

Psychology Today doesn't knock the idea of second-guessing, but it does have a few solutions when curtailing the significance

of your choices. The most logical question you can ask yourself is whether or not the circumstances have changed since you made the decision. If they haven't, your decision is still valid and there's no reason to second-guess it. That said, if the circumstances have changed and you're afforded the opportunity to go back and re-evaluate a choice, it's not a bad thing to do so.

Weighing your decisions beforehand against your values helps you understand how they affect your core values, and if you find yourself second-guessing decisions, you can refer back to your earlier process. Start by asking a simple question before the decision is made: Which one of these most honors the things that mean the most to me?

Of course, you can't really use this logic if you're second-guessing a retail purchase, but in the case of big life decisions like moving or a new job, it's a good idea to look at it through a larger lens both beforehand and in hindsight. Dr. John DeMartini's work helped me look deeper into my values and I was able to understand how my decisions affect my core values.

In my journey of "knowing thyself" I had to make a lot of decisions. With some I did a great deal of research beforehand. With other decisions I made I didn't, I made them instantly without any thinking on how those decisions would affect me.

At some point in my life I became more aware about how each decision affected my past, continues to do so in my present, and how it affects my future. One of the results of being aware and regularly making conscious choices was the understanding that true livelihood and spirituality are inseparable, in fact they are one. You are the decisions you make on a daily basis.

You have heard it many times that good things come to those who wait.

A well-researched decision can help you feel more comfortable in your decisions, which can prevent the eventual second-guessing.

Making a pros/cons list, calculating outcomes, and doing your research beforehand can help you feel settled in your decision.

If you've done all of these things, when you ask the question: Have I done enough research about how this decision affects me? you should be comforted by the work you've done.

According to a University of Michigan study, the physical act of washing your hands can help remove those niggling second thoughts about a decision you made. We've seen before that the simple act of washing your hands can help derail second-guessing because it offers the psychological effect of "washing your hands of a decision."

If you find you're the type to second-guess no matter what you do, *The Harvard Business Review* recommends scheduling time for doing it. You make a note to not question the decision when you're vulnerable, but instead plan on doing it after you've already had time to get used to the idea.

You can also consider interrogating yourself and giving yourself ridiculous, harsh criticism to put the whole thing into perspective. If you can acknowledge the fact you did your best in your decision making, it might help you move forward.

One thing I found particularly helpful is to recognize that "20/20 hindsight" is for the most part an illusion. At best you have a good view of how your life went after making the decision, but you usually have no better view (than at the time you made the decision) of how your life would have gone if you had chosen differently.

In other words, if you chose not to go to a concert and instead read a book, but the book ends up being terrible, "maximizers" tend to imagine that the concert would have been amazing and feel like they missed out.

However, the truth is you have no idea what the concert would have been like! It could have been terrible, or you could even have gotten into a wreck on the way, you never know.

The point is, don't let 20/20 perception make you regret decisions, because it's extremely presumptuous to think you know what would have happened if you'd chosen differently. On top of that you might still not have a good viewpoint on the course your life took with the decisions you made.

You might learn to like it more a little down the road. Although looking back later is a valuable tool to learn from past decisions, don't jump too easily to conclusions that make you regret your choices because you still don't know what really would have happened. So just try to accept, move on, and plan for the future, taking the bad or good decisions you made.

You know that there are many wonderful attributes – likely hundreds – that, without a doubt, are absolutely true about you. Reconsidering your finest aspects can be a rewarding activity.

Mistakes, Obstacles
and the Life Challenges

*"Life challenges are not supposed to paralyze you,
they are supposed to help you
discover who you are."*

Bernice Johnson Reagon

As you go through life, with difficulties such as redundancy, lack of money, relationship breakdown, choosing the wrong career, losing a loved one etc. it's extremely hard to recognize that being put out of your comfort zone might be the best thing that ever happened to you.

I used to work in the corporate world. I spent 12 years building a very successful track record working in IT for both private and public sector organizations, and my life was pretty much sorted. Well, that's what I thought until one morning in 2009 as the financial market crisis deepened, the company I was working for decided to make me and many other people around me redundant.

At the beginning it was exciting, I had worked all my life and it was time to allow myself to have a break. A few months passed and it was time to look for another job. Despite sending out more than a thousand CVs, I was constantly told there were no jobs for me as I was overqualified.

If I applied for jobs that were of a lower grade than my previous role, I was told I was a risk to them as I might move to another job once the market improved.

I spent more than 12 hours a day sending out on average 20 CVs. It became a full-time job to try and find another role. Six months passed. The pressure to pay my bills, cope with the family demands and the ones I had of myself, started to impact my well-being. Once again in my life I started to lose my sense of belonging and identity.

I realized my success, the way I was living my life, and the feeling of being secure depended on and was controlled by others, and by a simple piece of paper – the monthly pay check.

I had a moment of clarity. I knew this was not the reason I came into this world. I had survived much worse, and if this was another test that God, the universe, or my spirit gave me, so be it.

At the beginning it was very difficult for me to see a secure future in the midst of everything that I was experiencing. Daily I was hearing how unemployment figures went up, and spent hours sending thousands of applications to job posts that probably did not even exist. I had financial commitments, a mortgage and credit cards to pay, and at the same time I was worrying about how I would support my mum in Macedonia.

As time went on, I stopped looking for the needle in the haystack and instead I started to spend most of my energy focusing on what to do next. I had a window of opportunity to determine my core values and the direction I wanted to take my life in.

With all the obstacles presented to me, I started to ask how I could I use them to create opportunities and use them as stepping stones to the life I wanted to build. During this time I truly learned to see life with a different eye. As an experience in which there are no mistakes, only lessons and learnings that my spirit and I created to lead me to where I am today. I started my own entrepreneurial journey, and a few years down the line I built a very successful coaching company.

The lesson learned was that nothing I did or didn't do was a mistake. All the adversity I have had in life, all my troubles, challenges and obstacles, have strengthened me.

From my own personal and professional experiences, as well as from coaching, healing, and mentoring hundreds of clients, I know life will always present you with a challenge. You will make mistakes along the way and you will also have to face obstacles in any of the eight key areas of your life (spiritual, mental, emotional, physical, financial, career, relationships as well as love).

I also know parallel to facing challenges in life that you may feel are beyond you, you can create an opportunity to build on your faith, your understanding of the power you have within, and your courage. You have a choice in any given moment in time.

What I understood studying many universal laws is that duality exists in everything in life. I'm often asked to help people to always be happy. I start a dialogue with my clients and at the end of this conversation they themselves conclude that to think you can be 100% happy all of the time is impossible.

I personally have not met a single person that can claim he/she can do that. Let go of that illusion, accept that you will always face challenges, obstacles, and make mistakes. It is not the challenge itself that is the problem here, it is your attitude. The way you think about the problem, and how you face it plays a big role in your life.

I certainly don't regret the experiences I have created in my life so far. Without them I would not be the man I am today. As you overcome your obstacles you will see how life becomes a gift. Your attitude will change and you create inner peace.

Struggle, conflict, and many other emotions that are perceived as negative are built into us. Your challenge is to learn how to best manage them so that the way you experience life is more enjoyable, peaceful, and more loving. Conflicts and obstacles will always exist. You have a choice. You can decide to not let obstacles prevent you from pursuing the path you chose. As you do so you become authentic, someone who inspires others, and a hero.

Be that hero. Don't let the fear of self prevent you in this process. Real life isn't going to always be perfect or go your way. Focusing on what's working in your life can help you not only to survive but also to surmount your difficulties.

Your brain is chemically designed to find solutions to life's problems; you might wonder how you go about sorting them all out, and you might feel overwhelmed with the number of obstacles and challenges you might be experiencing right now.

You may feel your life is one constant struggle and experience times where you feel you are going against the flow, but what if there was a better way to understand all of this? What if there was a tool that could help you in your daily challenges and help you get your life back on track? Well there is. The path you are on led you to read this book and the powerful insights I learned over the many years.

Accept that there are many challenges you have faced, are facing and will face in life. All of those are part of the same source energy that is in you. You are human after all. Expect those things to happen and prepare yourself on how to best handle them with the resources you currently have available. Coaching can definitely help you tremendously in this process.

Let's now look at some of the most common mistakes, obstacles and challenges you might be facing in the eight key areas of life that prevent you from truly living your best life, listening to your heart's wisdom and trusting your own journey.

SPIRITUAL

One of the mistakes I made and you may make too is to not know how spirituality differs from religion. The two are sometimes used interchangeably. If you look deeper, they really indicate two different aspects of the human experience. You might say that spirituality is the mystical face of religion.

At some point in your life there will be a self-realisation that there is more to life. You start seeing yourself as consciousness, a spirit living in a physical form.

Due to a lack of understanding, various religious beliefs instilled in you since you were born, and the environment you grew up in, you might see yourself as a mortal soul. You are born, you live, and you die. The place you go is determined according to your religious beliefs. It might be either heaven or hell, and if you come from other religious beliefs you might get reincarnated. But even that comes with many conditions attached.

For thousands of years, knowledge was the best kept secret, only available to you if you were born into a privileged society, culture, or affluent family. For thousands of years, religion had power because it controlled the flow of this knowledge. Today, you have the world's information in your palm. Knowledge from the entire internet can be accessed from your cell phone, so you know you too are a powerful being.

You are here in this world to experience one of the greatest treasures of the soul. A life in a physical form where you have the opportunity to paint on a blank canvas the life you create.

For many this is the hardest spiritual challenge to overcome as their limiting beliefs prevent them from taking ownership of this God-given gift. Questioning the bigger purpose: where you came from, why you are here and where do you go once you cross over are great questions to start you on this quest.

As you discover more about your life, you start to accept that you are an immortal soul. A spirit that has lived and continues to live. You have gone through many experiences and have collected a lot of information along the way.

So what is spirituality? The common misconception people have is that they link their spirituality with religion; the two are very separate. Religions contain the doctrine and guidance that can lead to spiritual experiences.

People often become dogmatic in following scriptures, and lose the ability to experience the deeper spiritual purpose behind the initial teachings. Those people stuck in their literal interpretation of religion force many to separate out the deeply spiritual experiences that are available to us on a daily basis and get stuck in this physical reality. On the other hand, your spirituality is your connection to God, to the divine source of all that is and all that will be, it is the connection to this energy that today is commonly referred to as consciousness.

While the definition of spirituality is different for everyone, here are some common themes associated with spirituality:

- A process or journey of self-discovery.
- Learning not only who you are, but who you want to be.
- A higher power, whether rooted in religion, nature, or some kind of unknown essence.
- The challenge of reaching beyond your current limits. This can include keeping an open mind, questioning current beliefs, or trying to better understand others' beliefs.
- A connectedness to yourself and to others.
- Spirituality is personal, but it is also rooted in being connected with others and the world around you. This connection can facilitate you finding "your place in the world."
- Finding meaning, purpose, and direction in life.

So let's look at the most common mistakes people make when it comes to their spiritual path. To gain a better understanding, I went on a quest to interview hundreds of people including my senior executive clients, religious people, atheists, spiritual people and people from all walks of life.

I wanted to learn about the spiritual challenges people had. Interestingly enough, most of the people I spoke to first of all did not know the definition of it, and they could not tell the difference either.

Many of them felt a disconnection from their spirit. This was due to the challenges they experienced in life, their beliefs of what spirituality was, and not knowing the difference between religion and spirituality. The interesting thing was that none of them denied the existence of something bigger than themselves.

At some point in my life I too experienced a disconnect. I kept hearing the word spirituality though for me it sounded like just another religion.

When I was asking people about their spiritual challenges I often got the following answers:

"I am not religious, I don't believe in spirit, what do you mean what are my spiritual obstacles? I am not even sure it exists, this is it for me."

Others would say to me: "I can't accept others' suffering, I don't see how spending time on prayer and meditation time is more valuable than many other things I want to experience."

Another common obstacle you might face is finding it difficult to maintain your connection to your spirit when things get tough in your life. It becomes easier to blame something outside of you: God, the universe, people around you, religion. You become disappointed, disheartened, and rejected by your spirit as you feel your spirit was not strong enough to help you get through a difficult situation.

We live in a world in which measuring is a way of feedback to ourselves on how well we are doing when we do something. When it comes to spiritual work, it becomes a great challenge to forget about this and develop certainty, and trust yourself in this journey.

It's natural that you want to know and measure how well you are doing; however, if you don't trust yourself in this process it will prevent you from learning and growing on a spiritual level. Most likely you will end up being cynical, close-minded, not being true to yourself. You start to experience a disconnect. At some point in your life your spiritual ALARM will start to become louder and louder.

Often people go through life feeling great and positive. They make an excuse to relax spiritual discovery and practice, when in fact it's the best time to be even stronger in it and continue your journey.

You always interact with the outside world. Having family, friends, people you work and socialize with that are at a different stage of spiritual awareness and acceptance can hinder your spiritual development. You can end up controlling this process and want others to either adopt your way of thinking, or expect them to be at the same level of spiritual growth.

I learned to see spirituality as the wellspring of divinity that pulsates, dances, and flows as the source and essence of every soul. Spirituality relates more to your personal search, to finding greater meaning and purpose in your existence. Some elements of spirituality include love and respect for God, yourself, and everyone else. It also includes looking beyond outer appearances to the deeper significance and the soul of everything that is.

Religion is most often used to describe an organized group or culture that has generally been sparked by the fire of a spiritual or divine soul. Religions usually act with a mission and intention of presenting specific teachings and doctrines while nurturing and propagating a particular way of life.

If you choose to, religion and spirituality can blend beautifully. In my personal journey I came to an understanding that different religions can look quite unlike one another. Some participants bow to colorful statues of deities, others listen to inspired sermons while dressed in their Sunday finery, and yet others set out their prayer mats five times a day to bow their heads in prayer. Regardless of these different outer manifestations of worship, the kernel of religion is spirituality, and the essence of spirituality is God or the Supreme Being.

One of the great gifts of spiritual knowledge is that it realigns your sense of self to something you may not have ever imagined was within you. Spirituality says that even if you think you're limited and small, it simply isn't so. You're greater and more powerful than you have ever imagined.

A great and divine light exists inside of you. This same light is also in everyone you know and in everyone you will ever know in the future. You may think you're limited to just your physical body and state of affairs – including your gender, race, family, job, and status in life – but spirituality comes in and says "there is more than this."

Notice that spirit sounds similar to words like inspire and expire. This is especially appropriate because when you're filled with spiritual energy, you feel great inspiration, and when the spiritual life force leaves your body, your time on this earth expires.

Here are two main themes of the spiritual journey you can take yourself:

1. *Allowing you to be filled with inspiration: this also translates into love, joy, wisdom, peacefulness, and service.*

2. *Remembering that an inevitable expiration awaits to take you away from the very circumstances you may think are so very important right now.*

The study of spirituality goes deeply into the heart of every matter and extends far beyond the physical world. Spirituality connects you with the profoundly powerful and divine force that's present in this universe. Whether you're looking for worldly success, inner peace, or supreme enlightenment, no knowledge can propel you to achieve your goals and provide as effective a plan for living as does spiritual knowledge.

Go beyond the physical world

Perhaps the best way to think about a spiritual approach to the world is to contrast it with a more common materialistic approach.

The materialistic approach relies primarily on empirical evidence provided by the five senses – what can be seen, heard, tasted, touched, or smelled. This approach depends on the outer appearance of things to decide how and what to think and feel about them. A materialistic person fixes whatever may be wrong or out of place in his or her world by moving things around and effecting outer changes.

In contrast, the spiritual approach is to see beyond mere outer appearances and the five senses to an intuitive perception of the causes behind outer conditions. Someone with a spiritual approach may change and uplift their world by first transforming and improving his or her own vision.

Throughout this book I am taking you on an inner journey to help you transform your experience of your outer life. One of the main teachings of spirituality is to look within and find what you seek within yourself. The external world is ephemeral, temporary, and ever changing. In fact, your body will die one day, sweeping all those worldly accoutrements away like a mere pile of dust. Your inner realm, on the other hand, is timeless, eternal, and deeply profound.

Spirituality is going beyond all that is. Going beyond all religions yet containing all religions, beyond all science yet containing all science, beyond all philosophy yet containing all philosophy.

As one becomes more spiritual, animalistic aggressions of fighting and trying to control the beliefs of other people can be cast off like an old set of clothes that no longer fit. My personal journey led me to see and to feel that every soul on this planet and every image of divinity is just one more face of my own, eternally ever-present God.

Loving and respecting all religions and images of God doesn't mean that you have to agree with all their doctrines. In fact, you don't even have to believe and agree with every element and doctrine of your own religion! This goes for any teachings you may encounter along your path.

Everybody thinks that what they are doing is right. That's what's so fun about the world. Everybody is doing something different, and each one believes deep in his soul that what he believes is right – some with more contemplation and conviction than others.

There are many reasons why you should develop your spirituality; it can offer many benefits to your life, both emotionally and physically. Developing your spiritual life can give you a sense of purpose and help you figure out where you are most passionate in your professional, social, and personal lives.

Studies show that positive beliefs can comfort you and improve your health.

People who have taken the time to develop their spiritual life are also likely to better understand their needs.

MENTAL

Have you ever asked yourself a question: What is the nature of your thoughts? It would seem at first look that your thoughts are mostly structured in language. You may be aware of the constant internal dialogue going on inside your mind. In truth only 2% of your thoughts, experience and understanding is actually formed in words, this is the conscious part of your mind. The other 98% is made up of continual sensory impressions and associations in the subconscious mind.

Having and holding on to beliefs that don't serve you any more is the same as trying to put diesel in a car that runs on gas, and if like me you have made that mistake, you know what happens. It simply won't work and you have to take your car to the mechanic to repair it.

Take a rotten apple, put it in the middle of a pile of healthy apples and see what happens. In a week's time half the apples will have started to rot. In time no single healthy apple will remain.

This is exactly what's happening to your mind when a thought that pops in is unhealthy for your being. You would not expect the pile of apples to remain fresh, healthy, and not rot. Why do you expect that thoughts would not do the same to you?

In real life you would not go and put a rotten apple there so why would you put your mental health under the same risk by continuing to have thoughts that have the ability to damage your entire body?

Your paradigms, beliefs, and thoughts do exactly that to your life. They all have the power to slow you down, create inner conflicts, and infect your brain's operating system. They can influence your feelings. They shape and create your reality.

If negative self-talk is your current thinking, it is your dominant thought. What you think is what you emit into the world and into the universe and according to the Law of Attraction it's what you create.

You don't expect to have apples if you plant a cherry tree, so why would you expect something different from the universe if you continue to plant negative thoughts and keep negative beliefs?

Know this: whatever you think is wrong with you is emitted from your body into your experience of life. If you question your thinking and start planting new empowering thoughts, negativity naturally disappears. You don't need to do anything about it.

Your highest values determine the way you experience life. The way you make decisions, the beliefs you hold that you don't want to let go, and the quality of life you create and experience. Over the years you have learned to subordinate to those around you. You admire your parents, teachers, and those who are more successful. You start thinking that despite those who are less fortunate than you, you have to thrive to do better, and you enter the game of competition, comparison, and the "never good enough" mental loop.

Every experience you have ever had is the reflection of your beliefs, thoughts, and the values that are unique to you. The more you allow yourself to acknowledge the guidance, the more you can learn, grow and evolve.

Through your actions and emotions, you become aware of what is truly happening in the mental part of you. You can recognize the mental ALARM that consciously or subconsciously you might be putting on snooze or switching off while you continue to live your life without any significant changes.

These beliefs are your paradigms. They've been ingrained in you since childhood by your parents, teachers, preachers, culture and society. But do they really serve you?

One of the main mistakes we make is that you understand immediately the power of beliefs in your outer environment. For instance, when you observe conflicts in cultures that have different belief systems from yours, yet you don't readily apply that same clarity to yourself.

We function much like absorbing sponges, acquiring beliefs uncritically at a dizzying pace in order to take care of ourselves in the best way possible.

The onslaught of beliefs has become so steady in our culture that often you ingest beliefs and repeat them to others without questioning or reviewing them.

Some common ones are:

"I hate my job."

"This is the best country in the world."

"You are too young to understand."

"Education prepares you for life."

"Life is a series of ups and downs."

"Good health is often a matter of good genes and good luck."

"I am lost without you."

"I know I can't do this."

"I am stupid, lazy, not good enough."

"If I show my true self, no one would love me."

"It's embarrassing to behave this way."

"I have to do something in order to be loved."

"I must do something to make the other person appreciate me more."

The list goes on. If you spend most of your time in this state you forget to acknowledge and embrace your true abilities.

Overthinking and creating imaginary fears and possibilities are other great examples of mental barriers that you can create. They give you the excuse not to act. In most cases this is all due to a fear of letting go.

A challenge for most people is developing the ability to focus. Without this your mind can wander in all sorts of directions. It's like being on a little boat in the middle of an ocean that is left to the mercy of the sea currents, winds, and your ability to navigate toward a paradise island without a compass, engine, or sail.

I see people constantly being stressed by not feeling in control of what they are thinking, doing or feeling. This leads to exhaustion, physical illness, and lack of energy. If you start taking on too many things at once, you create imbalance. As the time passes by you start feeling resentful, more stressed, and you have less time to do things that bring you closer to your desired goals.

Not having a clear understanding on the different roles that your conscious and subconscious mind have is another mistake that people make. Some might set their unconscious brain to come up with the answers, and let go of solving problems using their conscious mind. Some might find it hard to trust either.

To learn more go to **http://www.apathtowisdom.com/resources**

A while back I coached a senior executive whose overthinking caused him a lot of sleepless nights. He turned to drugs to help him stay awake at work and be able to perform his role. Eventually the situation started to spin out of control and he was referred to me by a friend that I had helped a few years prior to overcome addictions.

One of the key problems he experienced was that because of the fear of losing his job he was not able to say no. He kept taking on more work and at some point this became a big issue and he spent a lot of time and mental energy trying to cope.

In one of his sessions I got him to write down everything he was thinking until there was nothing left in his head. It took a few hours and he felt exhausted at the end of the process. He went home and had his first great night's sleep in months without drugs.

The next step was to help him create a structure. We put everything that came out into an appropriate category. He listed the things that weren't an immediate problem or issue, and also created his list of priorities.

Once this process finished, he created some goals. He put time in his diary to handle the most urgent and high priority items and put the rest of the actions in the "parked" area that he could refer to at a later stage.

I taught him to meditate. At the beginning he started to meditate for five minutes daily, and a year later this increased to 20 minutes.

This helped him feel calm. He developed the ability to shut down the noises that put him in this position and let his mind rest. His self-confidence, self-respect, and self-love grew. He started to create the results he came to see me for and was able to say no without feeling fearful. He created a work/life balance and let go of his addictions as he started to love and accept himself.

Have you noticed most people are good at talking and bad at listening? As your mind is busy trying to think about what it needs to say, you develop mental laziness toward listening. This has a huge impact on your personal and professional life.

The other obstacle your mind can create is the game between the ego and the mind and the way in which it impacts all areas of your life. Seeking validation outside ourselves is a mistake.

This is due to living in a world that teaches you at an early age to seek some form of validation about how good you are. It becomes a challenge to reverse this process and accept your imperfections as part of being perfect.

What makes it worse is allowing past behaviors and circumstances to dictate responses, attitudes, and the behaviors you create.

To question beliefs like the ones listed above does not necessarily mean they are erroneous or invalid. However, questioning and inquiry opens the door to understanding more fully why you believe what you do and whether or not you want to continue believing it. Do the beliefs you hold serve you? Do they empower you or lead you to feel impotent? Do they lead to happiness or unhappiness?

You can change. You can be different. You can defy history. Your past is but a memory dragged into the present moment. That moment is no more important or significant than the next. And in the next moment you can change it all. You do it by consciously choosing to change your point of view, by changing your beliefs, as I have done and you have done too on many occasions.

Each and every one of us has the ability to shift these paradigms, otherwise known as conditioned habits stored in our subconscious – including you.

Of course I know that positive thinking doesn't come naturally to everyone. But kicking the ass of negative patterns of thinking is half the battle.

Later on, as you learn about the method I share with you, you will see how the self-talk and self-awareness (the way you talk to yourself and your awareness of what you're thinking, doing and why) is the key to learning how to be more positive. Allow yourself to be curious. Learn the method. Practice what you have learned. In time you will see it's well worth the effort.

This is how you then move away from reacting with What did I do? to understanding there is no blame. There is no guilt, only each individual's experiential journey which is uniquely yours to take.

Not only through personal experience, but also through many coaching sessions I have come to the conclusion that when you make decisions based on the opinions of others, oftentimes you wind up resenting them. "I did what so-and-so said and look where that got me!"

Yes, that happens because they are not you. They cannot know your truth. They do not operate from the same program that you do. They do not use the same perceptual filters and most certainly have not been brought up with the same values as you.

If you are someone who needs countless people to weigh in on every decision you make in life, well think again. You don't need to stop and ask for directions when you already see the signs! The more you keep asking – thinking the answers are outside of you – the more you walk away from the inner wisdom that is within. You may become more lost, insecure and out of touch.

Even with the advice from a mentor, friend, or family member, you want to allow yourself to imagine and actually feel the different options in your body. This can reveal which path is right for you.

By being still and silent, you allow your mind to delve beneath the chatter of fearful ruminating and projection and into a place of expansion and possibility. In that clearing, your route unfolds with clarity and becomes easy to navigate. You may not be able to stop stressful thoughts completely, but that doesn't mean you have to take them seriously.

The other important thing to remember is that you are perfectly capable of making informed decisions in your own right that align with your truth. Ultimately the only one who can do that for you is you.

For most of human history, in fact right up to the end of the 20th century, it was widely believed throughout the scientific and academic communities that it was impossible for someone to increase their intelligence, change their beliefs, and increase their mental faculty.

The experts in psychology and neuroscience thought that although you could accumulate large amounts of knowledge, helping you to put your innate intelligence to better use, the fundamental characteristics of intelligence were determined by genetics.

Their understanding was that although these factors could be influenced by a stimulating environment while growing up, once you reached adulthood your intelligence was locked into place, only to decline gradually with age.

Fortunately we now know that's not the case. Neuroscience research from the last two decades has shown there are a variety of methods you can use to get reliable and lasting increases in your mental faculty and intelligence.

By improving your mental faculty you can easily see more patterns, combinations, relationships and connections which improve your innate problem-solving abilities.

EMOTIONAL

*"One thing you can't hide -
is when you're crippled inside."*

John Lennon

Through some of my personal breakdowns I learned not to be at the mercy of my emotions. I learnt Daniel Goleman's framework of five elements to help me become emotionally intelligent: self-awareness, self-regulation, motivation, empathy and social skills. I also embodied this wisdom into my work and share that wisdom here with you the reader, as mastering your emotions is key to living a balanced, peaceful and successful life.

There has never been another time in history when we could experience emotions through sharing our personal journeys, our ideas and the content we create with billions of people around the world.

In my research to gain a deeper understanding of people's emotional intelligence, I interviewed hundreds of clients, friends, family and I also used Google, Wikipedia and many other websites where great content is shared.

Each gave me a different perspective about what emotions are, which creates a different challenge. Different sources tell you different things about emotions. You can end up being confused if you constantly search for something outside of you to make sense of the emotions that live inside you.

You experience reality through your own specific filters and the various levels of awareness you have of yourself and your five senses. Some of you might even have a natural aptitude in developing your sixth sense.

This influences the way you see your world, the meaning you give it, and the emotions you create as a result. All of that is carried through your energy field into your outer world. Commonly referred to as your aura, you may relate to someone who has a presence. You may have experienced being next to someone that you felt negative energy from.

You can start to see how easy it then becomes to transmit and receive emotions even when you're not consciously aware of this process. You can create great feelings in you and in others, as well as conflict between yourself and others.

The challenge then is in being able to express your emotions without judging yourself or others in that process, as they have their own captain and can steer you in any way they choose and you become emotionally vulnerable, unstable, and you lose control of yourself.

There is a lot of scientific research out there that links obesity with your emotional well-being. Not learning, understanding and conquering your emotions can have a knock-on effect in all areas of your life: your health, the way you feel about yourself, others, the way you see yourself fitting in the world and the way others see you. You start to experience a disconnect from within and with the outer experience of the reality you live in.

Take a moment and think of a specific situation in which you felt your emotions took control over you. How did you feel? What outcomes did you create? How were you perceived in that moment in time?

The word "e·mo·tion" is a natural instinctive state of mind deriving from one's circumstances, mood, or relationships with others. It can be any particular feeling that characterizes a state of mind, such as joy, anger, love, hate, horror, etc.

Emotion from a scientific perspective is an energy-electron in motion.

When you think about it, both meanings make sense. You don't need to be a scientist to know that you are an energy being. Each part of your body is energy; it moves, carries information, emits, as well as increases and decreases in intensity and density.

If you observe your emotions, they are doing exactly what they were meant to do. The problem is that most of us have not been educated to see them as natural. You learn to judge your emotions when you feel negative, or thank them when you feel great, when you feel loved, and cared for.

In my journey to understand my emotions I came across Wilhelm Wundt, a 19th century psychologist who offered the view that emotions consist of three basic dimensions, each one a pair of opposite states: pleasantness/unpleasantness, tension/release and excitement/relaxation.

Plutchik, another psychologist, suggests there are eight basic emotions grouped in four pairs of opposites: joy/sadness, acceptance/disgust, anger/fear, and surprise/anticipation. In his view, all emotions are a combination of these basic emotions.

Emotions exert an incredibly powerful force on human behavior. Strong emotions can cause you to take actions you might not normally perform, or avoid situations that you generally enjoy.

Emotion is a subjective, conscious experience characterized primarily by psychophysiological expressions, biological reactions, and mental states.

Emotion is often considered reciprocally influential with mood, temperament, personality, disposition, and motivation. It is influenced by hormones and neurotransmitters such as dopamine, noradrenaline, serotonin, oxytocin, cortisol and GABA. Emotion is the driving force behind motivation.

Although those acting primarily on emotion may seem as if they are not thinking, cognition is an important aspect of emotion, particularly the interpretation of events. For example, the experience of fear usually occurs in response to a threat, there is part of our brain that regulates this.

The cognition of danger and subsequent arousal of the nervous system (e.g. rapid heartbeat and breathing, sweating, muscle tension) is an integral component to the subsequent interpretation and labeling of that arousal as an emotional state.

Your behavior is affected by your emotions. Research on emotion has increased significantly over the past two decades with many fields contributing including psychology, neuroscience, medicine, history, sociology, and even computer science.

Many times when you felt emotional did you trust your internal wisdom to inform you of your next action? Did you listen to your divine, tricked-out Emotional Guiding System (EGS) that comes standard with the human package you were gifted at birth?

A main challenge you might have is getting to grips with your emotions as they have a massive control over you.

Emotions have the power to turn your world upside down. They affect the way you see the world, and the way you treat your body.

Have you noticed when you feel emotional how easily you reach for comfort foods?

Research shows that your emotions influence not only the level of happiness and joy we experience, but also have a negative impact on our eating habits.

When you are emotional you lose the ability to listen to the deeper intelligence within you that knows the limits. When emotions take control, you throw away the rational part of you that tells you to stop.

One of the key mistakes I see people making all the time is they try to make sense of their emotions through their rational left brain, the part of our brain designed to think.

I see others try to use their creative right brain to make sense of their thinking patterns. Neither will work, the reason being these two parts of our brain are very distinctive. Each part is uniquely designed to do a specific function. So what you need to do is to exercise both parts of your brain.

In your day-to-day life how do you respond when you don't know something? Take a moment and notice what answers you get.

With emotions, unless you have a good grasp of emotional mastery, at some point when faced with an intense emotion that you can't understand, you start to alienate yourself from it, you ignore and numb yourself. Your behavior, attitudes and actions follow. You pretend that everything is under control.

You find various distractions and you automatically start creating many coping mechanisms that become part of who you are without ever questioning them. You forget where these new coping mechanisms came from and what barriers they have created in you.

You become so accustomed to hiding your emotions that you don't even see them surfacing anymore. You give up on life and become a victim of circumstance in which you have no control. You might go on a journey in which you over-intellectualize your emotions.

In the same way we have a GPS chip for mobile technology to tell you where you are at any point in time, your emotions have the ability to do the same. They guide you, give you feedback, and keep you on track. Over the years you have learned how to hide them. The noise in your external environment is so loud that it prevents you from listening to your feelings and true voice.

This process handicaps your ability to understand, interpret, and effectively communicate in a loving, caring, and meaningful way the information that your emotions create.

There is no doubt that extreme emotions associated with a perceived threat, stress, or lack can impact your health and accelerates your physical aging. What you imagine to be a highly stressful event, like losing a job, losing a loved one, going through a divorce, having no income, or the discovery of a serious health issue impacts your entire way of being.

However, with the intensity of life today, it's almost irrational to believe that you will get through a day without some form of challenge, be it fears, things you need to do, or people you have to see and obstacles you have to overcome.

When you lack emotional intelligence your emotions take over. They are like water. Eventually they have the power to penetrate the deepest part of you that you never knew existed.

Think of a moment in your life when this was true. Times when you got snappy and angry, felt rejected, moody, or were feeling down. You may have taken things personally, and weren't even conscious of the responses you created as you might have avoided or suppressed "bad" emotions so that you didn't create further conflict.

Do you feel proud, guilty, ashamed, or out of control? What was the lesson you learned and what did you change as a result?

Recently I started working with a highly successful client who asked me to help him understand his emotional outburst and the stress he was experiencing. He was aware that his past feelings affected his handling of the situation in the present, though had no idea how to change that.

He took me on vacation with him, we spent seven days doing very intensive coaching sessions, and daily we addressed each situation that was causing him to feel emotional and stressed.

He started to look deeper into each cause of stress. Together we explored every part of his being: what was happening mentally, emotionally, physically, and energetically. As we dug deeper he started to uncover what the seed of stress was for him. He saw that the desire for that which is unobtainable and the desire to avoid that which is unavoidable was the source of his stress and suffering.

He started to accept fully that expecting life to be a one-sided magnet is futile. He realized the same applied to a one-sided emotion, or anything he experienced in life. By the end of the week he self-actualized to let go of the idea that life will always be perfect. He started to see, hear, and love the imperfections that existed in the broader meaning of what perfection is.

I will always remember the moment he gave me the warmest hug and said: "Thank you, you have freed me from the weight I was carrying." It was a moment I will always cherish. It was the same moment I experienced personally with a few of my teachers including Martin Brofman and when I did DeMartini's Breakthrough method. This is the moment when the emotional charge is dissolved and you experience true unconditional love for a person, situation, or anything that exists.

What holds you back is not committing your time and energy to the process until you go to the deepest part of you. You give up halfway when you experience temporary happiness, feelings of joy, or love. The other obstacle is your lack of trust in yourself. Making a conscious decision to overcome this, coupled with your fear of judgment and rejection by others when exposing your emotions and what hides in the depths of your emotional sea.

Any unrealistic expectation and unbalanced perception of life leads to an emotional rollercoaster. Your emotions bounce up and down like a yo-yo from one extreme to another.

This could be from love to hatred, fear to trust, exuberance to depression, madly infatuated to hostile. You are up one minute and the next thing you're down. It puts a huge strain on your physiology, adrenals and hormones.

These extreme emotions create illness, weight issues, and the stress ages you. As you accept and master the art of balancing your expectations, perceptions and emotions, you learn to live in peace. Free from emotional outbursts, you are no longer controlled by them.

You become emotionally mature and start to experience events without going through a rollercoaster where you lose control of your emotions and experience suffering. Sensitivity to the various degrees of emotions stagnates your spiritual, mental, emotional, financial and physical growth.

When you are feeling futile, challenged and stressed, cortisol and other stress hormones are released. Signs of this include thoughts that jump around, erratic speech and breathing and tense muscles, especially in your jaw, face, arms and hands. Stress may also lead to all sorts of physical symptoms such as stomach problems, constipation and high blood pressure which all lead to your body being overloaded, leading to premature aging.

Being oversensitive toward yourself and others brings a lot of pain into your life, and that holds you back from evolving. It also stops your true self from shining and blossoming.

Take a moment and think about your life and the role your emotions play in it. Would you go and see a movie that you know has very poor reviews and an actor who can't act? Probably not.

What you need to do is to make a conscious choice and a decision to be the best actor playing the lead role in your emotional movie. Be an actor that engages you, moves you, and makes you want to love for the rest of your life.

Think of your emotions as a movie that you love so much you can watch it repeatedly and never get tired. Each time you watch it from a different perspective, from another angle, another point of view.

So choose the best role for your emotions to play in your life. You cannot continue in life and be an observer. You need to participate, engage, and play your role.

Emotional maturity helps you participate in your movie but without the highs and lows of emotional intensity.

As you are about to learn **TJS Evolutionary Method** you will go on an inner journey to reach a high level of emotional mastery to help you stop the **ALARM** that keeps ringing inside. You can create an inner peace from which you can achieve higher states of consciousness. In this space you have the courage and the ability to do things even when fear is there.

As you've probably determined, emotional awareness, intelligence and mastery are key to success, balance, and inner peace, especially in your private and professional life.

The ability to manage people, relationships, and yourself in a very fast-paced, high-stress, high-demand environment is vital to any senior executive, leader, CEO, president, or even the Queen. Learning, developing, understanding and using your emotional intelligence can be a good way to show others the leader inside.

It is the reason why people follow them. They are perceived as a strong leader, and reaching this vibrational state you start to draw people naturally as your energy field starts to emit inner strength, confidence, love and you start to inspire belief in others.

Being the captain of your emotions tends to produce a charismatic effect. This charismatic effect results from the qualities which enable effective leadership. Some people are born leaders and some develop their leadership abilities. Most people don't seek to be a leader, but are able to lead, in one way or another.

You have probably come to the conclusion that your spirit, mind, body and emotions all form a unit. Almost every bodily symptom you have tries to make you aware that your expectations, perceptions and emotions are unbalanced.

Your emotions become electrical charges that influence your body and switch your cells, tissue and organs "on" and "off" or produce an "excess" or "deficiency."

Often when I coach clients I refer to a state called a "choice point", a place from which you can instantly switch your emotions on or off. A place in which you instantly dissolve your emotional charge and create unconditional love.

Perceptions and your response to them can be changed. You can set realistic expectations that are balanced. Prioritize your actions, delegate low priorities to others, chunk down large projects, objectives or goals into smaller bite-sized daily action steps to decrease procrastination. Reduce lack of clarity and frustration and increase your accomplishments.

As you do this, you start feeling more productive, efficient and have a greater sense of self-worth. As a result, your chemical imbalances become balanced, your cortisol levels go down and endorphins go up. You feel centered, poised, fulfilled, and you reduce your stress levels. You increase the speed at which your body heals. The quality of your life goes up and you slow down your aging process, adding years to life and life to years.

The pain of the above process is only temporary, but the feeling you get of mastering your emotions lasts forever.

CAREER

At some point in your life, in addition to wanting to look good, lose weight and spend more time with family, you will vow to improve your professional life in the coming year. According to research, one of the top 10 most popular New Year's resolutions is job-related. However, in the busy months that follow, many of these goals are forgotten and never achieved unless you are faced with a situation that forces you to make a decision on what career to choose.

It can be hard to choose the right career as our entire education system is based on going to university, gaining a degree and then into employment and starting the rat race. I see it all the time: the number of people who are doing jobs they simply do not enjoy, because it is what they learned, or to pay the bills, or simply the only job they found.

The common mistake here is that you become a victim of your own making. You create limiting beliefs around your capability of what is possible. You comfort yourself with the news that you hear, and tell yourself that you're lucky to have a job as all the news reports are of redundancies. You create massive fear and become your job.

The fear of change takes over, and before you know it you spend years being miserable, doing a job that only pays your bills, gives you a few vacations a year and keeps you just over broke: the acronym "JOB." Ask yourself why it is that you keep playing small. Why do you go about life making others big while you are living a life in someone else's shadow?

You might be a school leaver, a graduate, a PhD student, an engineer, a doctor or you might be someone who has already been working for many years but for whatever reason you are once again faced with the same process of which job to choose, what company, what industry, what role?

Looking back to when I started my career in the 1990s, the world we lived in then was a very different world from the one we live in now. The career choices you would have made then are very different from the career choices you would make now. The recruitment process was also very different then.

I came across many challenges and obstacles. Along the way I gathered the many insights that I am now sharing with you to inspire you to take full ownership of your own destiny.

As you may remember, in a previous chapter I shared my personal story when I faced redundancy in 2009. Nothing prepared me for the aftermath, the shock, and the emotional rollercoaster that I experienced.

Today, I say it was the best thing that ever happened to me, but back then when I was in the midst of it all, I could not see it. I was emotionally broken, hurt, and ended up being a very angry individual.

I was not angry at being made redundant or in knowing my employers could not pay me; I was very aware of the implications the financial markets had for my employer. I was angry with the manner they deliberately chose to execute the decision.

They do say pain is a great teacher. This process helped me take action and create the freedom, life and work that I have and love today. I decide how much money to make, what clients to see, and how much vacation I should have. The freedom I created through my entrepreneurial journey is priceless.

It made me reassess my own values, goals, and the direction in which I wanted to take my life. I am now able to see it from a very different perspective than four years ago. It was the best thing that happened to me. It forced me to take action and be proactive in creating the life I now have. Each obstacle that I now face, I see it as having its own learning.

It made me increase my understanding of self and the role I played in my life. It helped me gain the clarity I needed to see that I came into this world to deliver a vision that was bigger than me. Bigger than my family, friends, community, the religion I was born into, the city I lived in, and the country I came from. For the first time I was able to see clearly that I was born to deliver a global vision, one of a Heart Centred Approach (HCA) to living.

I learned that values play an important part in life. If your values are not aligned to the company you choose to work for, along the way you may experience a lot of pain that you could avoid.

You may get disheartened, disappointed, and give up in your journey to finding and matching a career you love and a great employer who provides that.

Sandra, a project manager working for a top consultancy firm in London, came to see me for career coaching as she knew it was only a matter of months before her company, like many others, decided to let go of staff. In our first session together she lacked clarity, felt stressed and fearful that no employer would be flexible enough to take her on board, being a single mother.

Despite all her efforts of talking to friends, using social media, sending CVs, and filling application forms there was little feedback or acknowledgment. This crashed her confidence and she started to feel insecure about the prospect of finding a job. Also she stopped enjoying the job she once loved due to the fear that soon she would be out.

I made her write down all of her work worries, issues, obstacles and challenges that she could think of. We then addressed each one of them closely and saw how some of her deep fears were unfounded. She started to become clear on what she wanted. Her list became smaller. Some items were parked on another list, and she created small goals that she was able to handle and could fit into her busy schedule.

As time went by, six months into coaching she got herself two part-time jobs that gave her the same level of income and job satisfaction. Her values matched those of her two employers who loved and supported staff who had children.

You cannot ignore it anymore. The world you live in has a massive influence in the way you live your life. You are part of a generation of a connected world in which from the palm of your hand you can find any information you seek. You can connect to anyone around the world, and you can also work from anywhere in the world. There are many successful people out there that live a laptop lifestyle and run successful businesses from the palm of their hand.

You are becoming more conscious of your choices, on how the choice of career impacts your core values, your health, and your world.

The traditional models in the way you would choose your career do not work anymore.

You may want to be an entrepreneur, or you may want to work for an employer whose mission and values support your values. Alternatively you may just want to have a job that pays your bills and offers you a security blanket in which you can feel warm.

We are all different. You are authentic. You are like no other human on earth, so when it comes to career choices, it is only you that needs to have the clarity on what to do. Once you do that, the path will open up for you to walk on.

A key obstacle that you might be facing now is how to keep motivated, make a good decision about your career and the process which you will have to go through to find the right job, the employer or the right business you might want to create.

This also requires sufficient time to devote to a thorough job search. Sufficient trust in yourself to overcome the fear that you cannot find another job. Not finding a balance between available jobs, your wants, and your qualifications, and the possibility that your present employer will learn that you are looking for another job.

For some people, financing additional training or education might be the challenge they face. You want that PhD but you don't have the support from family or friends, or the finances needed to do it on your own.

Another one could be the fear that you cannot succeed at the new job. This can crash your confidence, self-esteem, and can add additional stress to your life.

You were taught since you were born how to compare yourself with others. You learn to doubt your own abilities at an early age, and your vision of who you are is truly clouded with the experiences you have been through. So to embrace and trust a whole new vision of yourself can become a tremendous hurdle to overcome.

I worked with a client who was a finance director. His company was losing business and customers due to complex processes and procedures.

These were put in place due to a lack of trust amongst employees, executives and the different departments.

I delivered a custom workshop and created an anonymous survey to see how each layer of this small organization saw each other and the level of trust it had.

They were shocked at the report I sent. I was commissioned to deliver a few days' workshop on trust and help build trust amongst staff and each department.

Following the survey results, an order was issued to change some of the sales and purchasing rules. Each departmental head was empowered to make key decisions in the absence of a director, with clearly defined thresholds.

When a sales director needed to make an instant decision, he did not have to wait anymore for the FD to make a decision. What happened was that communication amongst colleagues became transparent, their sales increased, and the joy in the business increased.

The level of joy and success employees experience is directly proportional to the level of trust present in an organization. I invite you to measure this in your business and see how it impacts your profits, your customers, staff retention and everything else about your business.

When distrust is present, employees get involved in company politics instead of trying to resolve issues. Many creative minds in an organization start to lose their passion, ambition, and their drive to act as they start to feel that they are not trusted.

What prevents you from doing what you love is the lack of trust in your own ability to manifest income if you step away from a "false" sense of security and giving up your current income.

Looking back in time I faced this challenge as I learned to let go of this fear. I created the same level of income within a year working half the time – pretty impressive right? Well, it was not at the beginning, as lack of clarity also prevented me from seeing this.

Thinking that doing a good job is the fastest path to a great career is another mistake that you might be making, as later on you will self-actualize that you are not being fulfilled in the work that you do.

In business it has become a difficult challenge to maintain the balance between learning and doing. Most employees get bored quickly if day in, day out they are faced with tasks that are repetitive and do not motivate them. I have interviewed hundreds of my clients and random people on why they chose to leave their jobs and one of the themes that kept repeating was how they felt about work and the company they worked for.

Companies can no longer ignore the impact that feelings play in their organization.

Some companies have already started the process of creating spaces, offices, and a work environment that changes the energy of their employees. These have had a positive impact with their staff as well as gaining market share due to allowing their employees to work in an environment that supports their creativity.

Employees who work in such environments feel free to express their true potential. Others I have spoken to who work in companies where well-being and feelings aren't being integrated in the company culture feel they could offer more to the world, and at some point they choose to leave.

To know where to go is to go where you know. As each one of us becomes more conscious, the career choices we make will start to be increasingly aligned with our existential program.

The method you are about to learn will help you gain clarity in choosing the right career for you, by not getting dragged down by perceived failures, fears, and your perception of lack. You will learn about you at a much deeper level so that the choices you make are aligned to your values and who you are. You will be empowered and inspired to make the choices that lead you to a fulfilling career.

Career choice is also one of the main challenges of today's and tomorrow's leaders. The conscious leaders realize that if they want to go fast in life they need to go alone and if they want to go far they have to go together with the people they choose to co-create with.

The problem is that for leaders who have been with a company for many years, their values have been embedded into the organization's culture at a time when business and society were at a very different level from today's conscious evolution – for instance, at times when diversity and equality laws were not in place.

A new wave of conscious leaders is emerging and starting to work in companies where those old values are still deeply rooted. You can start to see how conflict can develop at an executive level and then filter down to the lowest ranks in the organization.

Leaders started to ask questions such as: How do we maintain the growth we have achieved so far, and what more can we do to go to the next level? How does each action we take impact our environment for the years to come?

They want to be free to make decisions that are heartfelt without three other people going over that decision. They want to have the freedom to be creative, be part of an organization rather than work for a business. A whole new shift is happening across all levels of the organization that has a massive impact across the business, its customers and the way it coexists with the environment in which it lives.

Exercise for you

Take a moment and before you continue further answer these questions:

1. *Why do I want to work?*
2. *What will work give me?*
3. *How will I feel about what I end up doing?*
4. *What contribution do I want to make?*
5. *What do I truly love doing? Why am I doing it?*
6. *As you dip a toe into the job market, what are the potential challenges you need to be aware of and what do you need to overcome?*
7. *What makes you happy?*

Think about the above questions at a much deeper level. See what truly brings the joy, the trust, and the happiness you want to have in your career.

Here are eight ways to help realize your professional objectives and take control of your career:

1. Know thyself

As you get to know more about yourself you will start to gain the clarity about the work you want to do. Know your values, know what you stand for, and know what you truly love doing.

Don't underestimate the power of your feelings. If you answered some of the questions above, you will start to have an idea of how you feel about you. Once you accept those feelings and know the information they give you, every time you apply for a job, attend an interview, or meet a prospective client, see how you feel about it. If you feel negative, most likely whatever you might be doing is not for you. I see many clients that I help reverse this process in which they go against what the feelings are telling them. It is not natural to go against you, it is a learned behavior.

2. Align your skills to your highest values

If you are an office worker, and your highest value is to travel the world, start thinking what skills would get you there. One route might be applying to any of the major airline companies. Another route might be while you are still working you start to learn about online investments and start making money online and create a lifestyle in which you can travel all the time.

On the other hand, if your career suits you, take time to better yourself at what you do. Stand out from other employees by completing the latest training and updating your industry expertise. Do this even if there is no training in your employer's budget. I self-funded most of the training I did. Years down the line this helped me create my own businesses and I now teach those skills to thousands. With an internet connection, skills development is at your fingertips. Online you can find the world's largest compilation of career training courses in a number of languages. From the comfort of your home find convenient options that will bolster your skill sets and strengthen your resumé.

3. Set TJS Evolutionary Method SMARTER goals

You might have been through this process before, but you might not truly know how to set Specific, Measureable, Attainable, Realistic, Timely, Empowering, Regularly reviewed energy efficient goals (SMARTER).

In one of my recent workshops I took a highly trained social media expert through this process. Although at his work he has been through this process with his managers, the problem is most managers do not know how to get you to be SMARTER about you and your goals. They are trained to embed the company's goals into you. Can you see the problem?

You would not be in control of your own career and goals. In time you can see where this would get you – a one-way avenue to being frustrated, unfulfilled, and unmotivated.

When you set your goals, knowing you at a deeper level helps you start doing the things that you love doing. As you do so, your creativity is engaged and appreciated. Learning is part of those goals and focusing creates the results you achieve.

As you go through this process you will know what you want to accomplish professionally in any given year and you can write it down in order of priority.

Your goals may include improving current work performance, being promoted to a job that you're qualified for or making a complete career switch. Just make sure each goal is specific, measureable, attainable, realistic, time bound, empowering, and constantly reviewed.

4. Create your plan of action

Your brain is designed to give you solutions and never stops thinking. Therefore it is essential for you to create a framework from which you can take actions. It is important for you to make one of the required steps you need to take to get your next year's goals and beyond career goals underway. Put them down on paper. Thinking about them will not deliver the results you are seeking. Once you have done this, and followed my plan, you will create goals and you will give yourself deadlines to follow, but keep them SMARTER. Remember that becoming the CEO of a company does not happen overnight, becoming a world top athlete requires a lot of training, effort and action.

5. **Stop thinking about tomorrow, and start thinking in the now**
Each day is a new opportunity for you to get a head start on your career goals. Make a list of career challenges to conquer and celebrate your achievements along the way. The small steps each day will lead to big accomplishments as the time goes on.

6. **De-clutter and get organized**
When I started to write this book I also started to decorate my apartment; in the first week when everything was a mess I couldn't get myself to a place in my mind to write. As I finished painting, reorganized things, cleared my desk, de-cluttered the space, the energy shifted and everything started to flow. Take time in the evening, early morning or during your vacation weeks to rearrange your space, files, as well as your work desk so that they are all more organized and efficient. Start by archiving anything you haven't sourced in the last year into a file cabinet further from your desk, leaving the files used daily closer and less cluttered.

7. **Get a good coach or a mentor**
Every athlete has a coach. Their success depends on it. In order to succeed you need someone to help you see your blind spots. If you want to outperform your peers, and want to accelerate your learning, you'll benefit from having someone support you in measuring your success, setting goals, and soliciting unbiased feedback. A good coach will also keep you accountable to your commitments, and help you stay on track.

8. **Follow through on actions**

Taking control of your career will not happen unless you follow through. Visualize your success regularly and don't be afraid to ask for help when necessary. More importantly, pursue your goals aggressively and resolve not to give up on reaching them.

Despite the fact I was a full-time student, I had no choice but to start my working life before I even started my university course. I did that as I had no money, family or friends that could support me. During the war I lost family, friends, and the sense of who I was. I simply had to take a lot of actions to get me where I am today.

I had no choice but to start working full time, save some money, and pay for the next five years of education. This was back in the early 1990s. Today, 23 years down the line, I am well equipped with the knowledge, the insights, and the strength required to help you get a head start on your career resolutions now. If you follow the method and insights shared in this book, and answer the questions presented throughout, this will be the year to reach your full potential and finally take charge of your career, your life and start doing what you love.

PHYSICAL

"To keep the body in good health is a duty...
otherwise we shall not be able to keep our mind
strong and clear."

Buddha

I have studied many disciplines, worked with many teachers, and read many books, and the reason I selected this quote is to inspire you, to start you on a journey to truly love, respect, and look after the body you are given so that it can serve you well into your old age.

When health is lost, we feel at our lowest. Sadly, for many it is only then that they start to appreciate their body and start telling themselves they will change. I would like you to imagine a moment in time when you too had a health challenge. Think about what you were feeling. What was happening when you could not do the things you wanted to do? When you could not love yourself because of the stupid things you did that led to the effects of your actions? Think of times when you experienced a physical illness. How did you truly feel?

With health, all taste of pleasure flies. You are vibrant, happy, and you feel you can take on the world. The problem is that you lower your natural defense mechanisms and start to put your body under unnecessary stress. You often start listening to it when it is too late, when the body has responded with an illness, or when you can't walk up the escalators as you exit the subway without losing your breath.

Did you know that you, just like the electric goods we have created, also run on electricity? You are not taught to think this way, though as you are about to discover, many different cultures across the globe name this energy: Electromagnetic, Chi, Prana, Reiki, all of which refer to your life force.

When you breathe, you breathe oxygen. Oxygen + energy travel together in the vehicle of the breath, hence breath is, quite literally, life.

Recently my path crossed with Alan Dolan, a talented man who teaches celebrities and many of his clients how to breathe. I was fascinated by his work as was he with my deep insights about life, the Elite Life Coaching and healing work that I do. He invited me to his Breathing Space retreat in Lanzarote for me to experience and learn his breathing technique and to do some coaching and energy work with him.

I learned quite a lot in a short period of time about breath and what was happening energetically in the lower parts of my body. Energetically speaking, you can have an energetic overload going on in the top half of your body when your mind becomes overstimulated. Simultaneously, you lack energy in the lower half of your body and become increasingly disassociated from the physical aspect of who you are. The less you feel and connect with your body, the less the body seems to be an integral part of you and the less attention and care you give to your body.

In our first breathing session together, Alan examined me and told me he would bring along Dennis to work on the lower part of my abdomen so that I could maximize the effects of Alan's breath work with him.

As I got to know Dennis better, I learned about his Dynamic Body release method, a way of repairing and rejuvenating the whole body. I felt I met two most amazing people who genuinely wanted to help me breathe better so that I could fully embody my healing gifts and help me unleash the power that was trapped behind my emotions.

What can happen over the years is that the muscles can become fused and the skeleton adopts unhealthy postures to compensate. This often results in pain. Pain can also be caused through the unhealthy build-up of toxins. This causes restricted blood flow, creating further pain.

Natural Dynamic Body Release works with a series of deep massage and movements that go deep into the body. As Dennis went deeper into my stomach he started to eliminate the build-up of toxins stored there over many years, and from what I was told it would stimulate blood flow so the body is able to repair and rejuvenate.

I learned this practice had been developed over 30 years. He began training and treating professional athletes who came to him with their injuries. Through my travels, my healing work evolved through gaining a deeper understanding of what creates and releases tension in the body. Dennis and Alan taught me another dimension to what is possible.

Not only does the technique help the muscle groups but also the nervous and lymphatic systems.

Being passionate about inspiring people to be authentic, reconnecting their body, mind, spirit and their hearts, when I met these two great individuals I knew they were equally passionate in what they did. They loved helping the body breathe properly and bringing the body back into a state of alignment so it could function the way it was designed to. I felt blessed that one coffee in King's Cross on a Sunday morning led to meeting, befriending and partnering up with two great health professionals. I love you and thank you!

As I continued to work with these two loving individuals, I had this moment of clarity when I could see how the combination of our skills could create a very powerful evolutionary retreat to help many around the world experience this transformation I was seeing in each one of us and the clients we were working with.

On my way back to London I felt rejuvenated, peaceful, and I could breathe deeper and better. At the airport I saw many people eating unhealthy food, feeling anxious, worried, and not wanting to go back to the places where they came from. It did make me wonder. We all came to the same place, but we all left the place feeling different.

I got inspired to do something about this. I partnered up with Alan and Dennis to create some powerful retreats around the world to help people create lasting transformational results in two weeks by bringing together our authentic gifts in one place.

Whenever you go on vacation you will see many people who don't take care of their body, mind or soul. The problem is when you neglect your physical body, you overeat. You make unconscious decisions that are viruses to your body, and start an emotional rollercoaster that takes you through places where you have access to all of your unhealthy eating habits, attitudes and behaviors.

In modern western society we deeply value good health, yet we have created a way of living so out of balance that damage to our long-term health is an inevitable result. You may rush around and push your body beyond its capacity. You might ignore your body's messages of pain and fatigue until they turn into serious medical problems. You seek quick fixes and ways to mask the symptoms so you can keep going, not wanting to lose an ounce of productivity.

I once worked with a very successful senior city executive whose life was so out of balance that he turned to crystal meth and cocaine to help him cope with the demands of his job, marriage, and his children. The day he collapsed at work and was taken to hospital is the day he called me from hospital and asked me to help him.

We embarked on a journey to help him get to the root issue of why he was doing this to his body. As we started to work on all of the issues that caused him to walk this path, he started to see how he did not love himself, and at the root of it all was his lack of self-esteem, self-belief, and his lack of confidence. He felt he couldn't be the guy that everyone perceived him to be.

As I helped him see this, he started to go deeper into himself and he started to address inner child issues that supported his attitudes, behaviors and the way he was feeling about himself.

In time he dissolved many of his emotions and we created empowering beliefs. I put him on a "body and mental" diet, and he started to appreciate and love himself more. We incorporated meditation into his daily routine and he started to change his attitude, his behaviors and the way he was treating his body.

Every time I would see him he would get excited on going deeper and learning more about his body's wisdom and how magically it integrated with his emotions, heart and spirit. A few months ago I received his email:

"Tony, the solution to my problems that you shared in our first consultation that 'illness is simply a blocked energy, and it manifests from not loving that part of ourselves, and the solution is a call for love' got me very angry that day as I could not see how I played an active part to bring myself to that state. Today a year down the line I am free from addictions, I have a new job, and I am consciously choosing how I live my life and what goes in my body. Your 'Illness=Lack of Love, Health=Call4Love' formula started to make sense. My family and I appreciate and love you for your wisdom and the healing you brought to me and my family. Thank you."

As you start seeing obstacles aren't there to be avoided but a great way for you to learn, shift and adapt to new ways of being, you will apply the right antidotes to help you get your body back to balance.

It seems you have forgotten the wisdom of the ages that good health is not just the absence of disease, but involves healthy lifestyle, healthy mental attitude, and healthy ways of relating to all living beings and nature.

Exercise for you

Take a moment and do a full inventory of your body. Be honest. Pay attention to that voice, and write down everything that comes up. Then score yourself from 1 to 10 where you are in the statements you come up with and create a plan that will support you to bring your body back to balance.

Be honest with yourself right now and ask yourself the following questions:

1. *What does it mean to be truly healthy?*
2. *Do I love, nurture, and look after my body?*
3. *How do I feel about my body right now?*
4. *What am I telling myself?*
5. *What excuses do I come up with when I am challenged to eat foods that I know are not good for me?*
6. *Am I exercising as much as I should?*
7. *Am I truly listening and acting on what my body is telling me?*

A full health check can help you see what your body is saying about you; it can be a harsh process to face the reality, though it is one that creates most shifts and results in your life when you face the problem head to head.

You can download a body awareness meditation to help you in this process at http://www.apathtowisdom.com/resources

Your body needs sleep; if you don't sleep well it's time to pay attention to why you are not sleeping well.

The way you feel about your body is another key obstacle to overcome. Looking after the body you need to support you through life is on its own a full-time job. Unless you start embedding in your day-to-day living behaviors and a mindset that support your body to function at optimum levels for the rest of your life, you will expose your body to a lot of unnecessary stress, illness and pressure.

Due to the body's ability to adapt, you may develop a lot of unhealthy habits which at some point in your life you will need to pay a therapist, doctor, or qualified professional to help you identify and bring your body back to its natural balance.

One thing that has helped me keep my balance is that I believe one third of whatever I take in is sufficient to maintaining my body to function at the optimum level. The rest, the two thirds that I take in, maintains the pharmaceutical industry, the doctors and the therapists. This has helped me over the years to eat balanced food, feed my mind with the right information, and be in environments where I feel great. I hope as you increase your awareness of what I have shared this will inspire you to act as fuel for your personal journey back to a balanced, healthy and purposeful life.

As a society we have evolved quite a lot and created many wonderful things, though at the same time we have also created many issues that can bring you out of balance in the way you live your life.

Look around you. Observe the many unhealthy people which is a global problem and one that many countries are trying to tackle. There is so much more obesity about nowadays than ever before. The foods we eat are full of chemicals. The jobs we do tend to tie us to our desk for over eight hours a day, and the way we feel about it all is what makes us increasingly do the things we don't want to do.

Your busy life takes over and you neglect the needs of your body. You stop exercising and you start taking it for granted. Before you know it you have created unhealthy habits, coping mechanisms, and you are constantly putting your body under additional stress.

As you do so, your body's intelligence will start the process of protecting itself as it is designed to do so by default. It has its own language, its own built-in alarm and self-defense mechanism to keep it safe. The problem becomes when you ignore this and you continue to be reckless with your body, when you don't truly listen to what your body's ALARM is warning you of.

Your body is trying to communicate with you so that you can change your behaviors, actions and your attitudes – so that you can keep your body at its optimum health. As you do so, your healthy body becomes a guest-chamber for the soul. If your body becomes sick, your soul becomes trapped in a self-made prison.

Listening to your body is all about acknowledging the feeling inside that knows this. If you are not feeling supercharged, excited and love yourself, then your body is not fully in that space. You know that you are not aligned to your optimum health. When you don't have that, that's when you have to look at your body's health and identify what requires attention on the physical level.

When you reach a point in life where you feel you are full of life, when you wake up feeling excited, energized, refreshed, and when you feel so full of energy and life, that's when you know you are perfectly healthy, looking after your body day in and day out, and have a zest for life.

I used to be one of those people who didn't put health as a priority in life. I was a workaholic. When it got to work, the things that were on my mind were:

"Oh... I have to finish this! It doesn't matter what time I have my meal and sleep."

When it suited me, on occasion I also used to be a lazy kind of person too. I was the kind of person who just didn't like to sit tight or lie about all day unless I had no other options. If I could, in every second of my life I wanted to do something. From hanging out, watching movies, talking – I did everything I could to avoid doing nothing. I never gave my body time to rest and recuperate.

Sometimes I would even wake up and not eat until midday, knowing I had a PT session booked and that my body required fuel. Even though I knew this, I still went ahead and had my PT session.

I would be asked to join friends in exciting activities and even if I felt very tired or I had just got home, I would still go. I could be sick, but I wouldn't care because my motto was "As long as I can stand, let's rock it!"

The only thing that mattered was my will. When I wanted to, I would work my body to the limit, so that I finished all my tasks and activities within a day!

Sometimes it would take more than eight hours a day to finish all my work. I would work until 3am or later, sleep for two hours or less, and the cycle went on and on. I knew my meals, working hours and sleep cycle weren't healthy.

At first, it was okay for me and it didn't matter because my belief was that if I got sick, there was always the hospital. It wasn't until I was made redundant that I had time to reflect. How over the years I had ignored my body. How I worked on average 14+ hours a day, and how I was eating unhealthy snacks throughout the day to cope. I started to realize how important it is to take care of your body. I started to love myself.

You know you only get one body, right? Unlike a computer, which if it breaks, you can fix it, or buy a new one. But your body, once it breaks down beyond repair you can't replace it.

Have you ever wondered how much the people around you love you? You might not realize it but it's true! Especially your family and your loved ones.

If you get sick, it will burden your family, friends and your employer. It may impact them physically, emotionally, or financially. Just one you could affect hundreds, thousands or even millions of people. So your body matters just like everything else on our planet.

A while back I saw a special screening of the documentary *Food Matters*. The gist of the film is that our medical system at the moment is not good at dealing with diseases. We focus on symptoms rather than the root cause of the problem. The main point being that doctors rarely consider nutrition as a cure or preventative solution. Instead it's often about cutting things out of the body, radiation treatments or drug therapies after the fact.

The drug companies like this because they can sell more. With a culture like ours, which reacts to problems after they occur and then treats them using drugs, we have created an environment for a billion dollar industry to deal with the symptoms and not address the illness. We tend to think about popping a pill when something is wrong, rather than tackling the root cause of diseases and maintaining a healthy diet.

Food Matters looks at nutrition – the food we eat – as the best prevention and cure for health issues. It's ridiculous how much sense this makes, yet people don't follow the advice.

Your body is also the key ingredient for business success. You might think the answer is marketing, customer service or a superior product, but for every business, the key ingredient is people. If you don't have healthy functioning people, then your business won't thrive.

For the home-based business, solo entrepreneur or professional blogger, it matters even more because you work independently as the main cog that keeps your business going. If you can't work, you can't earn a living.

The message in *Food Matters* is a simple one: eat organic foods. If you can, eat raw foods, and add superfoods to your diet too. Look to food as the best prevention and even the cure to any ailments you suffer from.

I'm not saying take on board the ideas in the documentary as fact; make your own mind up. The core message – you are what you eat – is so obvious, yet it needs to be stated. Even those of us with the best intentions have trouble sticking to healthy eating all the time.

Let me ask you a question: How hard is it for you to stay healthy? You can adopt healthy food habits, exercise regularly, eat the right food, and relax your body by listening to some meditation or classical music. Your personal development also plays an important part in this process. For example, as you manage your negative self-talk better, you are able to have a good night's sleep.

Balance is very important for your body. You can eat organic food, do yoga, Pilates, swim, meditate, breathe, go for bike rides and rollerblade. I like to get at least six hours of sleep and when I don't I make sure I don't feel bad about it. The way I do this is to use a lot of distraction techniques. One is to put on your favorite music and start dancing.

Recently I crossed paths with Adam Frewer, a vegan specialist who's inspired me to reflect upon my eating habits. He helped me see how I could further improve my health through adopting vegetarianism and being a vegan as a lifestyle choice.

All of this results in a productive work day and thus benefits my business too. I have plenty of energy, feel great, and my clients also benefit from my state of being.

Sadly, if you neglect your body, you won't live long enough to pay off the mortgage, or you will be selling the house for your medical bills. There's definitely a need to readjust priorities.

What's the point of working yourself so hard that you're unwell by the time you achieve anything? It's a lot smarter to invest your financial success first into your lifestyle. How you think, feel, live and what you eat must come before anything else.

The problem, as always, is that you sometimes don't see a correlation between eating healthy today and not getting sick tomorrow. You eat badly, don't feel 100%, but get by, popping a pill to deal with ailments. Do this long enough and eventually you get a major breakdown.

Stress is an issue too, hence that last point in my list above about balance is very important. If you don't take the time to become aware of your bad habits and force change, it might take something more uncomfortable for you to finally take notice.

When I worked in IT, my motto was always "prevention is better than cure." This kept the company operating at 99.99% of the time as it was always better than trying to fix something that was broken.

One of the key determinants for success with your business is your ability to work consistently and productively. The time you spend working should be purposeful, efficient, concentrated and focused. You enjoy leveraged outcomes from short bursts of high-return activities.

In order for you to be able to do this you have to be healthy. It's wise to adopt the motto above to maintain a healthy body. You need to be able to think straight throughout the day, avoiding a drop in energy by the time the afternoon rolls around. Your body can't be slowing you down with aches and pains.

You don't have to be perfect, but you have to make smart decisions when in a position to do so. Starting with what you eat is the easiest place to make an adjustment, followed by how you work and how often you exercise.

Exercise for you

Take a look at your day.

1. *What do you eat?*
2. *How often do you eat?*
3. *How long do you work?*
4. *What do you work on?*
5. *When do you exercise and how often?*
6. *Do you take time to relax?*
7. *Are you prioritizing material possessions over healthy eating and living?*

Sadly, a lot of people are driven by a mad scramble to accumulate as much wealth as possible. They are addicted to the short-term adrenaline rush that comes from making money or achieving a goal. Buying a car or house is a fine motivator, but it should not push you to the point of sacrificing your body so you can get to these goals faster.

If you feel a little out of balance, start by raising your awareness in the thing you feel out of balance in. Then stop for a minute today or tomorrow and take a look at your behavior – in particular what you eat. It's never too late to slow down and adjust your priorities.

FINANCIAL

"Don't stay in bed until you can wake up and know you made money while in bed."

Tony J Selimi

Life is indeed full of choices and illusions. What I know today is this: if you do not examine your choices and the illusions you create, they can take you far, far away from your intended path. They can take you away from living an abundant life, the life in which money does not cause you any worry. What do you think about when money comes up? Is money scarce for you right now? Or, do you have enough, perhaps wanting more?

If you look around you, the simple truth is money, as well as everything you want and need, is available to you. And there's always enough. Maybe you are at a point in your life where you can't see it, maybe you don't know how to earn it, or maybe you feel you have not got enough skills, experience or knowledge, but it is there. Do you ever wonder why for some people money flows easily and for you it does not?

You are the creator of your life, you determine how you live your life; you also play a major role in your financial success. Just the way you create experiences such as going to the movies, meeting a friend for a drink, or even booking a plane to go on vacation, you can create your financial success. The only truth here is that right now you may not be fully aware of how to go about doing it.

As you have learned so far, you are energy and you know this energy carries a lot of information including the information that gives and receives money. As you shift your frequency to the amount of money you want to attract, you will see how easily money starts to flow in your life.

You stop chasing money. You start doing things that bring tremendous value to others, and the higher this value is, the higher you start to vibrate. As you do so, you start riding the vibrational frequency in which abundance lives.

You have a set of values by which you operate. Beliefs that are deeply rooted in your subconscious mind, and feelings through which you interpret what money is to you. You always think about something, but you are probably not conscious about what you think. You don't truly pay attention to your thoughts and as a result of this, the way you see the world influences the way you think, act and create your world.

If you don't know what money truly means to you, what your own self-worth is, and you are not clear about the value you give to the world, you will not know how to go about creating it and will continue to experience financial struggles. Instead of remaining in this space you can increase your awareness, learn, and take command of your thoughts and actions so that you can change it.

You may want more money, though you never spend the time required for you to do a financial inventory of your life, both inside and outside of you. What I mean by this is how you feel and think about money has a knock-on effect on your financial future. By reviewing the spending and borrowing habits you have developed over time, you can see how you act with money. You may outwardly acknowledge your desire for great wealth but feel inwardly guilty about acquiring it.

Life obstacles or barriers can truly stop us from attracting money. Let's look and divide them into two categories: external and internal. External barriers are obstacles that exist outside of us. For example, recession, having little money, lack of transportation, no job opportunities, lack of time or being involved in unhealthy relationships are all forms of external barriers. They are things in life that get in the way of us building the life we want and meeting our goals.

In addressing any money obstacle, internal or external, it is important first to identify the barrier in question. This can be done through self-monitoring.

The best way to solve a problem is to break it down into smaller steps. For example, let's say that you want to have $5,000 a year in savings, but you notice that to begin with this feels like a large amount of money. The obstacle here is you don't feel like having enough money left at the end of the month for you to save.

To overcome this obstacle you might create a budget to see where you can save money during the week. You might explore other places where you can get cheaper (but still healthy) food. You might also find ways to make some extra money during the week (for example, working overtime or taking on an additional shift).

As you become clear where your money is going, you will also be clear how you can cut down things that can help you save $5,000 a year. You start a month at a time, and eventually this becomes your new habit. This leads you to start believing that this goal is now attainable.

Internal barriers are those obstacles that exist in us. You learn a lot about the world you live in from your parents, culture and society. Old conscious or subconscious beliefs that you hold on to, that you keep repeating to yourself over and over, is what keeps you in the "poor me" mindset and you continue to put your life on snooze mode.

Coupled with anxiety, the fears of not good enough, of there is not enough, unpleasant thoughts and memories, shame, sadness, hopelessness, your competitive or comparative nature or low motivation is what truly holds you back from living an abundant life. All of that is in the energy you carry with you wherever you go. This is all due to not knowing your passion, your self-worth, and your own authenticity.

You may notice some of the following thoughts such as:

"I can't do this, I am not worthy, money does not grow on trees, it's hard to make money."

"There is no point, things will never change, only rich people make money, I am not lucky enough."

"If I have money I feel I should hold on to it."

"I am scared to let it go."

"I have lived so far struggling for money, having bits of money, living day by day, pay check to pay check."

"I really want to quit my job, but I just can't afford to because I don't have enough money in savings yet."

Having those thoughts and beliefs in your head are at the root cause of why you may experience a lack when it comes to having and attracting money. Overcoming internal barriers that prevent you from being abundant is harder. However, it is important to remember that internal barriers aren't really barriers.

Even though emotions and thoughts such as those described above can be very frightening, unpleasant and uncomfortable, when it comes to what you truly think and feel about money, you are the one who is still in control of your behavior. Therefore, the best way to overcome an internal financial barrier is to move forward regardless of what you are experiencing on the inside. The more you can do this, the less those emotions and thoughts will feel like barriers.

Now, this is easier said than done. As you work toward overcoming internal barriers, start practicing healthy ways of managing your emotions and thoughts. Different coping strategies can be used to help increase your tolerance of certain emotions and thoughts. Use what works for you.

It is important to start moving toward your goals instead of waiting for the emotions and thoughts to go away first. It can take some time for our emotions and thoughts to change. However, we always have control over our behaviors, and most people notice that their emotions and thoughts change quicker if they take action first.

Addressing internal barriers requires a willingness to experience your emotions and thoughts about money. The more you do so, the easier it will become. In addressing internal barriers, you are essentially making a choice to let your goals and values drive your behaviors.

Let me share with you Ben's journey on overcoming the internal and external barriers he used to face that prevented him from attracting money. Our paths crossed during the time I was volunteering for the London 2012 Olympic Games. We connected instantly and kept in touch. One day I got a call and he was ready to start his coaching journey.

At that time he was doing some escorting work, he was also in a relationship which had a lot of conflicts, and it was the reason why he needed my help. He was ready to change his life around from being a struggle to creating a life that he wanted deep down but did not give himself the permission to have.

I remember in our first session together we took an inventory of the eight key areas of his life: spiritual, mental, emotional, physical, career/business, money, relationship, and love. His initial clarity discovery session helped him see the obstacles he was facing and how the problems in each area of his life affected the choices he was making. He also saw how he had adopted the "poor me" mindset to cope.

For as long as he could remember, money had always been a big issue for him. He graduated with honors in Nutrition. When he left university he struggled to find employment. Luckily at that time, the partner that he dated asked him to move in. Not only did he not pay rent, but also his partner was helping him financially. They do say everything has a start and an end. For him the lifestyle he was living ended when his partner moved back to Australia.

Suddenly he was left to his own devices. He faced many financial obstacles, and was afraid to ask his parents for help. He felt ashamed of his relationship failing and he couldn't tell his parents. He became withdrawn, felt embarrassed, and few people knew what was truly happening to him. He moved into a bedsit and started to panic about how he would pay his rent and how he would find money to live. He started to experience a social anxiety and the thought of going to interviews terrified him.

He knew if he wanted to remain independent he needed to come up with a way of making money fast. He was approached a few times to do some escorting work and this became the way he could pay his way in life. Years went by and he started to look for a way to change his life and move away from escorting. One day working out at the gym, a few people told him he would be a great personal trainer. He played with the idea and months later he became one.

Although he qualified, his next obstacle was he did not know how to build the business and he felt he needed to continue to do both jobs.

As we started to work together, he shifted the way he was feeling about himself. As his self-worth increased he started to see the value he brings to his clients through training them outdoors as well as through the boot camps he was delivering for other people.

In one of our coaching sessions as I helped him create the different products he could deliver, for the first time his eyes were tearful as he got the clarity of his earning potential. He felt empowered on how to go about it, and started to see he was able to create the wealth and the stability he so wanted.

Having created the vision, each time I would see him he took the actions that we discussed in each session and things started to move in his life. This led to him creating a clear plan of where he wanted to take his life and the Breakthrough Boot Camp was born.

As time went on, he felt empowered. His confidence increased. He could see many other ways to create an income. He let go of his escorting, and he focused on building his successful personal training business.

No matter who you are, you too can change your financial blueprint. I have seen it over and over again with many clients that I have helped become money magnets. When you don't anticipate, don't plan ahead, you can't potentially imagine your future.

Internal barriers are important to identify and address as they often feel overwhelming, insurmountable and can stop you in your tracks. As you overcome those, you start feeling a sense of purpose, direction, and worthiness.

On the other hand, when it comes to overcoming an external obstacle, you want to identify a number of small steps that you can take to make your way over the barrier and move closer to your financial goal. Some of the steps you take may produce immediate results; however, some barriers are larger and may take more time, such as going back to school and getting a degree.

Therefore, it is important to be patient. Trust and stay on task. It might take some time to reach your financial goal. With every step you take, the more you are living your life in a way that is consistent with your ultimate goal, the more you start manifesting the money that you need to fulfill that vision.

As I stated before, obstacles are going to come up, including money. Your goal is to have the best tool to use when those challenges arise.

You often measure your success through comparing yourself with others around you, through the amount of money you make or don't make, or through the things you may or may not have in your life. This creates a reality in which you start vibrating in the energy of perceived lack.

If you try to create from this space, you will always create more lack of what you are trying to create. You may have learned this when you were extremely young by observing your parents' behaviors, attitudes and beliefs. This then gets deeply rooted in your subconscious mind, and in line with the Law of Attraction you start creating a life in which you experience lack.

Deep down you may feel unworthy of receiving – something that could have been ingrained in you since you were a kid. You may tend to go spending money on things that you might think will make you feel happier, make you feel worthy, or feel loved.

The number of goods and services you have available to spend your money on is infinite.

When I met Tom, an entrepreneur who owns a few start-up companies, he spent most of his income on addictions, psychic lines and alcohol. He had little respect for the money he was earning. He had no financial goals in life, and he was in tremendous amounts of debt.

Using TJS Evolutionary Method he addressed his internal demons as well as the external obstacles that contributed to him creating the life he was living.

He self-actualized how all the external barriers he faced related to the way he was feeling in his inner world. The money he was making he was spending to overcome the nightmares and fantasies residing in his memory and his imagination. As he faced everything he did not love, he started to experience fewer and fewer obstacles until the time came when he embraced his true self and started to focus his thoughts upon balanced and loving actualities and moved away from unbalanced and elating delusions.

Attracting wealth and money is perhaps the most confusing subject to mankind ever. For most people it is also one of the key problems in their life. Just look at how most of humanity is poor, while a small group of people accumulates 90% of the wealth in the world (isn't this just ridiculous and absurd?!).

Making money is not just numbers or business acumen. If you understand metaphysics and are able to see how money is just energy, you can attract more wealth quickly and easily. The inner conflict between your desire to give and receive, as well as your spiritual and material beliefs of the good and the bad about money, stunt your growth in both spiritual and material matters. It creates an almost incapacitating poverty complex that may block your future opportunities and fortunes.

I hear many limiting beliefs about money. The one that holds most people back is the belief that you cannot make money doing what you love, and aren't able to turn your dreams into a reality!

Letting go of this perception can help you release your millionaire mind, simply by learning these golden secrets! Learning secrets you probably never even dreamed existed! Learning wealth creation secrets so incredibly powerful starts by truly knowing your self-worth and loving oneself. As you start loving who you are, you will feel more empowered to transform your financial life.

In 2009 I was going through a lot of changes in my personal and professional life. Although I was an extremely confident and easy-going chap, always helping everyone, when I faced my redundancy I realized my biggest obstacle. My entire life depended on the pay check I would receive once a month. I also realized that up to that point I was a giver and found it hard to receive when I would meet with friends or be out and about. I also had no clear financial goals or saving plans, and I was living my life according to my monthly income. It was the awakening that helped get me on my journey to create the freedom, the wealth, and the job I now love doing.

Asking for help can be humiliating, embarrassing, and you might feel you are a failure, although at some point in your life you must seek help. Over the years I studied many disciplines and I remember it was really hard to tell myself I needed help as I would often justify to myself that I could do it alone.

Yes, you can learn a lot on your own. But the investments I made, in training at the Smart School of Coaching (now the Animas Institute), hiring a life coach, attending DeMartini's Breakthrough Experience and attending Martin Brofman's Body Mirror System of Healing workshops, have been invaluable to my growth.

Trusting my decisions, letting go of the fear of not having enough money to pay for all of this set me free from the inner prison I was then living in. Synchronicities led me to meeting some amazing people. Each one helped me embrace my true potential and overcome the mental and emotional barriers that prevented me from seeing life and the bigger vision. I started to truly shift and change my life.

I remember one night I could not sleep. I was stressed and I spent hours in trying to understand why I was feeling the way I was feeling. Thank God for the internet and my big friend Google. I started to search online for some sort of meditation to help me figure out my feelings, create some sort of miracle that would get me out of the situation I was facing, and help me fall asleep. With the many solutions I found, I was presented with another obstacle. I could not make up my mind about which one to purchase.

Having used the Silva Method in my early thirties, I decided to purchase their full program. As I added it to the shopping basket I was presented with many more products to help me with everything I was experiencing that evening. It was as if they went into my head and knew all of my problems. For each of my problems there was another product, another meditation, and another book to buy.

When you feel desperate, hopeless, and emotional you would do anything to get you back on track, right? I can tell you for sure, pain sells. When you are in pain, you spend the money you sometimes don't even have to overcome it. Can you see yourself there?

I went ahead and bought quite a few products to help me get myself out of a situation which at that time looked like it was "mission impossible." By the time I clicked the checkout button I realized I needed to spend $2,200, and if I did not buy the products together they would cost me over $5,000. What do you think I did at 2am when I was at my lowest and had no one to call? Yes, you guessed it, I went ahead and purchased all the products that were going to help me "fix" my life.

I achieved my goal. Having listened to a few meditations I eventually fell asleep and felt better when I woke up. Although I remembered what I had done last night, it daunted me that I had spent so much money the night before and that I had no job to go to. The money I had received from being made redundant I had already spent on paying my credit card bills, family commitments, engagement, and vacations and I started to worry even more. How will I pay for everything that I had purchased? They do say a fortune is born out of every misfortune that happens to us.

This is the night that changed the way I looked at money forever. It made me realize that money does not mean doing a 9 to 5 job. The person who created the products that I purchased was sleeping at a time I was spending thousands of dollars.

This is the moment I said to myself: What a great way to live your life! You make money while you are asleep and at the same time you sell products and services to help people overcome their issues. At that point I asked myself a question: What do I have to offer the world? What solutions can I give that will help someone like me, and how am I going to achieve this?

I made a decision to learn, understand and change my own financial blueprint. I decided I wanted to create a life where I create wealth while I am sleeping, and do all the things that I love and enjoy when I am awake.

I promised myself that I would work as hard as I needed to until I achieved this. I decided I would not stay in bed until I could stay in bed and make money.

This moment in time changed the way I think about money for life. I started to learn, read, and understand how I too can make money while I am asleep.

In 2013 I decided to join Daniel Priestley's KPI Program which helped me clarify my pitch, write this book, create products, learn about the importance of your online profile and how to go about creating the partnerships you need to grow.

The KPI community helped me see the mountain of value I was sitting on. I made some great new partnerships, inspiring friends, and many of the people I met started to call me for coaching and healing work. Not only did I gain much from this process, I also saw great returns on the money I invested. If you are from the KPI community and reading this, I would like to thank you for your love, kindness, and for trusting me to be your coach, healer and inspired friend and teacher. Thank you for believing in me and my mission.

I believed since I was very young that the greatest wealth is your health. As I saw my own value, I saw the value I gave to others, and my business grew exponentially.

For many people, January is littered with a motley assortment of resolutions and it's the best time for you to also start thinking about your financial success.

Yet most likely January passes, other things take priority and you continue to live your life being careless about money. You make the same mistakes, due to the pressure of the vacation season and the need to buy gifts, you spend money you don't have, and you don't want to face this situation.

What happens is you enter a saving mode for the next few months and start denying yourself the things you want. What if you don't need to live this way? What if there was a better way for you to not make the money mistakes? What if you could earn money from multiple sources of income? What if you are the one who blocks your own flow of abundance?

One day I was talking to my very good friend Marcello about how upbringing, culture and parents play a major role in the way you make, spend and deal with money. Just like my parents, his parents instilled in him the following belief: "don't spend money you don't have." We both grew up with this belief to be the truth.

In his early professional life, this led him to work very hard and live his life according to his means. It also laid the foundation he needed for him to start saving money for retirement.

By the time he was 30 he had one year's net salary in his savings account. Achieving the financial goal he set himself gave him a good feeling of security and the freedom to not have to ask for money from anyone. This also helped him keep a simple lifestyle and he spent the money that only brought real value to his life.

He bought his first car in cash. Some years later he also bought his first apartment in cash. The belief instilled in his early childhood kept him from not living a life in which he bought goods by borrowing money.

Although at first this belief appears to be one that gave him the life he now enjoys, the same belief hindered him in making a choice and the decision that sometimes it's okay to borrow money. For example, if you want to start your own business, buy a second property, or help family and friends when faced with difficult situations. He realized that true value and how money can be earned or used does not necessarily need to be cash. It can also come from borrowing as long as there is the right balance between making, borrowing, and spending money.

As time passed by, he also realized that sometimes what you spend money on and the value you get from what you spend is very different. The most valuable lesson he shared with me is that money made, borrowed or spent is best when they are all serving a bigger purpose.

Money on its own will not make you happy; money in your savings account might give you some feelings of security. The greatest part of it is using it in a way to do good for yourself and others. This could be something as simple as rewarding yourself once a month and having a great massage. Maybe once a year you treat yourself to a great relaxing vacation, or even helping charities, family and friends.

As we finished our conversation we concluded that money matters. Keep it simple. Keep track of your income and expenditure. Increase your self-worth and the value you give to the world, and make sure you use the money to do good for yourself and others.

If you're ready to gain mastery of your financial success, the TJS Evolutionary Method: Money Magnet workshop will help you become the truth of your experience. You will hear the money ALARMs that are ringing. You will learn how to empower yourself, switch off the "poor me" button and switch on the "I'm a money magnet" button.

For more information about this and other workshops please visit **http://www.apathtowisdom.com/workshops**

This process will take you to your next level of financial success, prosperity, and abundance. The more you learn it, the more your journey to success becomes effortless, joyful, and trustworthy.

The world may revolve around love, but I'd be lying if I said that money wasn't important. Money is important. Money is how we can objectively trade value for value without resorting to bartering.

For some people more money may mean more problems, but most of us would rather have more of it than less. I imagine you know what it's like to not have enough for what you want to be able to do.

You've got bills to pay, mouths to feed, people to medicate, addictions to feed (I'm talking about cheese, cakes or chocolate of course!) and countless other little necessities that somehow add up to more than your income. At the end of the month you're left wondering where the hell it all went. (Ever done your taxes and wonder what you have left to show for tens of thousands of dollars?)

So when someone like me comes around telling you to quit your job and follow your heart, you want to drop everything you're doing and punch me in the face with the force of all the practicalities weighing down on you.

I know the feeling.

By all means I'm not a financial expert; however, I do know what it's like to be a regular person with little to no money. In 1990 I arrived in the UK with $400 in my pocket, no job, no education, and no friends I could turn to for help, and today I run a very successful Elite Life Coaching practice.

I know what it's like to want for more. I know what it's like to not have a job, no prospects, a poorly formulated financial plan, and not have enough in savings.

I also know what it's like to trust myself, to be all right, regardless of all the forces against me, regardless of the odds. I know what it takes to make it happen.

Intangible obstacles are those that live in our mind that are the most challenging to overcome. In my experience, these are the only real financial obstacles standing between you and the pursuit of living. Everything else you can figure out easily as long as your head is in the right place.

Adjusting your standards will help you determine where you place your priorities. And what takes priority depends on what you value the most. Whatever you value will be what's most important to you, and that's where you'll put most of your attention, focus and energy.

Imagine what would happen if you made happiness and/or fulfillment your highest value. How would your life change if your priority was always on your mental and emotional well-being? How would your decisions change? What would you start doing? What would you stop doing? What new attitudes would you develop?

This is fundamental to your growth. It's also really hard to do. It mostly has to do with creating a new habit and sticking to it. Over time, you will start to make decisions automatically based on your new set of priorities.

The best way to describe this mindset change is when someone has a near death experience, or when someone finds out they're terminally ill, and all of a sudden the things they thought were so important before feel empty and meaningless.

What really changed? Nothing changed. Only their attitude toward life changed and that's everything.

I went cycling around Vietnam and Cambodia to raise funds for Parkinson's UK and traveled through some of the most exotic parts of both countries and saw how people lived there. The level of happiness that children and the local people had who greeted us along the path we cycled was something to admire and enjoy.

I did ask the question: Why is it that some people are perfectly happy living in a metal hut on a dirty river with a lot of children while others would be miserable in anything less than a 400 square foot air-conditioned apartment by the river? They have two different standards. You can get whatever you want in life by raising or lowering yours. By changing what you value most in life.

I have had so many coaching consultations in which clients tell me "I want financial security." Creating a false sense of security by trying to get as much money as you can in order to feel safe is a mind trap that keeps you away from your true values. The fear of the future, not planning your life for the moment at the expense of future security, comes from not trusting your ability to manifest.

You learn to distrust yourself as you link the security of self with money energy. When there is a flow you feel secure about yourself, and then when there is a lack of money you start feeling badly about yourself. You start putting things off for another day, and the more you do that, the wider the gap you create between you and your financial goals.

You may not have been taught the importance of savings in your life, living a lifestyle beyond your capital ability, and the impact that living a lifestyle beyond your needs has on your life.

If you don't know this, then answer some of the key questions raised so far. Get to know what you truly want, then prioritize what is really important. Is a vacation or financial security more important to you? As you learn what you value the most through this process, you start to prioritize.

Being out of control and spending money you don't have on shopping, not knowing how to deal with that, can bring you to a range of financial problems. To create a balance and overcome the problem of being out of control with your spending, understand your feelings. Get to know your spending habits, and learn how to let go of the illusion that you would feel better about yourself by buying goods and services that you don't value or need. This will help you unleash your true potential.

You may experience that money seems to never be enough; it somehow has its own legs and escapes you. If you always feel like you don't have enough or that you want to be earning more, there is something deeper you need to uncover. You may have old beliefs and experiences that might be forcing you to operate from a place of "lack."

I have helped many clients raise their self-worth. If the service you provide is undervalued, you start to resent yourself, your client and what you are offering. I once worked with a personal trainer who delivered a lot of PT sessions for little pay. As we looked deeper into what was happening to him, he recognized that he resented giving his best to clients and not being paid a lot for his sessions.

As I helped him increase his self-worth, his net worth started to increase. He started to attract clients who paid in advance and promptly. He got to this place by putting money, self-love and well-being as his highest value.

The bottom line is, I don't know about every financial obstacle in the world. I also don't know about every single financial consequence. But what I do know is that money is energy. Everything around you is energy. Your job is to learn how to attract it in the form you want – in this case, money.

Most people around you rely on one source of income, one tap; when this tap dries out, the fear, panic and doubt kicks in. If you only have one source of income with no backup plan, and you experience a job loss or other emergency, your life could be turned completely upside down.

If you're a proactive person, you will foresee this issue and start creating multiple income streams, cutting back your lifestyle, or taking out more life insurance coverage. You won't always be able to prepare for everything life throws at you, but you can definitely prepare for it better.

Lastly, positive psychology has helped me a lot in focusing on the positives. When was the last time you counted your blessings?

Let me share with you a Chinese proverb that I love: "If you want one year's prosperity, grow seeds, if you want 10 years' prosperity, grow trees, and if you want a hundred years of prosperity, grow people."

Exercise for you

Let's look at how we can get you on track to a brighter fiscal future. You can use these powerful questions to create tasks that will set you up to have great financial success. There is no better day than today to start. What are you waiting for?

Let's go:

1. *What external financial barriers do you face in your life right now?*

2. *Does your job pay you what you are worth?*

3. *Do you need more money than you currently spend?*

4. *Do you feel your current financial situation interferes with you building the life you want to live?*

5. *Do you have a financial plan?*

6

6. *What do you tell yourself when money problems arise?*

7. *Are your decisions aligned with the money you want to make?*

8. *Is spending by borrowing money you don't have your way of living?*

9. *Do you easily get influenced by adverts to spend money?*

10. *Have you got any emergency funds?*

11. *Are you in a personal relationship where your values, beliefs, behaviors, and attitudes don't team up financially?*

12. *Who is making the buying decisions, your emotions or you?*

Here are some powerful affirmations to help you become a money magnet. Use these words of wisdom daily:

- I do what I love and love what I do

- I am worthy of love

- I am a money magnet, genius, and I apply my money magnet wisdom

- I pay myself first no matter what

- I manage money wisely, so I attract money easily

- My balanced heart and mind bring me financial freedom

- Every day I raise my standards and quality

- I plant loads of business flowers so there is no room for weeds

That's the key to conquering anything in life including how to make money from loving what you do: be someone who's a problem solver, who's proactive and not reactive, and someone who brings tremendous value to others.

RELATIONSHIP

"Truth is, I'll never know all there is to know about you just as you will never know all there is to know about me. Humans are by nature too complicated to be understood fully. So, we can choose either to approach our fellow human beings with suspicion or to approach them with an open mind, a dash of optimism and a great deal of candor."

Tom Hanks

Building a relationship with yourself and others is the fun and the complicated part of your life.

As I was growing up, my parents instilled a belief that helped me overcome many of the challenges you are about to read when it comes to relationships. They used to say to me: "If a window in our house is smashed, if a light bulb burns out, or when the washing machine stops working, we do not go and buy a whole new house to fix the few issues, we fix it. As you do so, you start to build genuine, real, loving, kind, and fulfilled relationships."

Your belief, culture, upbringing, and society influence the way you see your relationships. However, what matters is what you consciously choose to take and make work for you. When those beliefs don't serve you anymore, you do exactly what you do with your rubbish: recycle them.

Throughout your life you will have only two kinds of relationships: one is the one with yourself, and the other is the one you have with your outer world.

The relationship with others is extremely important to our day-to-day experience of life; however your relationship with yourself is what helps you dissolve the barriers that keep you from recognizing the love that already is, and expressing the love you ultimately are to yourself and the world you live in.

I have spent years in studying and understanding the hidden to the eye relationships that exist inside of me. I have also worked with hundreds of clients who find it hard to get to the root of the issues that cause them the most distress, conflict, or that they feel emotional about.

One thing you need to accept is that your relationships are just like the universe: they will expand and contract. What I mean by that is you may have times of growth where every relationship you have, internal or external, you feel is constantly growing, and then you may also have times when they are contracting, shrinking, or disappearing.

The other thing is that your relationships over a period of time will evolve and grow proportionally with your personal growth and your awareness of self and the world around you.

You may want to spend time knowing this about yourself, but your busy life takes over and you start to neglect this. The other problem is that the world you live in throws many good and bad things at you. You also came into this world with no instructions on how to build those relationships; imagine what your life would be like if you truly had a manual you could refer to?

No one taught you how to relate to yourself and gain clarity on how your body, mind, emotions, heart and spirit communicate with you and what they are trying to tell you. You cannot blame your parents, your society, or anyone for that matter. What you can do is take ownership of you, no matter what.

You spend most of your time communicating externally. No wonder as time passes you stop paying attention to your relationship with yourself. Just in the way you forget a language you learned at school when you don't practice it, in the same way, with time you forget to listen to your body's own communication with you.

This is one of the greatest obstacles to overcome, as when we were born we did not come with an instruction manual that we can refer to when we go astray from truly loving ourselves.

Having a great relationship with self is what love is. It is your objective, whether you are aware of it or not. Over and over when I coach clients on why they do what they do in life, as I go beyond any answer they give me, we end up with the word LOVE.

How much time a day do you spend learning about your relationship with your own spirit, body, mind, feelings, and your heart?

This relationship with self has a massive impact on your well-being. When you keep pressing the snooze button and you start to ignore all of the ALARMs that your body gives you, you have just broken this relationship. The result of your conscious or subconscious decisions to behave this way is that your spirit starts to distrust your ability to manage your body, the vessel through which your spirit manifests in this physical form.

The more you do this, the greater the level of distrust within you grows, which then reflects in your outer experience of the world and the way you build your relationships with people you love, and with whom you work and socialise.

The relationship you have with yourself represents your inner journey. Learning and getting to know you in the way your body, mind, emotions and heart operate, integrate, and communicate. Your body comes with great God-given intelligence. The question I have for you is: Why do you fear, ignore, and stop your relationship with you?

The problem is most people are trying very hard to build a happy relationship with themselves. If you only look for happiness, you are only looking for half fulfillment. If you seek the sadness and try to build a relationship with that part of you, you are still only chasing the other half of fulfillment. True fulfillment comes from you acknowledging both sides of yourself.

When you do so, your relationship with self becomes loving. You accept the good and the bad about you. The attractive and repulsive side of you. The pain and the pleasure relationship you have with yourself. If you think there is something wrong with you when you experience one side of an emotion, thought or a feeling, you are not seeing the bigger picture; it is the way you are designed.

I have not heard of or met any person who can claim 100% that they are happy, fulfilled, joyful, trustworthy and loving. Not even the likes of the Dalai Lama or people like him that you might imagine have something you don't. It is an illusion to think this way. Everything in this world has two sides. If we observe nature, we have drought and we have a rainy season, we have the sun and the moon, we have light and we also have darkness, and you could go on.

There is a greater intelligence that created who you are. Trust it. You are a part of it, and you have been made by the same energy that creates everything and nothing.

When you lose your relationship with yourself, you tend to ignore parts of you that you have disowned. People who push your buttons most are there to point this out to you, they are your teachers, thank them right now. As you get to own that part of you that you feel discomfort about – let's say anger, sadness, or frustration – each time you are being challenged, those emotions surface as it is the only way in which your body knows how to communicate with you to bring your unequal perceptions back into equilibrium.

Go within the next time you feel any discomfort next to someone – when you go on a date, when you are with your lover, family or friends – and see why it is you react the way you do. As you raise your awareness, knowledge and learn about yourself, you will stop blaming them as people who pushed your buttons and you will start to appreciate them for being your teachers. You will start loving them for increasing your awareness about you, and the parts of you that you have lied about and don't love.

Initially you may find it hard to change years of learned behaviors, thoughts, beliefs, feelings, and the residue that your experiences have left deep inside of you. As your relationship with you improves, and you take full ownership of your own ship – your body – you will learn how to navigate through times when you experience turbulence, distress, or any other perceived negative emotion, thought, or conflict.

It is likely you underestimate the power you have. You forget to nurture the relationship you have with yourself and start focusing on always giving your love, time, and patience to the relationships outside of yourself. When those break down you feel broken, betrayed, frustrated, stressed, and angry.

Your relationship with others is a mirror reflection of your relationship with yourself. As you accept yourself for who you are, increasingly you start accepting each and every being on this planet for the authentic self that they are. This reverses the process in you of trying to control the world outside of you. You start to build inner control of your body's built-in natural functions. Your relationship with yourself becomes stronger and stronger.

In my early days of coaching I learned many coaching models that I now integrate in helping clients build a great relationship with themselves and others. From the earliest days, psychoanalysts treated clients as though they were in some way broken and in need of "fixing." When I started my coaching journey I loved the fact that the traditional coaching world rejected this notion and worked on the assumption that people are essentially whole and perfect as they are.

This truly resonated with me and I started to learn more and more about a number of different coaching models. Using Person Centered Approach, Life Positions and Transactional Analysis Coaching, I have helped many clients improve their relationship with self and others, break different patterns and helped them in their journey to make conscious choices.

Through my self-healing journey and the many clients I have helped over the years, the biggest mistake you can make is to not have a relationship with your inner child.

You may not be familiar with Transactional Analysis in Coaching and the concept of Ego States, but let me simplify it for you. In each one of us there is a parent, a child, and an adult. The stimulus and response will both come from one of the Ego States, depending on which one the person is accessing at that time. So a stimulus will come from the Adult, Parent or Child state and the response will do likewise. For example, once I was working with a client to help him understand his reaction to his parents' response about his decision to become a vegetarian. The stimulus was his father who told him that he had to eat meat – a critical parent. His response came from a resistant child that disobeyed his father's wish if he decided to become a vegetarian.

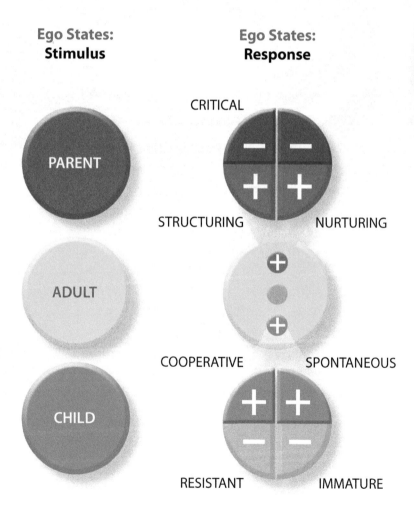

Working with a good coach will help you learn the three kinds of transactions which any transaction you do with yourself and others will fall into: Complementary, Crossed, and Ulterior.

As I learned, digested and integrated those models into my own methodology, I became extremely good at spotting them when I would engage in any form of relationship, whether the one with self, intimate, clients, family, or with anyone in my external environment. If you are a coach, a healer, PT, therapist, or simply want to understand the way you communicate in terms of stimulus or response, Transactional Analysis is a great way to start this process.

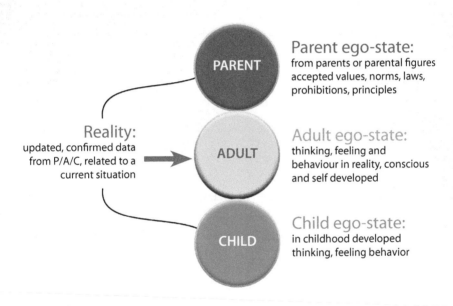

Parent ego-state:
from parents or parental figures accepted values, norms, laws, prohibitions, principles

Adult ego-state:
thinking, feeling and behaviour in reality, conscious and self developed

Child ego-state:
in childhood developed thinking, feeling behavior

Reality:
updated, confirmed data from P/A/C, related to a current situation

The knowledge of Transactional Analysis increased my awareness of self and helped me gain a deeper understanding of the way I reacted and communicated with myself, as well as with others.

It also helped me grow. As I incorporated this into my inner child healing, my clients started to stop judging themselves and others who, consciously or subconsciously, may have hurt them in the way they responded as a result of what was said or not said.

It helped me not only create a deeper bond with self but also with everyone around me. Naturally your energy increases as you start feeling great about yourself. You start vibrating at a higher frequency. You start to increase your state of awareness and you realize that anyone around you is simply another version of you on their own journey to fulfillment.

If you perceive that there is something wrong with them, this will be the version that you have disowned. Equally if you see them as someone good, this is the version of you that you have owned and now love.

Drita, a mother of two, was referred to me for some coaching as the way she was treated by her boss caused her stress, frustration, and a lot of negative self-talk. As I listened and looked at what ego state she was responding from, I helped her identify her underlying issues, the triggers, and see how she also played a part in the way her boss was treating her. As she learned this internal communication model, and how she engaged with her boss, she knew she had to break the pattern that she had learned when she was young and that it could not continue. Within 12 weeks of working together, she released this and she truly felt free.

When you remember that rule one of Transactional Analysis says that so long as the transactions are complementary, the communication can carry on indefinitely. When you master this, you become excellent at building a relationship with self and others.

You begin to step into your adult to achieve better outcomes for yourself. You might also look at which part of your ego state you're communicating from.

Perhaps, rather than operating from a structuring parent, you may regularly operate from the critical parent. Simple adjustments to the way you communicate will help you move from one to the other.

Julia is another lady who came to see me for coaching as she felt almost controlled by others in terms of their responses. At the beginning of our work together, she was unaware that the stimulus was almost forcing the response out of her. I frankly did not do much. I simply helped her see how she had a choice and how she could operate from the adult state and make choices which are more empowered. Within a two-hour session she felt free, smiled and left feeling empowered.

So transactions are a fundamental element of how you relate and build relationships with self and others. They form the basis for ongoing communication, be that effective or ineffective as in the case of games. But they also act, in the first instance, in a much more important manner. They allow you to know you exist!

They give you what are called strokes. I also use this to help people build a good rapport with themselves and their outer environment.

This does not mean that I helped them be perfectly happy. What it means is that they stopped seeing themselves as someone who is broken. I helped them to think, act and feel more or less effectively at any given time.

Now let's look at our relationship with others and your outer environment. The way you relate to yourself definitely influences the way you relate with others.

As in every area of your life, building relationships with others might be your biggest hurdle to overcome. You will come across obstacles. You will make mistakes. You will get challenged many times as you try to build intimate relationships, as well as with your environment, where you live and work.

Lack of self-belief, self-confidence, and a poor mastery of your emotional intelligence can truly prevent you from building lasting, loving, and fulfilling relationships with others and the environment you live in.

When you were a kid, you were completely absorbed in the moment and totally unselfconscious. You did not know how to be anything but perfectly authentic. No facades. Simply you were being you. It's a great reminder of your inherent ability to live this way. To build relationships this way with self and others.

So along the way, when did you lose it and how do you get back there? Parental influences may at times have elicited a feeling of "not okay-ness" leading to a variety of strategies being adopted in order to regain approval. The adoption of non-authentic behavior had a short-term gain. Over time however, it becomes the norm, leading you further and further away from who you really are.

TJS Evolutionary Method is your ticket back to the remembrance of your authentic self, to acceptance, and to building the relationships needed for loving you. This is a journey which will open you further than you ever imagined possible. Forget any exotic vacations you may have been on. Forget the money you may have. Forget climbing Kilimanjaro, visiting Machu Picchu or the Pyramids in Egypt.

Your journey to build relationships that bring you back to you is the most wonderful adventure you will ever have. Unlike even the most fabulous vacation, it doesn't stop when you get back home. It's literally the ultimate trip.

There is so much information out there on relationships. One of the things that the journey through the obstacles that I, and many of the clients I helped, has taught me (among other things) is: as you improve your relationship with self, the way you go about building relationships with others improves and changes. Just like you would do if you had a garden, you make the time to get to know each flower (relationship) and see what it is you can do to nurture them throughout the year so you can enjoy and grow your garden of beautiful relationships.

Relationships can drive your emotions flying through the roof. The way you do this is by not taking the time to listen to what is being said. What you tend to do instead is you listen to your own version of what was said. You may have been in a situation where your intended message is not what was received by the other person. Can you see the impact this has on your ability to create and nurture relationships?

When you engage in any form of relationship, you engage from the space you are at, so you bring your entire self into this relationship.

Let's say one day you felt emotional about something; the way you would speak if you met a close friend would be from your emotions. Let's not forget that emotion does not equal reality.

Another key mistake you may make is that you forget that relationships are also your building blocks to life, to all community organizing activities, and to your work life. You forget that the reason you need to build relationships with people is that you don't live in this world alone; you always interact and co-create with other people around you.

When you don't have good relationships, you feel isolated, and you stop trusting others and the world you live in.

Your relationships give meaning and richness to who you are, the work you do, and to your life. You all need a community of people to share the joys and the struggles of life. A little bit of camaraderie goes a long way. Do not make the mistake of trying to build a relationship from a place of need, want, or because you may get something back from the person you build a relationship with. These kinds of behaviors won't get you far in life and will leave you feeling alone, isolated, and not worthy.

A key mistake is to think and treat each relationship you have as the same. Of course I am not saying you should not be authentic. What I am saying is that over time I have learned that every relationship I have is different, and every relationship I have matters, be it with my family, my partner, my work, my clients, friends, or even with you the reader.

So far, reading through my book I have taken you on a journey and in that journey you have gotten to know the essence of me: my views, my opinions, and what I stand for. This on its own has created a relationship, a bond with me and the part that you see in me.

If you smile and say hello to a random stranger, homeless person, or the barista at your favorite coffee shop on your way to work every day, you have formed a relationship. That barista may be the one who will be watching out for your kids. He may end up being the top coach, teacher and healer who will inspire you, and who will help you be a better person.

When I arrived in London 20+ years ago, I was this homeless person, stranger on the street and the barista I am talking about. I worked in many coffee shops, restaurants, gyms, night clubs – you name it, I did it. This boy who served many people coffees, made sandwiches, smoothies, cocktails, and helped many people is now an Elite Life Coach, an author, a speaker, a healer and an inspired teacher.

The many relationships I formed over the years is what also helped me be the man I am today. And maybe your barista will be the one you eventually recruit to head up your IT department, lead your local school or become your representative in government.

The relationships you have with your family, friends, your staff, with members of your board of directors, and with your spouse will all be different but they all play an important role.

The more relationships you have, the better. You never know when they will come in handy. A murderer might be just the person you need to help you organize a rehabilitation and educational program for the prison service. Whether they are government officials, school teachers, business people, the elderly, gardeners, children, people with disabilities, homeless people or whoever else, building friendships in a co-loving way will pay off in ways you may never have anticipated.

You must be at the center of your relationship; if you are not, this will throw you out of balance and in many directions.

Imagine a wheel in which you are at the hub or center and each spoke represents a relationship with another person. Does that sound egotistical? It doesn't need to be. It takes a lot of spokes to hold the wheel together and the wheel is what helps move the initiative along. There is enough room in the group for everyone to create their own wheel of strong relationships.

The point is that you have to take the time to set up and sustain relationships. If you wait for others to establish relationships with you first, you may spend a lot of time waiting.

One reminder: it doesn't make sense to form relationships just to get people to do work for you, to like you, or to recommend your business and clients. You must be authentic, genuine and loving. If you are not this way, it won't work because eventually people will feel used and see you for who you are. So, be honest, be loving, and be kind.

If you observe people who work in your community, you may be able to see how they approach relationships with integrity. When you do this, you form relationships because you genuinely like someone, because you have something to offer that person, or because you share some common goal, activity, or life interests.

Another obstacle you may need to overcome is to know when to build and sustain those relationships. You do it all the time. If you take an extra five minutes to ask the person who is stuffing envelopes how they think their son is doing this year, you will have built a stronger relationship.

Some relationships require more time than others. You may want to meet for lunch once a month with all the other directors of youth organizations in your town. You may need to meet twice this week with a staff member who has some built-up resentment about their job. You may want to call your school committee representative every now and then to check in about issues of common concern.

If like me you are an entrepreneur with few available resources to help you grow your business, you are often under enormous pressures that distract you from paying attention to relationships. You may feel the urgency of achieving important goals.

You mistakenly feel that spending time on relationships is the fluffy stuff that makes a person feel good, but doesn't get the job done. Often, however, relationships are the key to solving a problem or getting the job done. Building and sustaining many solid, strong relationships is central to your work as a parent, friend, leader, or as a monarch to the throne.

I am amazed when I observe how the Queen, the Prime Minister, top lawyers, bankers, world leaders, and every individual I come across does this. Your vision, your purpose, and the value you bring to this world also determine the relationships you need to build to help you get there.

I am truly grateful to the entire world, to our universe, to whatever created us to be able to have this innate gift. Often building relationships is the groundwork that must be laid before anything else you need to do. The bigger your vision, the more relationships you will usually need as a foundation.

Ask yourself: Would I be more persuaded by someone I know, or by a complete stranger? Then be guided by your own answer.

In my last job, working for a key government department, I had to deliver a program to tight deadlines, with limited resources and at a time when many of the people in the team were facing redundancy and were not motivated.

The mistake I saw in many of the roles I used to work in is that managers would not make the time to build relationships. Some might want to do that, but the fast-paced nature of work has forced many to work from a mindset that does not give enough time to build strong relationships.

If you are a project manager reading this book, when you plan a project you need to include the time it takes to build relationships into your plan. People need time to build trust. Whenever people work together, they need to have trusting relationships. When trust is missing, people usually have a difficult time functioning cooperatively. They worry about risking too much.

Disagreements seem to erupt over no important reason. Investing time, resources, and one's organizational reputation can be risky. At the least, people want some return for their investment. They have to feel like you know them as a person, understand their interests, and will not let them down when the going gets tough.

One route to go about establishing relationships is to start building them before you need them.

When I moved away from working in the corporate world to start my own business, I already knew many people with whom I had formed deep relationships. It's always better to build relationships before you need them or before a conflict arises.

If you already have a good relationship with the HR director of a major global company, you will be in a better position to approach him/her about a possible joint venture. If you have already established a relationship with a friend who is a web designer, she might be more willing to help you when you have no money to spend on building your website, or help you learn how to do this yourself.

I have built so many relationships that with every obstacle I faced I had friends, expertise, and a lot of people who were willing to help.

Everyone who helped me on my journey, who came to the workshops, to the charity events, the social parties, and the retreats I organized did so because of the relationships I had built over a period of time. Many of my clients have enriched my life in so many ways and have also become friends and people who I consciously choose to have around. I nurture these relationships.

Don't make a mistake and try hard to establish a relationship when in crisis. That said, it is not impossible as often a crisis can bring people together. I have seen it in my own family, time and time again. While it may seem unusual, make the most of your life crises. Call for help and people will rise to the call. You can build relationships when you are in need, because people often want to help.

Let's look at the challenges you may have in building intimate relationships. We all are built with the same dough, and we all have an animal instinct built in ourselves. It is easy to go astray, to have a one-night affair, or simply forget to say "I love you" every day to the person you are intimate with.

The relationship you have with a partner represents the opportunity to learn and grow with someone opposite or different from you.

Optimum relationships thrive when two individuals who come together share common values, have a mutual desire to learn and grow from each other, while being willing to engage in the effort required to see a different perspective.

In every individual there is an overwhelming desire to express love fully, and sometimes you may go through life and bang your head against the wall because you can't figure out how to express this divine energy that is inside of you. You go in the mind and start using rational thoughts to justify that it wasn't meant to be, that you don't know what it is, or you are not satisfied the way things are.

Your soul's purpose is to experience, feel and express this love. When this energy stops flowing, the relationship you may have starts dying. I often ask people who come to me for healing or coaching after a break up: "What happened to the love you initially had with this person?"

I am often told the story, but never both sides of the story. The client rarely consciously starts to take any responsibility for the part they played when their relationship started to break down. Usually what happens is you start to ignore the ALARM bells. You go on living on snooze and before you know it the time comes to press the stop button.

Every relationship you build being intimate or with others around you provides the stability and foundation needed for your soul to take a next step toward fulfilling its own existential program.

You can learn about where you are in your relationship by doing an analysis of Maslow's hierarchy of needs. Where the journey is about survival, the partner will provide those basic necessities. Where the journey is about emotional maturity, the partner will provide a challenging diversity of emotions. Where the journey is about spiritual development, the partner will support and guide as needed, staying close, and creating space as required.

There is no right or wrong, better or worse, there are many different relationships you learn from, and experiences of intimacy and closeness that support and nurture you during your lifetime.

In many of my female clients I have seen a correlation on how most women tend to attract partners who remind them of their fathers. This happens when women don't own the parts that they do not like in their fathers and they will keep repeating this pattern until they become conscious enough to own the disowned part of themselves.

The truth is that this kind of behavior is not sex or gender based. I remember the times when I was not fully embracing or accepting myself for the man I was. I got married in the hope that it would help me fulfill mine, and my family's expectations of what my life should be like while suppressing the disowned parts of me.

As time went by, I became rotten inside of me. Inside I felt like I was killing myself, by not accepting the truth of who I was. I knew a heterosexual marriage wasn't for me, and that I had to leave. I simply did not listen, love, nor did I have an authentic relationship with myself.

Unfortunately, when you are in this state of being and don't love yourself, you can't receive and give love to someone else. Being in this situation caused me to lose the relationship I had with myself. My feelings were telling me one thing, my mind something else, and my heart was stuck between the two and couldn't make a decision.

I felt paralyzed. Surrounded by a culture and people who I could not be authentic with, communicate my pain to, and where I could not move forward in peace. Despite how much I tried, deep down I did not honor my true self. Everything started from a need, from a place of wanting to have something so badly that I forgot to honor my true feelings.

Eventually I had to face the truth. I came out to my family, I got divorced and I let go of the fear that stopped me from living my own authentic life. I invested a lot in this journey, worked with many healers, coaches, and inspired teachers that helped me get back to loving me for who I am. Some of the people who helped me through this challenging time include my teachers, Martin Brofman, Parag Pattani, my friends Marcello, Stuart and Mouna. Thank you and I love you!

The relationships I had built from the disowned part of myself needed to be rebuilt. I needed to spend time nurturing my relationship with the family that I had lied to for so many years about my true identity, so they could take the time to adjust, learn and grow to love me for being me.

Having lived for so long in fear, lying, denying, and being ashamed of who I was, I needed time to rebuild the relationship I had with myself and embrace my true identity. Not knowing yourself at a deeper level can have a tremendous impact in all areas of your life.

I hope this book inspires you to upgrade your life to first class, and start living a purposeful life.

You may feel trapped in loving the idea of a relationship, not the actual relationship; this infatuation can truly throw you off balance. If you see yourself in this picture, do something about it right now, not tomorrow, not in a month.

The need to control plays a big part in the way you form relationships. For some people this is a huge obstacle to overcome, as all of your life you have learned how to control and let others control you.

You create many fantasies and illusions about what relationships should be. By all means I am not an expert in this field. But what I have learned so far and through the experiences of the many people I have helped, it's important to stop chasing happiness in a relationship and start building and looking for a relationship that is fulfilling.

Fulfillment comes both from being supported and from being challenged. From seeing the positives and the negatives in the person you love. In accepting the person you love for the person they are.

Once I was listening to a friend of mine who was telling me her problems with her husband. Toward the end I asked her if I could give her some feedback. As I summarized the fantasy she had built around what her relationship meant to her and asked her if she knew anyone in this world who would have that, she started crying and told me: "You are right. I love my husband. I am going home now to tell him that."

The next day she called me to thank me for breaking her illusions, for helping her feel free, and for helping her let go of the need to control the things she did not like in her husband.

I interact with many people on many levels, be it professionally, personally, or socially, and one of the common themes I hear frequently is "I lost my passion" or "I don't have that kind of passion anymore, it is impossible to have it as we have been together many years."

All I know is that at some point all these people had passion. The part they are not telling me or not being honest about is how this passion disappeared. Perhaps they don't see it, that even when they tell me about it there is passion, even in the arguments they have there is passion. Just in a different form that they don't recognize it.

Remember the two sides of emotion come together as pairs, and if you start to infatuate you will pay the price that resentment brings. When you embrace both sides of the relationship you will start to embrace the entire person and you will be one step closer to having a fulfilled relationship.

Exercise for you

Through answering these questions you'll be able to identify which relationships you focus on the most. This can help you bring the focus back into building relationship with self, which in turn helps you build better relationships with others, and the world you live in.

1. *If you think about relationships, what does it mean to you? What is the first thing that comes into your mind?*

2. *Notice what thoughts pop up. Are those thoughts about personal intimate relationships with someone you love, or your relationship with your family, friends, or work colleagues?*

3. *Now identify what percentage of your thoughts is about the relationship you have with yourself, your spirit, your heart, and the way you relate with your outer world.*

If you discover that you spend most of your mind energy thinking about others, you need to refocus, and start spending more mental energy on building a better relationship with self.

LOVE

"If we make our goal to live a life of compassion and unconditional love, then the world will indeed become a garden where all kinds of flowers can bloom and grow."

Dr. Elisabeth Kübler-Ross

If you think about life without love, you will know instantly that it is meaningless, purposeless, and for sure unimaginable. Deep down you also know that when you experience a lack of love you do not feel fulfilled. A lack of love makes you do all sorts of crazy things. Your life becomes filled with all sorts of problems, and when your body is starved of love it becomes weak and illness takes over.

You are often taught to deprioritize your own needs in favor of assisting others to meet theirs. God forbid you should be seen as selfish. This is seriously flawed programing. It took me years to overwrite this program in me. Working on yourself doesn't mean you are self-obsessed or self-indulgent. It makes perfect sense to love you.

There seems to be a lot of confusion regarding love, self-love, and self-worthiness both in terms of what it constitutes and also how to effect it. It is in fact an incredible and worthy skill that takes practice. It is often used as an excuse for self-indulgence and self-deception (the extra slice of chocolate cake, glass of wine etc.). It takes awareness and possibly a large number of questions to be able to differentiate, and then make love a choice.

You often follow the path of least resistance to get to this place. Apathy and being in your comfort zone is really detrimental to travelling "onwards and upwards" which is why so-called breakdowns often become breakthroughs.

You eject yourself from your familiar zone into a place of newness and possibly hardship, at which point you are able to perceive your situation from a point of greater clarity.

In this new place, you start to be aware of the mistakes you make, the various obstacles you may need to overcome, and the challenges you may face.

Exercise for you

Let's begin this journey by answering some simple questions:

1. *What does love really mean?*

2. *How does it help you in your day-to-day existence?*

3. *Why is it that you feel hurt when relationships break down?*

4. *Why do you use love to control and get what you want?*

5. *How can you apply that understanding to your present state of living on this planet?*

6. *What can you do to live your life from a place of choice in which you choose love?*

7. *Is love that permeates your very existence truly destined to remain elusive to your individual and collective expression?*

For me love is such an amazingly simple, elegant and universal expression of the very nature of life itself. I see it present in every life-giving heartbeat, in nature, and it is intrinsic in nebulas swirling with potential in faraway distant galaxies. You feel it in the beauty of each sunrise and in the gentle embrace of a smile. It is the sublime connection that does more than connect. Love is the essence of all that we experience and in that which we have yet to imagine. Love knows no bounds and creates no conditions. It is what it is.

Somewhere along the way you may have forgotten (or ignored) this innate wisdom and awareness of love. Your present world is seemingly filled with an absence of love when viewed from a singular perception that you are somehow separate from love. Nothing could be further from the truth. Yet, for reasons you don't even remember, you strive to maintain this well-established stance and continue to find or invent ample evidence to excuse your disconnection from that which you ultimately are.

Quite the contrary, love is such an essential part of your life that it is impossible to separate yourself from it; you only create the illusion that you do. If you look back in time you will see how love was always there, present. You may not have seen the form that it might have manifested in, but at a closer look you will see it was always present.

As you are reading this book, you may also notice shifts already happening to you as you have been reading through the different chapters and going deeper into who you are. As you do so, then the sense of separation is rapidly departing as you are (re)awakening to your fundamental loving spirit. One by one and around the globe we are turning within and comprehending just how magnificent each and every one of us is at the core of our being.

The more you embody this love right where you currently are in your life, the greater your capacity to encourage and inspire love in those around you. Love by its essence needs to flow, be shared, and put to service. This accelerates the recollection and cultivation of your universal love and restores your collective potential that has always been rooted in this same love. Individually and together you are acknowledging the reality of love and know that each perspective and experience is an opportunity to expand ever more love.

Think of times when your life was being turned upside down. When you felt love left you, times that no matter what you did you could not feel, receive or give love. The truth is love never really left you. It was only the one-sided perception of what love is that created that separation and the feeling of "lack."

As you raise your awareness of your immortal existence, you start to accept that you are the love you seek in the darkest night of your journey, just as you are the reflection of love to others that encounter you in your brightest moments. Love awaits you long before you arrive and remains with you in every step you take. It asks for nothing and provides everything.

Love is unconditional in nature and eternal in presence, it is who you are, and through your expression of it, love continues to expand, evolve, and express the many facets it has.

The mistake you may make is that you don't see love as jealousy, control, anger, frustration, hatred, judgment, fear and many more negative associations with love. Most people I know tend to see only the positive qualities of love, such as freedom, trust, honesty, beauty, harmony, joy, peace, wisdom, compassion. Love is the fusion of them all and the point at which two opposites come together into a singular point.

Don't be fooled, love was born even before mankind was born and it still exists in all kinds of organism, including you. You know you were not born to be anything but love. The further you go away from love, the less fulfilled you will be in your life. The problem you may face is that you stop believing in this innate energy that makes the world go round.

One of the main problems you face is that relationships, culture and religion all teach you something different about love. As you grow up, you inherit those beliefs about what love is to you depending on where you came from. The family you were born into, the culture you grew up in, the many relationships you might have had, as well as every experience you have created, all contribute to the meaning you may have attached to love as a result.

This can cause that inner separation you may feel. It may also lead you to a lot of misconception, confusion, and idealizing about what love is and then you start to judge everything that love is not.

Modern authors have distinguished further varieties of romantic love. Non-western traditions have also distinguished variants or symbioses of these states. This diversity of uses and meanings combined with the complexity of the feelings involved makes love unusually difficult to define consistently, compared to other emotional states.

First of all, I found that by bringing my awareness to the recognition of unconditional love for "self" as the beginning point, I can actively observe and comprehend how love is a natural part of my life. The declaration that I learned from DeMartini – "No matter what I have done, or not done, I am worthy of love" – was a life-changing and transformative experience for me and everyone I have taught this affirmation to for the many years I have worked in the personal development industry.

However, getting to that understanding, let alone applying it in the midst of chaos, stress and fear, can seem like a monumental task. Just for fun, and as a way to explore love, let's set aside the common sentiments that loving yourself is a "task" for some future accomplishment or "hard" or even "impossible" and allow the possibility that you are "worthy of love" to enter your being right now, this moment in time, just as you read this book.

Let's take a moment to consider what unconditional love means. Of course it will be interpreted and understood on an individual basis; personally, I like Harold Becker's contemporary definition that "unconditional love is an unlimited way of being." To me that means that love exists as an energy and ever-present experience in all levels of physical, emotional, mental and etheric life. Love is freedom, it exists inside of us and outside of our time and space reality; love is infinite.

By embracing that stream of energy and removing your self-imposed restrictions, belief systems, etc., you become more unlimited and more capable of handling life in its myriad of expressions. What stops you is your willingness to forgive, release, change, grow, and explore who you really are. As you open up to acceptance of self, you become more than you thought you were and have more love to offer the world.

Almost everybody thinks that love is hard and relationships take a lot of work. In actual fact, the easier you make love and the less you "work" on your relationships, the more love you get to experience.

If you're single, your objective is to attract the love you want by effortless shifts of consciousness, not by stressful pursuit.

If you're a couple, your objective is discovering how to open and maintain a flow of love by effortless shifts of consciousness, not by doing more of what already hasn't worked.

I have coached many individuals and couples to help them move from having conflicts almost daily to a new way of being in which all communications come from a place of love, understanding, and learning.

As you were growing up, you didn't have any mentors so you had to figure out a lot of things "the hard way." Now, as you open yourself to love, you start going back to your authentic self. You discover your life purpose, and you start sharing this love to help people experience more love than they ever imagined possible... and to have it be easy. If you learn how to make love easy, everybody in this world can benefit.

A mistake you might make is not educating yourself about how Maslow's hierarchy of needs truly impacts your inner world, and how all relationships go through five stages:

✓ Romance
✓ The Inevitable
✓ The Choice-Point
✓ The Result
✓ The Re-Kindling

Nobody ever told you that creating the kind of love you want is an inside job. In fact, your parents, family, relationships you may have had, the society, advertising and media teach you the exact opposite: to look at the outside, the superficial aspects such as clothing, cosmetics, hairstyles, going to the gym and building muscle, and much more.

The more I got in touch with loving and accepting myself, the more I realized how easy it is to love and have a relationship. Almost everybody tells you the exact opposite: that love is painful and you have to work hard on your relationships.

If you are willing, by overcoming those limiting beliefs you can prove to yourself once and for all that lasting love is easy.

The best lesson I've learned in this walk along my spiritual path is to get out of my head, my ego, and my emotions and get into my heart. Since childhood I cultivated and cherished an intellectual understanding of spiritual teachings and practices without really living them and without taking them into my heart. The teachings of Sufism, dervishes, and a whole lot of mystical knowledge I got from my family I only embraced fully once I embraced my authentic self and got to know myself at a deeper level.

It never really sank in properly until the day came when everything made perfect sense. Although it may seem it was an overnight thing, for sure I know it was a process of many years of self-reflection, inner work, and opening up my heart to acceptance and love.

Let me tell you something: even for people whom you perceive to be extremely enlightened, it's not always easy to love. The ego is very tempting. However, I've learned that love really is the healer and that we can have a healing even in our most difficult relationships and circumstances. That healing won't happen unless you move into your heart. That's what family, friends, animals and nature can be for you if you take advantage of the opportunity.

In our family dynamics, in our friendships, and in our communities are the perfect opportunities for us to practice compassion. Compassion *is* love in the form of understanding.

As the civil war broke up in former Yugoslavia, I started to believe less and less that being loving and compassionate would serve me and the people around me. The only thing on their mind was survival, it was you or them, one had to die, one had to be killed, one had to win.

I learned to withhold love as a form of punishment. I didn't realize that there is only one presence and that I was only punishing myself. Years later, having come to the UK and rebuilt my life, I began to wake up and realize the mistake I was making.

I once again began to look for opportunities to be compassionate. If there was agitation or frustration or perhaps a "stand-off" with friends or relatives, I began to say: "I'll go first. I'll make the first move to release the judgment, forgive and be compassionate."

I began to go first, not so I could show I was better, but so that we could get to the loving sooner. Love is the healer and I was truly interested in that healing!

During the vacation times, if you find yourself withholding loving kindness and patience, if you find yourself wanting to hold on to judgments, if you find yourself wanting to be right and not caring at all about being happy, I invite you to practice the Presence in this simple way:

If you feel agitation or discord, be grateful. That feeling of upset lets you know that you're out of your heart and you're probably in judgment, in your ego state. Place your hand on your heart. Take four deep breaths. With each breath, say to yourself: I'm grateful that love is the healer. I'm willing to choose love. I am love.

I have been on many rollercoasters, and what I realize is love is always the same. Once you have completed the ride, you want to go again.

Before trying to get someone to love you, make sure you are aligned with yourself and that you love yourself. Love can sometimes be temporary. You never know how long it may last. So cherish each day and make each moment count. Loving yourself is self-worth and that can last forever.

To get to this place where I now see love as something easy to give and receive, I went through a lot of life challenges, experiences, and had to overcome many obstacles. I also invested a lot in my personal development. In the early 1990s as I was going through an emotional rollercoaster, I came across Harold W. Becker's work. He developed a unique, and perhaps unconventional, contemporary definition for unconditional love and shared it in his first book *Internal Power - Seven Doorways to Self Discovery*.

He chose to understand and evolve each of the two words "unconditional" and "love" to their core essence of meaning. This resonated with me, as I have always known the power of the words, our thoughts and the vibration they produce. As he combined them into one idea, he realized a useful insight for applying this profound perspective found in this unique combination of two words. Harold's definition simply stated: "Unconditional love is an unlimited way of being."

This definition doesn't necessarily speak to the typical expected response or popular collective understanding of most cultures. Instead it reveals something more important: the individual potential that resides within you every moment in time. It merely asks that you approach each moment with clarity and right perspective and recognize the vast unlimited possibilities to choose a new way of thinking and feeling.

You may have read many books, learned many tools, and are aware of this, but the sense of profound love comes when you first truly forgive and accept yourself for all your limiting beliefs, mistakes, judgments and misunderstandings and apply the "unconditional" to you personally. You recognize your self-worth, value your talents, and allow yourself to be who you are rather than what you think others wish you to be.

> *"You yourself, as much as anybody in the entire universe, deserve your love and attention."*
>
> **Buddha**

Self-love is about your being. It encompasses more than just doing. Hence, to truly love the self is more than a physical act of self-care, having material goods, using mental force to will yourself or having the day off to rest. It is also more than saying positive things to yourself. Self-love necessarily involves the mind-body-spirit. It incorporates an inside-out approach.

For one, holding on to myths can prevent you from loving yourself more fully. If you believe that self-love is simply about having a long bath, a manicure, massage or having your hair done, then you are sadly mistaken. Sure, these self-care activities make you feel good about yourself. Buying a branded handbag or expensive car may be able to give you a high. However, these are just externals. The satisfaction that you derive from them does not last long. The excitement dies out – fast!

Hence, it is possible to be engaged in years of self-care but still face difficulties with loving yourself. In fact, by keeping yourself endlessly occupied with forms that engage your senses, you may even miss the whole point about what it truly means to love yourself. And so you get an instant perk through these activities or material possessions but they do not transform you from the inside. The rush of energy fizzles out rather quickly.

You will eventually discover that you are the one that you seek. Answers to having a more successful life do not lie outside but can be found within. It is only when you search inside your heart that you will realize who you really are. Your inner being shines with luminescence, touching and inspiring everyone around you. You become alive and very much awake.

Martin Brofman and his Body Mirror System of Healing helped me tremendously in my journey to awaken myself to this state of awareness and open my heart to the power of acceptance. DeMartini's Breakthrough Experience was the last missing piece of the puzzle that helped me see the healing power of love. Each experience I created helped me be at the point where I am today where with the power of unconditional love I now heal many people around the world.

I had to make some difficult choices in my life, but what I realize is that when you commit to your mission, in time everything makes sense.

I now feel free to love. Free to live the life I always dreamed of. I am living my dream: I heal, coach, teach, speak, inspire and contribute toward unleashing human potential. I gave myself permission to be the infinite love I am talking about in this chapter. I am asking you right now to do the same. Give yourself permission to open to this infinite wisdom of love.

Loving myself for the infinite being I am, in turn I now naturally understand those around me and extend my helping hand without condition, judgment or expectation to shine the light that is required to find your path back home. Back to love through the journey of acceptance. It is what my gift is to you, the quiet space that you need for you to transcend to the next level of consciousness.

Today I live my life by seeing myself in the reflection of another and I know that without a shadow of a doubt everyone deserves to love and be loved without condition. This way I have opened my heart to the infinite wisdom of love. We are all teachers and we are all students to each other.

By embracing the present moment with openness, you realize and know you have the solutions and answers already within you. You begin building a reality that is based on love, wisdom and power in perfect balance. For each step you take personally, you impact the world with this amazing energy of love.

Unconditional love turns hope into knowing in a collective reality that is often seen as hopeless or seemingly impossible to overcome. When you know something is possible, you empower this to manifest with your very being. So know from now on that you are loved and loving and see how the world responds to your light and knowing.

Watch how your peace and strength is sought out by others and how the limitless love you have to share is the love you receive in return. Being deeply loved by someone gives you strength, while loving someone deeply gives courage.

You might be extremely sensitive to the outer world, you may be subconsciously living in the response-reaction mode you read in the previous chapter, and when someone does something that hurts you, you lose the trust you may have with that person.

Your internal feedback mechanism takes over you, it puts you on a carousel and starts spinning you without any control. Naturally you feel out of control when events like this happen. Although the resentments you may have built also serve a purpose to get you out of the carousel onto a stable ground in which you can walk again and continue to grow emotionally, physically, mentally, financially, and spiritually.

If you live your life looking at hurtful people you may have come across in your life, you are not seeing the other side of the coin. As you come to accept life, your existence, and that you will always be challenged and supported, you start learning the lessons and enter the realm of unconditional loving.

You will stop living an unrealistic world in which the illusions you created of the meaning of love start to disappear. You get out of your bubble, and you start living life from a place of gratitude. You open your heart to all of the awful, unkind people who have come into your life, and you will have huge compassion toward them and start being grateful for the lessons they taught you.

You know you are at this space when at each moment in time you are present. Present with yourself. Present with anyone who you interact with. You see love in everything you experience.

You live in a world where you are taught, encouraged, and you learn since an early age to compete and compare yourself, your success, your love and your life with that of another. When you start your professional career you are also taught to crash your competitors. To learn their weaknesses so your business can strive. To see success as a comparative measure.

This is no one's fault. The primary function of the reptilian part of your brain is to help you survive. It is your animal instinct. Humans are really competitive and competition has the element of war inside it. You battle against yourself as well as somebody else.

Once I worked with a very successful trader who came to me for spiritual guidance, healing and to help him deal with stress. He was excellent at competing. It is what made him so successful. Though as I took him on an inner journey to reflect on his experiences, he realized the same energy was also what made him stressed, ill, and restless.

As he opened his heart to love, he saw how this had served him to be where he was. He started to be authentic and knew his self-worth, the value he brought to clients and he did not need to compete anymore. He could do his job by simply being loving.

A year down the line he took me out for an amazing dining experience at one of my favourite Gordon Ramsay restaurants. He ordered a bottle of champagne, raised the glass and said: "Thank you for being patient, kind, and for helping me see the love you saw in me in our first consultation." At that moment both of us had tears in our eyes. It is that moment that I call the moment of unconditional love.

This is unconditional love in action. The more you understand yourself and acknowledge love, the more you naturally love your neighbors and the world around you. You too can become a living example of unconditional love in action.

The TJS Evolutionary Method you have been so patiently waiting to learn will help you know this. It will help you get your life back on track, and you will learn how to identify, listen, and use the built-in intrusion prevention ALARM as a way of creating the quiet space within you so you can listen to the voice of the spirit that lives in your heart.

As you do so, your actions, attitudes, your language, your results, and your motivation to do things all lead toward the same destination. A life in which you are fulfilled and are consciously making decisions that support you and your work toward your own existential program.

The better you become at listening, the better you become at being in the right place, right environment, with the right people. You become a love magnet; you continue to improve your ability to hold the love and light frequency.

Years of struggles, criticisms and hurtful experiences you have gone through can make you create a Swiss-made internal security system. You become guarded, and you stop letting people in. You become standoffish, selfish, and insecure. You start creating many processes, systems and beliefs to support you in this state of being.

This creates the perfect environment in which the virus of distrust lives, breeds and spreads. It takes you over, and as it becomes resident, you have already forgotten what your life used to be like without having to be this way.

Through the ages, mystics, sages, singers and poets have all gone through stages like this and come to a place of awareness from which they can express love through their work. This vision "A Call for Love" came to me last year. I started to mediate each day. I got in touch with my true spirit, and saw visions of my future and what it is that I needed to do.

I knew the answer was that I needed to create something that would help humanity shift their consciousness to the next level of awareness. It is what I saw in my dream. That any illness is an alert that your body gives you so you can take action to bring it back to its natural state of being. The cure is this call for love that I saw in my vision.

This clarity has given me the energy, the vision and the motivation I have to be of service – not only to you the reader, but also to the world. My mission is a global vision and a universal one too.

The key to higher states of consciousness is the understanding of the power of love you have in you, the acceptance of who you are, and consciously choosing day-to-day decisions and taking actions that lead you toward higher states of vibration and awareness.

My mission is to empower, inspire, and teach this methodology to all the continents around the world. Work with world leaders and key persons of influence to maintain balance, the present state, and work toward what more we can all do to improve, learn, and share this infinite wisdom of love.

As humans, we have searched endlessly for the experience of love through the outer senses. Great nations have come and gone under the guise of love for their people. Religions have flourished and perished while claiming the true path to love.

You, as a person of this planet, may have missed the simplicity of unconditional love. You are this love, and you have in you infinite ways of being. You are built without any limit to your thoughts and feelings in life and can create any reality you choose to focus your attention upon. There are infinite imaginative possibilities when you allow yourself the freedom to go beyond your perceived limits.

If you can see it in your mind, you can have it in your palm. If you can dream it, you can build it.

Life, through the filter of unconditional love, is a wondrous adventure that excites the very core of your being and lights your path with delight.

The key that opens the door to more love than you ever imagined possible is something that sounds so simple but can actually be so hard to give yourself in real life: willingness. Your own willingness is the key that opens the door.

I now invite you to allow yourself to understand the impact your actions have not only on yourself but the planet you live on. As you do so you may realize the necessity to take loving action. You have the power to correct conditions within as well as to affect the world you live in. We are one!

Despite what you may have been conditioned to believe, there is nothing that you have to do or achieve to be worthy of love. No matter what you say or do, you are love and you are worthy of love. Your true self is pure love and you are already infinitely precious exactly as you are.

This awareness of who you really are connects you to your true self-esteem. This esteem is solid and unwavering. Your soul loves you unconditionally. The approval rating of your ego, in contrast, is fickle and forever shifting. Your ego may approve of your performance one day and then the next day judge you as inadequate or lacking.

As you shift from identifying with your ego's insecurities and fears, you open to the gifts of the soul. It all begins with self-awareness. Each day as you spend time in the inner quiet of meditation, your awareness will expand and awaken you to love. Come on, confess it, you would love it! Who wouldn't, right?

Love, the word that has the power to change you in so many ways, is used on a daily basis, but do you truly know the meaning of it? Do you apply that to every thought? Every feeling you have? Every decision you make? Or any action you take?

If you are like me, no matter how hard you try there is still so much you can do to gain that deeper understanding of the unconditional love that we all want to experience, hear about, see around us and know that it exists in abundance.

I'm not talking about the kind of love that comes in passionate sweeping ecstatic bits. I'm not talking about the love that leaves you breathless with hormonally-infused and socially projected chemical responses that you're doing something right.

I also don't mean the love that takes you far from where you started, but that which brings you back, and that which acquaints you with who you are. Not the outbursts of passion that drive you to madness. Not the false pretenses under which you fall into believing you'll never survive without someone – not the love you attach yourself to for the sake of self-assurance. Not the feeling that drives you to the obsessive and compulsive withholding of someone, but the love that fills you up and lets them go.

When you love yourself deeply and completely, you open your heart to love others genuinely. You start to love the funny little things about you and you appreciate this about them. You start to reassure yourself in the same way you would reassure someone you love.

You let your time with yourself and with others be an experience, not a chore or a social staple proving your worth.

Love is not within itself a nasty, manipulating thing. But you become nasty, manipulating yourself and other people when you hold on to the kind of love that you falsely believe is the only way you can feel that sense of worth.

You have to love yourself for who you are, this will help you love someone for who they are. See yourself for who you were and you will see them for who they were; and for who you have the potential to be so that you can see in others the potential they have to become.

Even if you don't always love yourself or all of those different people you may feel you are, even if you don't agree with what you or they have done, and even if you're not sure about where you or they are going, make sure you love yourself and them because your and their souls are all worth loving.

Reach inside of yourself and them and make yourself feel and see love in them. Show yourself and them the unhealed parts of you so they reveal that part of themselves to you and themselves, and hold their hand while they start the journey to accepting themselves.

We think of love as though we are destined for a happy ever after, and that it's only a matter of finding someone else to give it to us. Happy ever after will be infiltrated with illness, death, suffering, sadness, but also great achievement, excitement, adventure and growth.

Love without reason, and love without condition, is the stuff you're looking for. Love is a constantly flowing, understanding and patient equilibrium. Learn to see love not with your mind or feeling, but with your soul and your heart, and give it from there as well.

Love yourself with the same forgiving, honest, vulnerable rawness that makes you lose your breath a little. Love yourself because your soul inspires you, not because you're interested in the relief from loneliness.

To step into your power, your greatness, you need to be prepared to step outside your "familiar zone", the space in which you know how to think, feel and react to any given situation. As you get challenged to step outside this familiar zone, a whole new world opens up for you. This is what Hera experienced; a glimpse of what is possible once you allow yourself to love. To stretch your mind to new horizons, a new awareness, and a new way of thinking.

Understand that your unconscious mind is not logical, it's purposeful – and its number one purpose is survival. It will always aim for your today to be as similar to yesterday as possible. It wants you to stay within your comfort zone because it's safe. The challenge is to override it, to hear your heart's voice, and push yourself toward greatness anyway.

Look Inside

With so much distraction, years of conditioning, as well as through years of learning many coping strategies, mechanisms, and building security walls to protect yourself, no wonder that when something does not feel right you naturally look for solutions outside of you.

You learn how to hide behind the many facets your ego creates to protect its own mortal existence. Your immortal being who knows of the infinite wisdom of love also has the ability to tame the ego so that you can allow love to flow through you.

Your body's built-in feedback mechanism does exactly what it is there to do: to let you know that you are entering "protect" mode and that you need to hide. You are building a barrier to stop the overflow of emotions from taking over. You hide from being seen, from being discovered, and from feeling not good enough.

As the time goes by you learn to forget the love you are. You learn to forget that everything about you is there to serve you – the good and the bad.

The way in which your body communicates with you is extremely complex, yet it manifests in the simplest form that you can recognize. You may start to gain weight, easily become emotional, or be unable to stop your negative self-talk.

When you feel incapacitated by all of the information your body is communicating with you, instead of turning within and digging deeper in yourself to start learning to work with all of this body intelligence, you turn outwardly for solutions.

Initially it looks like an easy way out. In time, as the pain, the shame and the feelings intensify, you turn to addictions: drugs, alcohol, sugar, nicotine, sex, shopping, drinking – you name it.

I believe you can heal your body from any illness; medical science and western medical knowledge has not even reached 1% of what is possible.

If you look around you, everything you see has been created by the human brain. Yet you believe solutions to your problems in life are outside of you. Just in the same way that we create solutions to any of life's problems, your body, mind, spirit and emotions have the wisdom to do the same with whatever your body needs to bring itself to its natural state of balance, health, and love.

Exercise for you

Take a moment right now and write down your answers to the following questions:

1. *Why is it that you stop trusting yourself in your ability to find solutions to life problems you created in the first instance?*

2. *Why is it that you acknowledge everything you see around you, yet you deny to see all that you create inside of you?*

3. *Why is it that when you are hungry, you know how to find food, yet when you are ill you turn to medications and don't even question why you came to that state in the first instance?*

4. *Why do you choose to stop believing in your ability to heal and find solutions to your life problems?*

If you look at the fact that everything in the universe is based on energy, mass, light, various particles that vibrate and can exist in two places at the same time, you can start to see a whole new world. A world which you know nothing about. A world that you come from.

You become humble, you start to know that you know nothing of who you are, and what you are capable of. Your ego becomes your teacher, your spirit ascends to your heart, and you start to live, create and do actions that lead to living a fulfilled and purposeful life.

As you acknowledge, learn, action, recognize, and create a mindset that is infinite in its ability to think, create, and generate solutions to any life challenges, you enter a new paradigm in which the impossible becomes possible. That is what TJS Evolutionary Method is all about. It's a deeper exploration of self.

Hera, a successful lawyer and venture capitalist, came to see me when she was so stressed, frustrated and anxious that she could not take it anymore. She was even thinking that the solution was in moving to another country, away from stress, away from demanding family duties and from the busy city life.

During the next six months I took her on a journey that at the start was alien to her. She could not even believe she was capable of bringing her life back to balance. Her mind, her body, her emotions, and her heart were all mixed together and could not differentiate what was what, as this space was far too dark for her to see.

She was withdrawn, lifeless, and experienced a lack of energy when she wanted to do anything. She was prone to infections, and illness became the friend that created the time for her to be able to listen. And as we started to peel, organize and learn from each layer, she started to see the wisdom she had. She started to see the decisions she had to make, and how her inherited beliefs, the thoughts she was thinking, and the things she was doing caused her to be in this place.

As she let go of each illusion that she had lived with for many years, and gave herself permission to be, by the end of six months she had created the most amazing vision board I had ever seen. At the beginning I was doing most of the talking. At the end of six months I was simply listening. It was a moment where light and dark became one. The moment in which you experience the glimpse of what love can do.

The affirmation she adopted to help her in this journey was: "I am open to love, I remain open to learn, I accept everything about love, I am wise, and I apply my wisdom." The work we did on learning her limited beliefs and creating her personalized empowering language paid off.

Without exception you are part of the same make-up, same universe, same intelligence that created it all. In this respect, you and everything else around you are all strolling "bodies of rotation-vibration" differing in forms of compactness and frequency – and also everything is connected with each other by impulses. It is therefore no longer amazing that all information, including the information that we produce ourselves, enters our cells from outside or inside the body through special receptors and gives rise to effects which impact our well-being or ill-being.

From a physical point of view, you are constantly broadcasting electromagnetic or acoustic interferences that are constructive or destructive. Every thought you may have and any words you speak have resonance, a frequency, and a vibration that lifts you up or brings you down. TJS Evolutionary Method helps you transcend what prevents you from seeing this and you start seeing that they are all qualities of love. They are what you truly yearn for in life.

These words are more than the qualities they represent; they symbolize a feeling that resonates deep within and brings you a sense of completion and oneness. From your outer personality standpoint, you often think in terms of happiness, personal success and accomplishment.

Yet as a result of your best efforts you may feel only a moment of peace and contentment. However, you rarely feel complete in these areas or remain content.

What you desire is a deeper sense of knowing that all is well and you are loved. You look endlessly to the outer world of your daily experiences hoping for some glimmer of this feeling of love. As you let go of the need for the outer world to validate the love you already are, you will open the gates of instant love.

TJS Evolutionary Method teaches you how to listen to those ALARMs that prevent you from looking within and beginning your inner journey. You learn to turn the outer focus inwardly, and the more you do this, the more you start to live a healthy, balanced and fulfilled life.

You start the process of becoming consciously aware of your thoughts and feelings, language and beliefs, motives and intent, actions and attitudes, reasons and resistance. TJS Evolutionary Method is about this inner awareness through which you get back to your point of power. It is also where you find the love you seek and the opportunity to share it with others. It is the journey that makes you see that love with its all facets is right here and available in this current moment.

Know Your Limits

Anything you may use, see or has been created has its conditions under which it operates; one of these conditions is the limits under which it must operate otherwise it stops working. Just like your iPhone, your car and your relationships, your experience of life has limits, so does your body.

To remain at your body's optimum operating conditions you need to learn, acknowledge, and respect your own limits. The challenge you may have is how do you decide if you have breached those conditions? Another challenge may be at what point do you say "no, enough is enough"?

You also may notice changes in your behavior. You become irritable, withdrawn, snowed under with work, have sleepless nights, you crave food and drugs that give you a temporary relief. Yet you continue to do things without consciously being aware of those limits and the damage you do to your own being.

Everything about you is designed to help you keep within your operating limits. What stops you is the lack of self-worthiness, self-love, and self-awareness that is required for you to make a conscious decision. A decision that helps you know your own limits. Know that for you to remain healthy, balanced, and fulfilled you need to respect the body through which your spirit manifests and the body that you will need until the very last breath.

Your environment, the people you interact with, and your body's own feedback mechanism are all there to support you in knowing your limits. You are the only one who can invoke or deny those limits that serve a greater purpose.

Through your willingness and determination you can reconsider your limiting beliefs about what is possible and what is not.

Simply go within to realize why you feel, act, think and often choose to go over your limits. You can then choose to change your perspectives if need be and take action accordingly so that you can respect your limits.

In this process of getting to know your limits and how they serve you, you also start to understand other people's limits and why they also can be your teacher.

You are born with a very sophisticated feedback mechanism to help you know when you are off limits. I have worked with a number of clients who experience body weight issues. They go through periods of being super active, dieting, and fitting into that dress or pair of trousers they bought last year. And then they go through periods when no matter what they do they start to put it all back.

Weight fluctuations are a very good indication of how you feel about your life in general. In many healing disciplines they see weight problems to be an imbalanced sacral chakra. Also as western medical science becomes more aware and learns more about the human body, it too is now starting to acknowledge the link between feelings and weight.

So at some point, consciously or subconsciously, those limits are breached, and eventually your body responds to what you are telling it to do: store. Your body then stores everything as it requires extra "moral support food" to deal with the ocean of your emotions.

Weight is an ongoing cycle that you might be facing right now. I hear people blaming genes, parents, work etc. though most people never take responsibility for one very simple truth, and that is you are what you eat.

In scientific terms your body will only spend the exact amount of calories it needs, so if you don't know your limit, you will be eating more than you are spending. It is not rocket science what the outcome will be. It gets transformed into another form of energy – body fat – and gets stored in your body.

The question for you is why do you breach your limits? Why do you keep doing what you are doing to keep yourself in that state?

Your emotions also have limits; they are a great feedback mechanism. If you dig deeper into your emotional self you will start to learn your threshold, you start to understand the messages that your emotions are telling you.

Exercise for you

Let's explore more deeply some of the emotions you might experience in life.

1. Make a list of emotions you might experience in the following environments/situations:
   a) when you go to a wedding
   b) at a funeral
   c) at a job interview
   d) when meeting someone you might be interested in dating
   e) when going to work
   f) when you learn something new for the first time
   g) when you observe a sunrise
   h) when watching the full moon

2. What do you notice about the limits you keep breaching?

You know that your mind, thoughts, emotions, your heart and your spirit have a way of communicating with you. Sometimes you may feel that you simply cannot stop your thoughts, they flow like a river. It is not knowing your limits in whatever experience you may be creating that your body will fire triggers to tell you when you breach your limits.

Your mind gets busy analyzing and you simply forget how to be present, how to calm your mind, and how to respect those limits that keep you loved. Each part of your brain has its own function. The left brain is in charge of your will and your right brain is in charge of your emotions. You may know that the cerebral cortex is the part of the brain that houses rational functions. It is divided into two hemispheres connected by a thick band of nerve fibers (the corpus callosum) which sends messages back and forth between the hemispheres.

And while brain research confirms that both sides of the brain are involved in nearly every human activity, we know that the left side of the brain is the seat of language, and processes in a logical and sequential order. The right side is more visual and processes intuitively, holistically, and randomly.

It seems that our brain goes on autopilot to the preferred side. And while nothing is entirely isolated on one side of the brain or the other, the characteristics commonly attributed to each side of the brain serve as an appropriate guide for ways of learning things more efficiently and ways of reinforcing learning.

Just as it was more important for your purpose to determine that memory is stored in many parts of the brain rather than learn the exact lobe for each part, likewise it is not so much that you are biologically right brain or left brain dominant, but that you are more comfortable with the learning strategies characteristic of one over the other.

What you are doing is lengthening your list of strategies for learning how to learn and trying to determine your limits and what works best for you. You can and must use and develop both sides of the brain. But because the seat of your preferences probably has more neural connections, learning may occur faster. This section will look at some differences between left and right brain preferences. Be on the lookout for practical strategies that work for you.

Know when you breach your limits, you are built in with a threshold. Have you noticed when something goes out of your threshold how your behavior changes? You become irritable, withdrawn, frustrated, you suffer anxiety, lack of sleep, you are more prone to addictions (alcohol, drugs, smoking, sugar, gambling, shopping, or simply becoming addicted to someone), and if you look around at work, people who work long hours tend to have issues that are making them stay longer at work. They have forgotten their limits, the effects are instant.

While it's good to stretch yourself in order for you to grow, at what point do you say no? Do you know your own boundaries? For instance, when you do things that lead you to put your body under tremendous amounts of stress, you expose it to all sorts of chemicals, and then you expect it to work at its optimum.

Relationships tend to stretch us quite a lot, be they personal, professional, family, or even our friends. Your attitudes have a massive impact on this; if you love someone, your experience and the perceptions you may have toward any issues you might be experiencing with this person can determine those threshold limits.

With people you care more about you seem to have a shorter threshold limit, and for the people you don't care about this threshold is much higher as they are not as close to your personal/professional space. These people tend not to preoccupy your thoughts, have an impact on the way you feel, or force you to operate outside your guidelines.

You learn to let them go much faster than when you are hurt by a close friend. Lisa came to see me after she confronted a guy that she was dating about a girl she saw him with. In her heart she felt it. She instantly knew that there was something going on between her boyfriend and this new girl, though she chose to ignore it.

Your feedback is the doorway to your inner world, you hold the key to using, respecting, and knowing your limits.

Once I worked with a client who came to see me to help him do something about the guilt he was having as a result of having sex outside his marriage.

As I took him through this journey, we uncovered the seeds he had subconsciously that fuelled the need to express his anger, disappointment, and distrust he had with his own mother through having sex with other women.

As the year went by, his attitude changed. He started to align his life with his values, spoke to his wife, and started to have a massive love for his mom. As he saw this love in himself, he saw it in his wife, and his relationship transformed. He saw through his own experience how when love is present, there is no room for any one-sided way of living.

You may have gone through times when you told yourself: I don't need anyone to tell me what to do, no one knows better than me, who are they to tell me how to live my life? Trust me on this, while I agree with you that you are the one who knows what's best for you, I also know and believe that each one of us also serves by being a mirror through which we can reflect and see our inner world.

The people closest to you are excellent feedback mechanisms that you can also use to learn about your own limits, when you have breached them, and how to raise your awareness so that you don't keep repeating the same mistakes over and over again.

Exercise for you

Take a few moments and make a note of the answers to the following questions:

1. *Always doing things, rushing around, always trying to get somewhere, do you ever stop long enough to question your reality or that of the world around you?*

2. *Think for a moment: is what you are experiencing real or just a limited view of a much larger picture?*

3. *How do you act and react to daily situations?*

A PATH to WISDOM

4. *What are your limits in terms of thinking, feeling, sensing, touching, and hearing?*

5. *Do you know everything you need to know about you?*

6. *What does your being tell you about you?*

7. *How often do you listen within to your own thoughts and feelings about life rather than reacting or responding to outer suggestions and conditions?*

These questions can all help you realize where your focus is: on the outer or the inner world. The idea that you are the creator of your own reality may be difficult for you to accept. The truth of the matter is that you use the energy of your mind and feelings to generate the life you see in your outer experience.

8. KNOW YOUR LIMITS

TJS Evolutionary Method

This chapter is where it all comes together. If you have paid attention, done all the exercises so far, and you continue to follow it to completion, I guarantee your energy would have already shifted to higher states of awareness and you will have had many experiences filled with "aha moments."

After years of absorbing the best ideas of great teachers from around the world, I went ahead and put together this wisdom into a simple method you can learn, use, and apply in your day-to-day life.

The TJS Evolutionary Method was born through synthesis of all the above teachings and life experiences that helped me and the many clients I have worked with to acknowledge, listen, change and transform the unresourceful states that we have been exploring so far in the eight key areas of your life.

You are about to learn one of the most powerful yet simple processes you may ever find in your life that brings you to a level of awareness in which you say, believe and know that you are in control of your life. The levels of awareness in which you keep growing, reflecting, expanding, and transcending.

As you learn this method, its tools, and do the various exercises, you will find it difficult to deny the hidden truths about you. That you are indeed the designer of your own life, that you have the same qualities of the intelligence that governs us all and going through an inside revolution helps you to create an outer evolution.

You can use this method to heal emotional and physical issues, achieve excellence, balance, and inner peace. The method can be applied to any issue in your spiritual, mental, emotional, physical, career, financial, relationships, and love life.

The method gets you to acknowledge, listen, act, and respond to your inner guardian, your sophisticated intrusion detection system that constantly learns and evolves through your experience of life.

You will know how to acknowledge, listen to and silence the built-in ALARM system that is keeping you safe in your journey to fulfilling your soul's existential program.

Living your life on snooze becomes a thing of the past, you start to recognize, understand and learn to navigate through your body's own intelligent feedback mechanism. As you do so, you increase your awareness of who you are, how you can reconnect to your own higher self.

Get ready to hear your heart's true calling, to listen to your heart voice that knows, the voice that helps you transcend the inside revolution and create the evolution you seek.

TJS Evolutionary Method: The ALARM is a fusion that derives from the teachings of the western psychology about the body embedded in the acronym ALARM, and the eastern methodologies of natural healing of the body represented through seven main chakras.

This method will help you expand and develop to higher states of consciousness to such an extent that you in turn will inspire others to walk *A Path to Wisdom*. You become the light that others need to self-reflect and see the magnificence that they already are and have forgotten. This process will take you through an inner revolution, through a cleansing process that is required for you to evolve to higher states of being. So what are you waiting for? Let's go and start your journey.

ALARM

So what is this ALARM I have been talking about? I bet you are curious to know how you can finally learn about yourself from listening to this ALARM and use it to open your heart, the place where the true soul's voice resides.

The ALARM consists of five main pillars: Acknowledge, Love, Achieve, Results, and Miracles that help you create clarity, purpose and vision in your life. In the process you become authentic, trustworthy, and start to work from a place of acceptance and unconditional love.

Each of the main pillars consists of four subcomponents – the essential building blocks that make each of the main pillars.

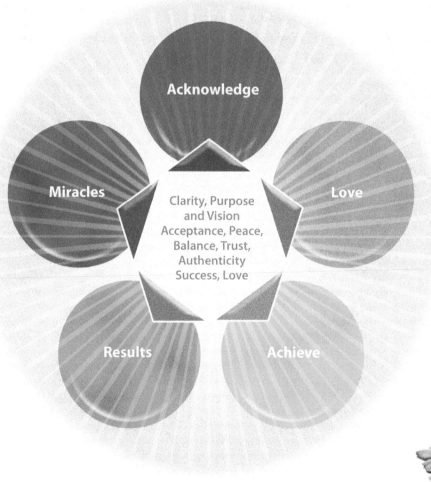

ACKNOWLEDGE

Building blocks of this first pillar are Awareness, Awakening, Alertness and Attention. For you to change any of the unresourceful states that you have learned about so far, first of all you need to become aware of the state, situation or problem that you wish to change in your life. As you do so, an inner awakening happens almost instantly. You have learned so far through everything I have been sharing in this book and from your own experience that the body you have is the most sophisticated piece of technology known to human kind.

The body has its own feedback mechanism to alert you to what is truly happening inside of you so you can pay attention to the changes that this awareness brings to your inner world – positive or negative. Here the goal is for you to get to a place in which you truly acknowledge the changes that are happening inside your body as well as acknowledge the unresourceful states I have been explaining so far.

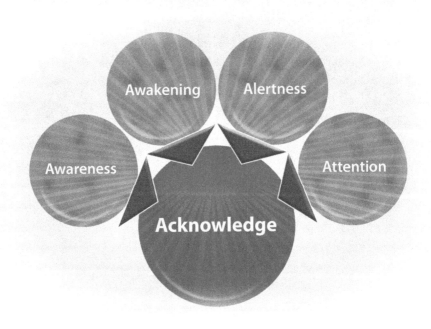

ALARM - *Acknowledge*

AWARENESS

To change any of the eight areas of your life discussed so far in any way, you need to know yourself before you can truly acknowledge what it is that you wish to change. You need to know what you need to do to head in the right direction and you can't do that until you know yourself.

People are using this term all the time though it seems that its full meaning is unclear. For example, you woke up in the morning, stood in front of the mirror and said to yourself: my face looks tired, I look ugly today, or my teeth could be whiter. Does this really mean that you are self-aware to your looks?

No it does not. It means that you are looking at the world through your fears. Comments like those above have a direct relation to your sense of self-value and self-esteem.

Being self-aware means looking *at* those fears instead of looking *through* them. So a self-aware way of looking in the mirror would be more like: I feel bad because I hold a belief that I'm ugly.

In addition, being self-aware will mean that you will be better at choosing and making decisions. Self-awareness can enrich your life because you can then move closer to living your values and realizing your dreams.

Becoming self-aware does not mean being selfish though. Discovering the inner you will enable you to give more of yourself to others and this will benefit your relationships as well as helping to build your self-esteem and confidence as you become truer to yourself.

Being more self-aware is knowing:

- ✓ how you see yourself as a person
- ✓ what you want in your life
- ✓ your strengths and weaknesses
- ✓ what motivates you and makes you happy
- ✓ what you want to change about yourself or about your life
- ✓ your achievements so far
- ✓ how you relate to others
- ✓ you need to improve as a person
- ✓ your most important beliefs and values

Go ahead and make your own list now. There are other factors that could be added.

Everything I have shared with you so far and much more helped me become more aware of who I am so I can develop physically, mentally and spiritually. Everything you have gone through has helped you to become more self-aware.

In science fiction, self-awareness describes an essential human property that bestows "personhood" on to a non-human. If a computer, alien or other object is described as "self-aware", you may assume that it will be treated as a completely human character, with similar rights, capabilities and desires to a normal human being. If you are a *Star Trek* fan like me, you will know I am talking about Data, the human android aboard the *Star Trek: Enterprise* ship.

At the base level, self-awareness begins with self-reflection, an intellectual search for reasons for one's own emotions, beliefs about oneself, actions and a study/learning session involving consequences. Furthermore, self-awareness can be an understanding of one's own knowledge, attitudes and opinions.

The next step in self-awareness leads to the search for answers to existential questions: Who am I? What is God? What is my relationship to the Self?

This is the time when you start searching for answers, finding out the relationship between the Source and the whole of humanity. This leads back to the Self and its realization that you are connected to everything and then searching for what that truly means when translated into action. All paths lead back to you. It is a process with every new Now.

When all paths are taken, all processes done, someone can truly say they are self-aware. We are all self-aware to some degree but it hasn't come to completion. True self-awareness is like enlightenment, it is like a light bulb that always shines without having a switch to turn it on or off.

You may think being self-aware is a goal for you to reach. Self-awareness is not a goal, but a continual learning process. Understanding yourself can help you during arguments, in choosing friends, and in finding general peace and joy in life.

It sounds straightforward, but it is a journey that lasts throughout your life; it takes some people years before they understand what this concept means, and how to apply it to their lives. You normally spend most of your time and energy living from an unconscious mind.

You get caught up in your own little drama and not actually paying attention to what is truly happening in your inner world and in the world around you.

Talking on your cell phone while walking on a busy street is an obvious example. You may think you are aware, but are you? Being fully aware is known as being present. This does not imply that you sense everything, only that you are processing as much sensory input as you are able to.

One sure way to determine if you've got an issue with self-awareness is that you feel everyone else is always to blame for things, you argue with others as you may feel threatened by their tone of language, transparency or you may feel you are being questioned and put on the spot.

Once I worked with a client who was unaware that she was making nasty comments to her daughter. Her daughter would ask her to please stop and she would become irritated with her for accusing her of what she as a mother should or should not do, and no matter what, her daughter should listen.

Without self-reflecting at all, she could not see how she would ramp up her negative jabs until she said a few horrible things she couldn't take back. Her daughter would then become hurt and would say she wouldn't see her again unless she stopped.

She would blame her daughter and tell others she didn't understand what's gotten into her, and that out of nowhere she threatened never to see her own mother again.

As I took her through the method, I helped her see that at the root cause of this situation was her need to control. Her approach was one from a critical parent, and we also uncovered the underlying cultural belief "I am a mother and a child should always listen" that caused her to remain stuck. As she acknowledged all of that, the situation with her daughter transformed into a nurturing, loving and trustworthy relationship.

Your inability to give and receive apologies keeps you in the "unaware state." When someone apologizes, you either may not accept it at all or believe that the person needs to keep apologizing. You don't understand what it means to truly accept someone's apology and move on. As a result you continually harm the relationship by rehashing old arguments.

By contrast, you rarely apologize when you should, and if you do it's a non-apology instead of a genuine acknowledgement for how you acted. Your focus stays on what someone else did instead of your own contribution to the argument.

When I moved to England I noticed how people here apologize to you even when you bump into them when you are walking, when you are on the bus, or when you are on the subway. At the time I thought how nice it was, but whether they truly mean it is another matter altogether.

Self-awareness means that you have a solid understanding about who you are and how you relate to the world. This means being mentally and emotionally present in situations, and understanding how your actions affect people. It also means you're clued into what you really enjoy and dislike.

Self-awareness is important in all areas of your life, but you also have to balance it. The act of self-reflection should be to determine how your actions affect your life and not to act as a martyr or take the blame for everything. Understanding your role and acknowledging the things you do wrong will help you keep a balanced life

Being aware is the act of looking at your feelings in real time, every day of your life, every present moment, instead of being them. Your feelings flow from the unconscious part of your brain to the conscious part of your brain once they are recognized by awareness.

To be aware is to perceive both the outside world and the inside world at the same time as being one. So you're aware of the environment you are in, and aware of what alters the perception of it. As an example, you may be aware that you're not clean inside, that you're not in pure awareness, but are feeling an emotion of jealousy. So come back to the present moment and be aware. You know how to lie to yourself and you can deal with the ego the moment it arises.

However, this concept is not as simple in practice. Many things in life can change you, for the good or bad, and these changes cloud self-awareness.

Awareness Exercise

Becoming self-aware is an ongoing process. Make it your priority to get to know yourself, your dreams, achievements, strengths and weaknesses. Here are some suggestions; list all of the things in each point that can wreak havoc on your awareness. You can start with the list below and add your own points:

1. **Your upbringing.** You are taught to behave a certain way and also that some things are good or bad for you. This means that you may get stuck in a rut or fail to try new things to see if you really like them.

2. **Your religion, cultural beliefs.** Although you may have moved from home, country, friends, school, etc. your religious and cultural beliefs reside deep in your subconscious mind. List the ones that serve you and recycle those that don't.

3. **Society.** You understand what's acceptable in society, learn social grace, and live by the golden rule. But unless you really have a grasp on your self-awareness, any changes will be on the surface and not .. at the emotional level where they need to be.

4. **Media influences.** You're being bombarded with images and messages telling you how to be and many of these can change your perception of what you think or should act like.

5. **Friends.** You choose friends that you think you should be like, or you look for approval from them. Dig deep and become aware why you are having the friends you have; you will raise your awareness and you may learn some invaluable lessons about yourself by doing so.

6. **Past experience.** Look at past issues you've had with people and be honest with yourself. Sometimes it's so hard to think you might have messed up that you don't allow yourself to reflect on the actions you took to help prolong or cause an argument.

7. **It takes two to tango.** Admitting and accepting that you have a part in how people treat you is a hard concept to embrace at first. The following thoughts can act as a warning sign for better self-awareness: Our friendship ended and I have no idea why. What's wrong with them? is a common one I see day in and day out. Another one is: They did this to me for no reason... and so on. When you think these thoughts, turn the focus back to yourself and see if there was something you did to push someone's buttons, start an argument, or prolong a disagreement.

8. **Know your emotional pain.** This is a bit more challenging as your emotions are trapped in all of your body, in every organ. My recent visit to Lanzarote and working with two great professionals, Dennis Smith and Allan Dolan, through a series of breathing and body work, helped me release deep-rooted and forgotten pain in my body. You can for sure do a lot to identify it, it is just harder to locate because – believe it or not – you actively hide it from yourself even as you search for it. This is why your problems can be so frustrating and confusing to you, yet obvious to others, and vice versa. The challenge with long-term emotional pain or self-sabotage is that a part of you wants to hang on. When the pain is so familiar to you, it can be scary to let it go.

You create an identity attached to this pain and you fear to let it go as you would feel lost without it. You would not know who you are without this pain. This is called a psychological attachment. We become attached to emotional pain, deprivation, rejection, being controlled and other psychological states. If that was your childhood programing, then that's what you've come to expect in life.

So, you hide the emotional thumbtack because you can't imagine a world without it. Welcome to Earth. We get attached to pain around here. We really need to learn why and let it go.

9. Know the difference between being aware and not being aware. The only way to tell the difference is to actually be aware, because it's not a thought. If you're so used to thinking, then you can easily just think about awareness, so what you have to do is to practice being aware. Try doing something where you just concentrate upon being aware. For example: go for a walk and just practice and feel what it is to be aware, to feel through your five senses. It really is a matter of practice, because the mind can't give the answer – it's something different to the mind.

10. Play with it, investigate it, and when you do, try to feel it. What I wanted to add on this is that we go through many tasks in our life and we bypass them without paying attention to them enough anyway. Maybe that is what we are talking about by being aware and not being aware? This is what I understand about being aware, because if I go past a human being having a problem and I don't pay attention to it, I'm not being aware of something happening.

AWAKENING

Let's now look at the importance of the second subcomponent that is needed to get you to the place of truly acknowledging everything about you in the present moment.

Being aware does not mean you are awake, so the next step that needs to happen is to look at what it means to be truly "awake." Together let's explore how your life would be if you were to live from an awakened state. What it is that stops you from being awake about everything that is happening inside of you and around you, and look at what you can do to be awake in each present moment.

Now, what do you think it means to be "awake"? Does being awake have anything to do with realizing that there is more than the physical 3D reality you experience every day?

The idea of being "awake" or "conscious" means that you are a person who truly thinks about your own life, what you want to accomplish and you actively seek to achieve your goals.

This is compared to a person who is "asleep" and keeps pressing the snooze button, who may not pay much attention to improving their life and they just kind of live and die, going through the motions. Your built in ALARM that you are learning is there to awaken you from this unresourceful state.

Most of us live our lives through a bit of both being awake and being asleep states. It seems kind of dumb and pointlessly narcissistic to think about it this way; I've known plenty of people who call themselves "conscious" yet their actions and the way they live their day-to-day life is totally opposite, because there is no congruency or consistency in their actions.

There is nothing that can be pinpointed insofar as truly being awake in an ultimate, universal sense. You can be relatively awake with regard to the things that make your existence, such as the kind of awake you're experiencing now while reading this, your everyday matters, the degrees of focus that you bring to whatever is at issue, etc.

"Awake" is of course a term that implies by its opposite not being awake – a condition where awareness is less than optimal. Much has been written for example as to a large sector of society that is basically sleepwalking through their existence, that they're "hypnotized", "brainwashed", and conditioned in a way that shows them not to be on the ball when it comes to awareness.

Even on the individual level you can recognize this when you catch yourself for whatever reason not being as attentive – or not even aware – of some of the things you should be.

After all, the best wakefulness that you as an individual can achieve is a state where your personal dealings and perceptions return results that facilitate objectives, rather than leave them suspended in some mental operational ambiguity.

There is of course the aspect of wakefulness as referring to a transcendent kind of lucidity. I'm sure many of you have your opinions on that. My own view is that it is possible and indeed one that I in my own way seek and aspire taking my life toward.

But as with all things, I believe there needs to be a balance, and so without getting into the maze of particulars on that, let me just say that I have to make sure that the ship and the masts that I am, have to be in top shape – the ocean is not going to be adjusting its demeanor just for my sake or lack of forethought.

Being conscious means that you have created and use a model of the world around you. This allows you to consider options for action before actually doing them. In the strictest sense you can be conscious without being aware, but usually some amount of awareness is implied.

Being awake also means that you realize the true nature of reality – that the world you see or believe you see or want to see is merely an illusion which is heavily influenced by what you believe to be true about the world.

Being fully conscious, also known as fully realized, means that you have a comprehensive grasp of the nature of reality which allows you to do anything possible, or even extend reality.

You realize that you are on your own and that nobody is here to help you find your way – that only you truly know your own way and what you should be doing. When you ask for advice, you are merely asking for input, for a validation of that which you already know and then do your own thinking before you decide what to do.

You learn to trust yourself and to do things that feel right rather than doing things that somebody else considers to be right for you. You recognize that social conditioning is a mirage that has been put over your eyes to stop you from seeing the world as it truly is.

In short, when you are awake you become one with your inner self.

Exercise for you

Go through each of the points, experience them by closing your eyes, take a few deep breaths, repeat the sentence and let your imagination take over and guide you toward what those statements mean to you, make your own realizations and see how you too can awaken to your greatness. The conditions listed below must actually be truly internalized, not just known about.

1. *Experience the notion that behind the veil of the physical illusion, all things are connected.*

2. *Let go of the need to compare. How would your world look if you did not need to compare yourself with others or subordinate to others?*

3. *Accept the world of "drama and trauma" (emotional angst) is created by you. Though triggered by events external to you, it is entirely an invention of your own making.*

4. *Accept and realize that there is more to you than simply your body, there is something beyond the physical "illusion" that exists and that you are part of. You may call it your Spirit, a higher consciousness, or God.*

ALERTNESS

Now that you know what awareness and being awake-conscious is, let's look at what alertness is about and why it is another important subcomponent of the first main pillar Acknowledgment.

You were built with a very sophisticated feedback mechanism and you also were given the knowledge on how you can use this sophisticated feedback mechanism to heal your body. Your body alerts you so you can quickly notice any unusual and potentially dangerous or difficult circumstances that might be happening inside of you.

Alerts that your body sends you teach you how to be vigilant, and how it helps you by putting you in the state of being watchful for possible danger.

It is a warning mechanism that tells you of a danger, a threat, or a problem, typically with the intention so that you can avoid any experience that you may be subconsciously or consciously generating which is not aligned to your true being.

Your body, just like a computer, has its own software to send you virus alert messages when it's under threat; your body has the same intrusion system and it uses everything we have discussed to warn you about what viruses really do to your body.

We get amazed by the different products we use on a daily basis that alert us when we are in danger, when we need to be on time to attend a meeting or even if someone hacked our computer. Yet we ignore our own intelligent built-in alert mechanism.

If you reflect right now, you know that your body alerts you in so many ways: it uses all of the five senses to give you the feedback you need; it also communicates to you through your intuition, and most of all your gut feeling.

If you think about it, your body alerts you 24/7: it tells you when you need food, it wakes you up while you are sleeping if you need to go to the bathroom, when you need certain vitamins, and it also tells you when you have ignored it, not loved it, and not paid attention. It simply creates something to alert you; when you are not listening, it will do it in form of an illness.

The quirky urge, a funny tingle, and that little voice in your head are your gut feelings talking. But what are they telling you, and should you listen? Here's how to make the most of your own innate alertness wisdom.

Most of us have experienced the sense of knowing things before we know them, even if we can't explain how. You hesitate at a green light and miss getting hit by a speeding truck. You decide on a whim to break your no-blind-dates policy and wind up meeting your life partner. You have a premonition that you should invest in a little online start-up and it becomes Apple, Google, Amazon, or Linkedin.

If only you could tap into those insights more often, right? Well TJS Evolutionary Method: The ALARM enables you to do that, especially if you learn to identify which signals to focus on – whether they're sweaty palms, a funny feeling in your stomach, or a sudden and inexplicable certainty that something is up.

According to many researchers, intuition is far more material than it seems. Hope College social psychologist David Myers, PhD, explains that the intuitive right brain is almost always "reading" your surroundings, even when your conscious left brain is otherwise engaged. The body can register this information while the conscious mind remains blissfully unaware of what's going on. Isn't that amazing?

Another theory suggests you can "feel" approaching events specifically because of your dopamine neurons. The jitters of dopamine help keep track of reality, alerting you to those subtle patterns that you can't consciously detect.

So how do you choose which gut feelings (body alerts) to trust? I believe it's a matter of combining the linear mind and intuition, and striking the right balance between gut instinct and rational thinking. Once you've noticed an intuitive hit, you can engage your rational mind to weigh your choices and decide how best to act on them.

Did you know that the immune system's command center is housed inside the gut? An ecological imbalance of organisms in the gut means the body can't defend itself against unfriendly microbes. The result is you get sick a lot.

Ironically, I believe that often medicine, such as antibiotics, wipes out the gut's supply of good bacteria. When you wipe them out again and again with antibiotics and then eat a poor diet, it's a disaster for the gut. That, in turn, can spell trouble for the rest of the body. In my own journey I learned to listen and adopt the eastern teachings of the healing powers of the body.

The experts agree that one of the easiest (and most delicious) ways to restore the gut's healthy flora is to eat more foods rich in good bacteria, such as miso, sauerkraut, kombucha (a fermented Japanese tea), yogurt that contains live bacteria, and kefir (a fermented milk drink).

Oh, before I forget, I wanted to thank my friend Stephen who grew some kefir for me that I now use on daily basis, and grow it with love. It's amazing what you find in nature if you look, question, and believe in the healing powers you and nature have.

Although many of the body's messages can be decoded with a little guesswork and a lot of active listening, it's important to remember that some of these same symptoms can be signs of more serious illnesses.

If, after a couple of weeks of self-care, things don't improve or resolve, it's best to consult a health care professional.

A chronic ache or pain is an invitation to stop and take a look at your life. Your body is telling you it's time to make a change. Respect its request, listen to this alert that it is producing, pay attention to it, make the necessary changes, acknowledge them and you will see how quickly you can restore your body back to balance.

You might struggle to know the wisdom your body is giving you and not know how to get to the root cause. What helped me in the process of fully healing my life was a multipronged approach to health care, seeking advice from both alternative medicine practitioners as well as western doctors. Being curious to get to the root cause of your illness by many different approaches helps you decode your body's warning signals before they cascade into something more serious.

Western medicine has many strengths: stamping out infections, treating emergencies like heart attacks and swooping in with trauma care after an accident or disaster. But when a condition is hard to diagnose, or is chronic or nagging, like poor digestion, insomnia or general fatigue, going outside the doctor's surgery may be your best bet.

Through my personal experience, and now as both a coach and a healer, I see limitations in the way that western medical practitioners typically try to snuff out the body's attempts to heal.

Many symptoms, such as sinus congestion, allergies and excess mucus, are ways it's trying to rid itself of excess toxins; they are feedback to you to tell you to look within and identify where there is no flow of energy and awaken you to that part of self you have not loved. They are a wake-up call for love.

On the other hand, western medicine tries to control these symptoms by suppressing the fever or drying up the congestion, instead of supporting the body's natural means of elimination and detoxification.

In addition to your primary care there are many alternative practitioners you can seek help from. Here are some of the ones I used and trained for: EFT Reiki, Body Mirror System of Healing, Reconnected Healing, Theta healing, life coaches, NLP practitioners, hypnotherapists, Chi-gong, yoga, breathing, body dynamics, etc.

Adelina, a city professional, came to see me for healing to help her get a good night's sleep. She was exhausted, and the only way she could function was drinking a lot of coffee. As she was talking to me, I was listening to her voice, observing her energy, body language, and started to embody her and see what signal the body was telling her that she could not see. Fatigue was what came up.

As we worked together, I took her through this process you are now learning, we spoke about how the Starbucks caffeine fix trip every morning was going to an already low energy bank account and she was trying to lend it a little extra energy for the short term.

I took her through a guided meditation and she was able to see where her energy was being depleted. She realized through her healing sessions that she was living in a bubble that had many holes through which energy escaped.

Those holes were overthinking, taking responsibility for other people's actions, pressure, and long working hours. She realized that she had ignored her own needs, her body's signals, for so long that it became easier to reach for a caffeine fix than face the situations in which she put herself.

As she created some clear goals about her next steps, let go of some of her beliefs, and restored her work/life balance, she stopped drinking coffee and started to tap into her own infinite energy.

Know that your body alerts you in many ways; the above examples are just a grain of sand in a mount of a desert. Its feedback mechanism is complex; it is more than a gut feeling. Intuition is another feedback mechanism for your body to alert you about what's happening inside and outside of you. Try some of the exercises below to kick-start your own intuitive powers.

Alertness Exercise

1. When your body is telling you something, carve out a space and time to clear your mind and get beneath all that noise to see what the body is telling you. Let's say you have a headache; sit down quietly and see what in your real life is causing you pressure that might be leading to you having headaches, migraines, etc. Always look within for solutions.

2. If you feel tired every day, make a note of where you spend most energy. If time is spent doing things or being with people that do not support your highest values, your body is telling you that.

3. If your mind is full of noise, those noises are alerting you to something. When I started my healing journey I learned to meditate to help me shut down this noise and go beyond my current awareness. Meditation is like the bench press for strengthening your intuitive muscles. Sit quietly, breathe deeply and notice if any thoughts or images come to you.

4. Make a list of any symptoms you may be suffering right now, spend time to get to know what each symptom is telling you about you. Do you feel a sensation in your stomach, bones or chest? Do you have a sense of "knowing" or hear the answer inside your head?

These exercises will sharpen your intuitive skills and give you a sense of your intuitive style and you will become an expert in listening to your body's language to yourself.

ATTENTION

> *"Often the body speaks that which the mind refuses to utter."*
>
> Mabel Todd

Now that you have learned more about the three subcomponents Awareness, Awakening, and how your body Alerts you, the next thing you need to do to come to that place of true acknowledgement is to truly start paying attention to all that you have learned about your body's communication to you.

By bringing the feelings of your body to your conscious attention, you begin to access a source of wisdom that knows a great deal about the life you were meant to live.

Would it surprise you that your values and beliefs communicate more authentically from felt experiences than from the rational mind? For example, when you think of different possibilities or choices in your life, notice how you're feeling when you think of each one. Is there resistance in a part of your body or is there an energy or flow?

People say the most important thing in life is your health, because without it you can't enjoy what life has to offer. So why do so many people pay so little attention to their bodies: physical, emotional, mental, astral, etheric, or even the spiritual?

A logical answer to the reasons why we do not pay attention is the illusion of feeling disconnected within ourselves and the greater part of you, your spirit, your consciousness.

In order to become in tune to your body's wisdom, it is important to pay attention to it. Of course, proper sleep, healthy eating and exercising will create more balance for you to stay "in sync" with your body.

But you can also practice right now as you are reading this book. Take a moment and notice how you are sitting in your chair. Notice whether any part of your body hurts or feels uncomfortable. How are you breathing right now? What are your emotions telling you right now? How do you feel? What are you prompted to do? Simply notice, and see if you truly paid attention.

The more you notice what is going on within your body, the more you will know yourself better, and in this way you will become more focused, conscious and efficient.

By checking in with your body many times during the day, you will start developing an innate intuition where you will take productive action more naturally, and you will spend less time spinning your wheels regarding decisions that are important to you.

Many of us live our day-to-day lives taking our bodies for granted, without a real appreciation for what your body provides you in every moment. Most people are unaware of the many influences on the shape and state of the physical body, particularly the mind and the emotions.

For most people, their body remains a largely untapped resource because they have forgotten how to pay attention to the communication and the messages of their own body. By learning to reconnect with your body's wisdom, you can tap into the healing resources of emotion, sensation, intuition, imagery, memory and mystery.

The awakened sense of wholeness that results from this body-mind-spirit connection helps to activate your immune system and promote healing.

So, take a moment right now, sit in a comfortable position, take a few deep breaths and listen carefully to what your body wants to tell you. Every single cell in your body is full of inherent wisdom and communicates with you constantly. All you have to do is learn to listen, pay attention, and honor what your body is telling you to begin this reconnection.

As you quiet your mind and deepen the intimate connection with your body, it is absolutely amazing what you can experience if you only pay attention and listen with greater awareness!

No matter what the nature of physical, emotional or mental illnesses in general, and pain in particular, these can be ways and means of your body to send you messages.

Chances are high that your body has already been trying for a long time to communicate something to you. Noticing these signals, feeling your energy levels, and adjusting your activities accordingly are essential steps in the healing process.

Because your body constantly reflects your thoughts, feelings, emotions, and beliefs, and reacts on them, the state of the body provides insights about the deepest realms of your hidden self: your truest convictions, loves, and fears. The body is a powerful, honest (and often literal) mirror, one that isn't always easy to face.

Listening and engaging to the signals of the body is exactly the opposite of what most people are prepared to do. Instead, we tend to strive to hide, ignore, push away, or numb these unpleasant sensations.

However, the more you ignore them or actively numb them, the "louder" your body becomes – you know what I am talking about. As long as these signals stay unnoticed and no appropriate attention is granted to the affected body part, no real healing can take place.

I have seen it in myself and in every person that my path has crossed. No matter what medical treatment you may receive, your underlying problem can worsen or reappear at a different body area until you give your body your full attention and understand what it has to tell you. As soon as you give your body the opportunity to be heard, it can start to relax and healing can begin.

Paying attention, listening to your body and learning how to work cooperatively with the body's innate wisdom is the first step in understanding yourself.

Learning how to reconnect with your own inner nature is a major leap in entering a stronger relationship to the needs, weaknesses, and unlimited potential of your integral self.

Here, within each and every one of us, is a highly potent system with intelligence far beyond what we might imagine, yet actualizing this potential to create solid foundations for health and recovery is only possible when you learn to be aware, awaken, listen to the alerts your body is sending you, observe, pay attention, and engage with the most advanced single system in the world: you.

Keep in mind that you can communicate with your body at any time. Your body does so every single day.

ACKNOWLEDGEMENT

You may have learned so much about yourself already through the process I have taken you, and gone through so many life experiences, but do you truly acknowledge your body's wisdom?

Did you know that the word itself stems from the Old English *oncnawan*, meaning "to understand, to admit the existence, reality, or truth of something"?

When we think of the word acknowledge, we often use acknowledge to understand our outer world. For instance, in your day-to-day life you think about thanking someone for their hard work, express thanks or gratitude for something they may have done, shower them with overdue praise, or perhaps honor their achievements in a formal ceremony.

You also use it to express recognition of a friend's smile, their feelings, or obeying the different rules imposed by your family, relationships, work, or even authorities of the country you live in.

I'd like to inspire a revival of Pure Acknowledgement – acknowledgement of you, of everything that is happening inside of you, and everything you have learned so far about you: the good, the bad, the emotions, your thoughts, the things you may have said and done, and the things you have not done.

The promises you have broken, the people you have wronged, the people you have loved. Take a moment and acknowledge everything about you, your existence, your spirit, your infinite capacity to create, love, and be loved. Acknowledge you, and that you are a magnificent being, you are a creator of your world.

These days, we rarely take the time to acknowledge ourselves or someone without expecting (or at least, quietly hoping for) something in return.

It's not enough to simply tell a celebrity you admire: "Hey. Your work moves me" without an accompanying photo to "prove" to your "friends" on Facebook that it happened. Why would you think that it is enough to tell yourself "I love you" without accompanying positive feeling, thought, action, behavior, without truly having to "prove" that you do so?

It's not enough to simply send an email to a writer whose work you cherish and say "Hi. You are magnificent" without asking for a few words of advice, a promotional tweet, some form of energetic payback.

There's nothing wrong with reciprocity. There's nothing wrong with seeking support. And there's certainly nothing wrong with wanting things.

As you acknowledge more and more of who you are, you increase your awareness, you start to awaken yourself to new ways of thinking and being (new paradigms), you start to listen to the alerts that your body sends you, and you start paying attention and truly acknowledge the infinite wisdom that exists in you. You start taking care of you.

As you implement everything you have learned so far and start to acknowledge that, you will start experiencing what mindfulness truly is: reflexivity and enhanced self-awareness that helps Buddhists root themselves in the moment.

Once you have truly acknowledged everything about you without any criticism, expectations, hopes, dreams or strings attached, you can sweep away your negative thoughts, illness, and emotions from you like the fallen leaves from a tree.

You start to listen to your body's ALARM that tells you about the different types of intrusions that are happening in your body, mind, emotion, or in your spirit-consciousness. You learn to deeply acknowledge the power of you.

When you acknowledge you, first and foremost, you are saying to you and everyone around you: I love you, I see you, I get you, and I thank you.

Acknowledgement Exercise

Let's start the exercise with you; once you do that for you then choose four people you want to acknowledge right now as you go through this process. Send them this note, or a delightful variation of your own devising. Hope for nothing and see what happens.

I want you to know that...
- tick all that apply, or add your own -
( )　You are amazing.
( )　You are wise, and you apply that wisdom.
( )　You are a force of nature.

( ) You are doing such a good job at life.
( ) You are a spirit living in a metaphysical form.
( ) You are hysterical.
( ) You brighten up the room.
( ) You are my teacher.
( ) You lighten my spiritual load.
( ) You make it an absolute joy to come to work.
( ) You make me want to make art.
( ) You are trustworthy and I trust you.
( ) You make my life sweeter and easier – and you don't even know it.
( ) You prove that my dreams are delightfully doable.
( ) You remind me what's possible.
( ) You are authentic, you are a gift to this world
( ) Your ideas are spot-effin-on.
( ) Your support alters my world.
( ) Your words delight me.
( ) Your work moves me.
( ) You are born from love, you live to give and receive love, you ...
     are going back to love.
( ) I see and understand what you're trying to add to the world.
     I get it. I adore you. And I applaud you.

I hope you tuck this note in a top-secret file, where you store the bits of appreciation for rainy days when your spirits may be sagging.

Thank you for existing. That is all.

Awareness Awakening Alertness Attention Acknowledgment

LOVING

Now that you have come to a place of true acknowledgment, let's look at the next important thing that you need to do to help you get back on track and overcome any of the issues that you have identified so far – Loving, the second main pillar of this method.

To truly love yourself you must change the language in which you speak to yourself and others around you. You also need to know and overcome your own limited beliefs for you to change any of the unresourceful states that I have been talking about. Then you need to learn to listen, and I don't mean just with your ears, what I mean is listening to everything you have learned about you.

Here the goal is for you to truly love and accept all that you are so that love flows in you and through you. This is the state in which you are always switched to the flow of love and the light in your life.

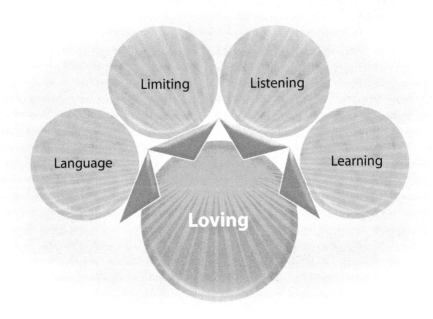

ALARM - *Loving*

LANGUAGE

"When there is no enemy within, the enemies outside become your friends."

Tony J Selimi

Language is one of the four subcomponents that form the second pillar of the TJS Evolutionary Method and it looks at the importance of understanding the language that you use and how it impacts your way of being and the state you are in.

Here, as you practice and learn to cut out all of the outside noises, you truly start to listen to everything that is going on inside of your body. As you do so you start learning more about who you are, and the body's way of communicating to you when it is out of alignment.

Negative self-talk is one of the most common issues and a recurring theme that comes up in a lot of my workshops and with the private clients I work with. They all want to get rid of their negative self-talk, or reduce it, or make it less intrusive, or be in charge of this internal dialogue that is the bane of many people's lives!

If you pay attention, you will see that everyone around you is looking for ways of dealing with negative self-talk because it features so strongly in negative moods such as anger, anxiety, guilt, and panic; in fact, negative self-talk is often the principal way in which we maintain and exacerbate these moods.

On average you are 50-75% water, daily you think 75,000 to 120,000 thoughts, and statistics also show that for most of us 70-80% of our daily thoughts are negative. Those thoughts influence the way you feel, behave and act. They also create the attitudes you have about life, and the outcomes you create.

Knowing that, and observing everyone around us, it would seem that the human mind is wired for neuroticism. A healthy first step to alleviate this problem, therefore, would be to acknowledge this, to acknowledge the science that already exists about how to maintain a balance between the negative self-talk and maintaining a positive mental attitude.

I have never met a person who does not have negative self-talk; there is no statistic in the world that will show you that you will never have it, so let's break this illusion right now and remove this expectation of yourself of the need to be positive.

You know what I am talking about: the internal commentary that goes through our heads non-stop, every day. You know you do it, right? We all do it! We talk to ourselves so often that we don't even realize we're doing it!

Self-talk isn't a problem when the commentary is benign, but when it turns negative it can have a huge impact on your overall well-being. It controls your health, the way you feel and the way you behave.

Let's face it, you can really be your own worst enemy and the truth is that most of your commentary consists of cruel, inaccurate, unhelpful, unsupportive, negative statements about yourself and others.

How many times have you said to yourself: I will never be rich; I will never fall in love again; I am bad at writing (this one I said to myself so many times); I'm never going to be good at this; this person doesn't like me; you're such an idiot, how could you have locked your keys in the car?

You can be really hard on yourself, and when you are hard on yourself on the inside, it shows on the outside, you cannot hide it as you are like a TV transmitter that always sends waves of information in your environment.

Think of a moment in time when you went somewhere and you did not like the energy of the room, or the person you came across. Something inside of you told you that it did not feel right, without even speaking or being close to that person. The reason you know this information is that you are energy being, everything that you think and feel travels through your energy field that you radiate into this world that other people pick up, and vice versa; you are both transmitter and receiver.

You don't deliberately set out to exacerbate your negative moods in this way. That would be daft. It happens because you don't know how to manage this form of negative thinking and, as a result, believe that you are stuck with it and it's just a reality of life.

Once I was coaching John, a city trader who was experiencing a lot of anger issues. John was having a disagreement with his work colleague Dan in which Dan insulted him and then stormed off, leaving John feeling hurt and fuming – and without the ability to have his say. This created an awkward situation in his team and had a massive impact on him. They no longer spoke unless it was absolutely necessary; they would deliberately ignore one another, even though they work in the same place and the disagreement occurred weeks ago.

What was happening was John continued to have imaginary inner arguments with Dan, saying all of the things he meant to say at the time – over and over again, day and night. These inner arguments or tirades would erode his peace of mind, ability to concentrate and, of course, his sleep.

Anything which reminds him of Dan will restart the inner fuming: he'll typically visualize him, feel a rush of anger, rerun the original disagreement, hear him being insulting, criticize himself for being ineffective in dealing with him, criticize himself for not being able to "let it go", and on and on. Every time he does this it feeds his anger.

And the inner self-talk and visualizing winds him up physically, too, producing a state of neurological and chemical arousal. His heart rate increases and his muscles become more tense which, of course, is likely to add to his inner turmoil since he is also likely to be angry with himself for not being able to control his own moods.

You can see how just 10 or 15 minutes of this kind of inner activity caused him to be emotionally aroused as if he were face to face with the person. And when this occurs during the night, it removes any chance of him drifting back into sleep for an hour or two. And, ironically, when I asked him if Dan thinks about this while John is experiencing this turmoil, he answered most probably not as he is probably sleeping peacefully and soundly in his own bed!

Self-talk is a normal and important and valuable part of our inner processing, as long as we know how to use or manage it. But because few of us receive lessons in how to use and manage our inner thinking-feeling process, let alone our inner self-talk, we end up developing our personal ways of dealing with it through trial and error. And rarely are these trial and error results even reasonably effective in putting us in the driving seat of our emotional lives.

Over the years, I studied many disciplines; for me Neuro Linguistic Programing was the driving lessons I needed for understanding the mind-body interface. It is a "model" that gave me valuable insights and helped me examine how my clients use their minds and bodies and how they can manage their lives better.

Excessive self-criticism tends to backfire, because it leads us to focus on our so-called failures instead of the small ways that we could have improved. And over the long term, studies show, negative self-talk is associated with higher stress levels and even depression.

The secret here is to embrace your imperfections. I can tell you from personal experience and the many people I have helped do this that it's enormously freeing. It is also a huge stress reducer, and it helps you stop holding yourself to insanely high standards.

Perfectionism can be great, but it is also destructive. I've spoken to over 5,000 people, interviewed CEOs and award-winning athletes, and not once did I ever hear someone say "I achieved everything I have because I am a perfectionist."

So re-evaluate, rethink, and relax your standards just a little. If you give yourself the same empathy you'd show a friend, it will be so much easier to take on The Nag, and win.

The truth is when "used" effectively your self-talk is a wonderful competence: a gift which enables you to think creatively, realistically, analytically, thoroughly, critically, etc. Without these abilities you would not be able to function very effectively in everyday life.

The problem with negative self-talk arises from the fact that you may not know you are doing it, or make a conscious decision that you can manage it. Or, if you do know this, you don't know how to manage it. It's a bit like having a pet dog. If the dog has been trained it can be a wonderful companion, security assistant and playmate. If it has always been allowed to do as it wishes it can wreak havoc indoors and outside – and even endanger the safety of friends and family!

So, it is never what happened to you that matters. It is how you perceive it, what decision you make out of it and how you act on it that matters.

Happily the old saying "you can't teach an old dog new tricks" doesn't apply. Here the analogy falls down because it is perfectly possible to learn to manage your self-talk; this is where NLP has helped me and many I have coached overcome this limiting belief.

So before you go any further I challenge you to get your negative self-talk in check!

Happily, there are many ways to muzzle that inner critic for good. Here are some NLP techniques for improving and managing your negative self-talk:

- ✓ Block it: so that you actually inhibit your own ability to self-talk.
- ✓ Replace it: similar to blocking, here you are replacing one stream of inner self-talk with another.
- ✓ Inhibit it: by paying attention to things which either do not require self-talk or which strongly call upon other senses such as sound, vision or physical sensations.
- ✓ Redirect it: using your self-talk for more positive purposes.
- ✓ Negotiate with it: do a deal with your own self-talk using an NLP technique.
- ✓ Make it unnecessary: often our self-talk is a means of figuring something out or clearing our mind. So here we use better ways of achieving this result.

✓ Reduce it: use awareness, plus some of the other methods, to reduce it.

✓ Modulate it: change the manner in which you talk with yourself so that it has a more supportive and calming effect.

✓ Manage it: **develop the ability of deciding to not "entertain" certain trains of thought.**

✓ Own it: **as a result of using the other methods, the self-talk ceases to be an "it" – we recognize it is simply something we are doing, and which we can do differently.**

LIMITING BELIEFS

The second subcomponent of the second main pillar Love is your limiting beliefs that are stored inside of you and remain there without even questioning if they are true or not, or if they are serving you in your day-to-day living or not.

Much like a computer, you too are literally "programed" with beliefs and feelings. The negative ones create blocks within your life and illnesses over time. Core beliefs are very deep emotional beliefs that often you are not even aware of and were created when you were very young.

It is now understood that you can inherit beliefs and emotions from your parents and ancestors, because they are passed down to you in your cellular memory. This is often the reason for inherited physical illnesses and diseases that are passed through generations. It's pretty amazing when you think about it, though they can hinder your personal development and influence the way you live your life.

During the first six to seven years of your childhood, many negative beliefs are also created within you, which cause you difficulties in later years and if ignored in the longer term will eventually become blockages in your body and, in time, illnesses. These beliefs are deep within you and you are generally not aware of them as they are hidden in the subconscious mind.

Here your mission is to eliminate old beliefs that limit you, such as lack of ability, intelligence, competence, not being good enough, not deserving good fortune and the like.

A good way to determine a possible limiting belief is by becoming aware of the statements you make that contain the word "but". "I want to be healthy, but with this illness, it'll never happen." "I wish I could make more money, but with my education that's impossible." "I would love to find the perfect partner, but all the good ones are taken." "I really do want to be happier, but my past gets in the way." "I dreamed of success, but I was born on the wrong side of the tracks."

Now, before you continue further take a pen and paper and make a list of your own buts.

Beliefs are thoughts associated with experiences that have energy attached to them. Many of your beliefs are from your early years and are frequently associated with experiences involving peers, parents and education. These experiences may be either of a positive or negative nature. Most often they operate at the subjective level and exert tremendous impact on your life.

When you have been told that you are intelligent and creative, then your experiences are characteristically of this type. On the other hand, when you have been told you are clumsy, dumb or not good enough, then these programs often shape your experiences.

Programs operating from the subjective level are very powerful. Once the program is installed, there is no evaluation of positive or negative. The belief is accepted as true and never gets questioned until you have a major breakdown and you seek professional help.

Your personal beliefs are perhaps the most important aspect of how you have lived and how you spend the rest of your life. When you want to change a current belief, you must first examine the beliefs you currently hold and those new positive beliefs you want to create. Then use some of the techniques you can find on my website to eliminate the negative belief and create and manifest the new positive belief, and it will be so.

All emotions and limiting beliefs arise from such disturbances in the body's subtle energy system. I will be going into further details about how you can use the second core element of TJS Evolutionary Method: The Rainbow Zones in my next book.

Exercise for you

Create your "I believe ..." note cards, they will help you bring out the true believer in you. The cards can be placed in your wallet, pocket or purse as a daily reminder of how strong your internal belief system is.

You will need a pack of small index cards, scissors, and a pen or pencil. Write the statements on the index cards, here are some for you to choose and start the process:

1. *I am wise and I apply my wisdom.*
2. *I am the creator of my life.*
3. *I believe that I can achieve any goal that I set for myself.*
4. *I believe that I am valuable.*
5. *I believe that inside of me lies an enormous amount of strength to withstand any obstacle that I have to face.*
6. *I believe that I should only speak positive words about myself to build myself up.*
7. *I believe that I have total control of my life.*
8. *I believe that I have to love myself from the inside out.*
9. *I believe that within me lies a survivor.*
10. *I believe that I am succeeding in following my dreams.*
11. *I believe that my past doesn't predict my future.*
12. *I believe I am powerful.*

Continue and add your own beliefs to the list above.

Carry one of these cards in your wallet, pocket or purse every day, and read it throughout the day several times (say out loud when possible). These cards are meant to be used as a constant encourager, and as a tool to replace the incorrect beliefs that you may have about who you are and what you can be.

The more you read and repeat the words on the cards, the more you will start to believe the statements. You can also record them on your cell phone and listen to them throughout the day; it is the repetition that creates the memory.

LISTEN

Listening is the third subcomponent that is required for you to reach a state in which you truly are in the flow of love. This is your ability to receive messages accurately in the communication process that is happening inside and outside of your body.

You use this skill daily, and you know that it is crucial to all effective communication; without the ability to listen effectively, messages are easily misunderstood, communication breaks down and the sender of the message can easily become frustrated or irritated.

Listening is so important that many top employers give regular listening skills training to their employees. This is not surprising when you consider that good listening skills can lead to better customer satisfaction, greater productivity with fewer mistakes, and increased sharing of information that in turn can lead to more creative and innovative work.

However, you might not listen to the signals your body is sending you every millisecond of your life. The good thing is as you start liberating yourself from negative self-talk, limiting beliefs you may have, thoughts, and feelings that take up most of your time, you start the process of becoming intrusion free, and as you do so, you strengthen your ability to awaken to higher states of being.

Good listening skills also have benefits in your personal life, including a greater number of friends and social networks, improved self-esteem and confidence, higher grades in academic work and increased health and well-being. Studies have shown that whereas speaking raises blood pressure, listening brings it down.

But what about your ability to listen to your body's built-in ALARMs you have been learning about, to all the alerts that your body is sending you, to the messages that each illness carries? What would you discover about yourself if you listen to everything that is happening inside of you with the same degree of integrity?

Part of the awakening process is learning to listen to the inner guidance that is never wrong, not for you. All the advice from your friends is just not going to do it. For sure, you can talk about it, but the very best advice is going to come from you to you.

Have you ever felt uncomfortable being in a particular place or with people where your stomach is tense and you get that "I feel I should not be here" feeling? This is your inner voice's way of telling you to move on or get out or it's not the right time to be here. Doubt the self and the inner feelings and you are likely to find there is a valuable lesson coming up in listening to your inner voice.

I experienced this recently; I attended a workshop and was approached by a guy that my entire being was not feeling comfortable being around. On the surface he seemed very pleasant, although my gut feeling was telling me that something did not feel right.

It did not take long for my gut feeling to be right, it only took a day. The next morning when we met for breakfast I got to know the victim mindset through his argumentative conversations with the entire group. He saw himself as a victim of circumstances and that the world around him was responsible for the situation he was in. My own inner voice and divine guidance told me this, not in the format I saw the day after, but my entire energy field spoke to me, so did my gut.

Your gut feeling is in the solar plexus area, this is where your anger and your power live.

When this knots up and you feel tense, more than likely you are coming into contact with beings that are negative or an area or person or persons that is sucking your energy or power from you, and by you being there this is just what happens.

Learning to listen to your inner voice includes knowing what is going on in your energetic field. This is an easy process once you know how. Just don't let the head get in the way and tell you that you are "being silly."

Your inner voice and clairsentience is your higher self communicating to you loud and clear and trying desperately to get your attention which the head is desperately trying to avoid.

Listening is not the same as hearing. Hearing refers to the sounds you hear, whereas listening requires more than that: it requires focus. Listening means paying attention not only to the story, but how it is told, the use of language and voice, and how you or the other person uses his or her body.

In order to listen effectively you need to use more than just your ears; in other words, it means being aware of both verbal and non-verbal messages that are happening simultaneously.

Your ability to listen effectively depends on the degree to which you perceive and understand these messages. The most basic and powerful way to connect to you or with another person is to listen. Just listen. Perhaps the most important thing we ever give each other is our attention. Effective listening requires concentration and the use of your other senses – not just hearing the words spoken. All of the five senses can be deployed to help you become an effective listener.

A good listener will listen not only to what is being said, but also to what is left unsaid or only partially said. Effective listening involves observing body language and noticing inconsistencies between verbal and non-verbal messages.

For example, if someone tells you they are happy with their life but through gritted teeth or with tears filling their eyes, you should consider that the verbal and non-verbal messages are in conflict. They maybe don't mean what they say.

Another example is your best friend calls you and invites you to go out to the most amazing event, and although your inner voice was telling you to have a bath, chill and relax, you make the decision and you agree to join him. Are you truly listening?

Maria came to see me for help with shoulder pain, lack of sleep, constant migraines, and low energy levels. She had tried the medical route for a few years, and although it helped a bit, it did not cure the problems, so she decided to try alternative methods of healing.

I remember our first session together: she talked so much that at some point I asked her to stop talking, to go within and listen to her body and point out to me where in her body those symptoms appeared. As she relaxed more, she could focus more on what she was ignoring and not paying attention to.

She started to put other thoughts out of her mind and concentrate on the messages that were being communicated to her through her feelings, her heart, and her gut instinct.

She started to get a clear idea of how much she had ignored herself for the sake of others, and in that process totally forgotten about her own needs. I asked her to empathize with herself as she would do with a friend, to be patient and let her body speak in its own time, and to listen deeply.

As the time went on, in each session she started to get the whole picture that was causing her distress, not just isolated bits and pieces. She learned that one of the most difficult aspects of listening is the ability to link together pieces of information to reveal the root cause of the symptoms she was experiencing. With proper concentration, coaching her to let go of distractions, and helping her with her focus this became easier for her.

Her health returned to normal, her energy levels increased, and so did her ability to listen truly to her body's wisdom.

Why is listening important? If you listen to yourself with full attention, conviction, commitment and support, you will feel affirmed and important and have a sense of value and the validity of your feelings, ideas and experiences. You start caring for your body, for yourself and you start to experience loving yourself fully.

When you listen to all of the dialogues that are happening within you, you truly start to pay attention to you. You take an interest in looking after your body, you take care of your heart, and you validate, acknowledge, and appreciate yourself.

When you accept and recognize yourself for who you are, you may feel freer to express your feelings and explore deeper and understand better who you are and how to make good decisions for issues you may be facing in any of the eight key areas of your life.

You must be fully connected with what your body is saying and how it is being said.

Good listening requires being totally present and aware and keeping an open mind without judgment.

And finally, it is extremely important to love yourself, as it is the only way that feelings and thoughts can be shared comfortably, and you can be free to be who you really are.

When you listen and hear the voice that comes from your heart, you can access your greatest potential joy and desire. This is the heart's vision – the personal dream that will allow you to accomplish the things that bring happiness and fulfillment.

As you become master at listening and hearing your heart's voice, fling your deepest longings and desires toward that heart vision, the body and senses merely follow the heartstrings that are made from your faith.

This is the magic of personal creation and manifestation that marks the wholehearted seeker who knows that miracles are real. You create the miracle of cooperation through the faith and willingness to be a partner with the Great Mystery, allowing personal desire to manifest in its own way.

The universe is a changing place, changing into a wonderful place of light, and it is through your heart that you have to learn to listen to yourself and the universe you live in.

Exercise for you

It's fascinating to become familiar with your inner wisdom and start the process of truly listening from within – you can learn so much about you. Here are some ways to experiment.

Take a moment, close your eyes, and start listening to what is happening within. Bring your awareness to your toes, and make your way all the way to your head. Pay attention to what you can hear and listen as you move your attention from one part of your body to another part of your body. At the end ask yourself the question: what is my heart saying?

Do not be surprised if the answer comes in an indirect way, for spirit has vision and the answer or guidance needed just for you can come in the form of being guided to a particular book, or movie, or you may find someone may just come up to you and say "I just have to tell you this."

So do not short-change yourself in receiving the guidance. Be open and attentive to the voice of spirit for it comes in wonderful ways – spirit is never boring and always full of passion.

You will find that your heart knows, it is never wrong, for the heart is the place of divine guidance. The head is the place of human reasoning and always challenges divine guidance until you have worked out the issues that need healing over those for which you need guidance.

> *Follow your heart and it will take you on a journey to a star. The way to know when truth is talking is by asking a simple question: is this moving me toward love or away from love?*
>
> **When the truth is talking, there is no sinking feeling that something is wrong. The body unclenches. There is a sense of clarity, excitement, or relief, an undeniable knowing.**

The true path for your life cannot be figured out or created. Your job is simply to listen, and in the listening you will be given all the guidance you need to do exactly the right thing. When you listen, life unfolds mysteriously. You get out of your own way and allow the still, small voice to be heard.

LEARN

> *"Intellectual growth should commence at birth and cease only at death."*
>
> **Albert Einstein**

I am certain that so far you have come to self-realization on how have you turned away from your inner wisdom. So if you asked yourself the question What did I learn? what would be the answer? What is your experience so far doing the exercises to get to know you at a deeper level?

As you accept that there are no mistakes in life, as time passes you start to free yourself from these limiting beliefs, the mistakes of the past become lessons of the present.

By now, if you have been following me through every chapter and through the second pillar of the TJS Evolutionary Method, Learning is the fourth subcomponent.

You may have gone through the first pillar of the ALARM methodology, but unless you truly learn from everything you have gone through, you are not likely to experience the shift from one state to another that I have been describing.

But how do you get true value of learning?

Simply, I believe it is the consistent and deep engagement of the mind and body in the active pursuit of knowledge and experience from birth to death.

Now, science is helping to support the importance of learning in keeping brains active and healthy for a lifetime. Mental exercise, especially learning new things or pursuing activities that are intellectually stimulating, strengthen brain-cell networks and help preserve mental functions. Let go of any illusions you may have about your learning ability; the brain is just as capable of learning in the second half of life as in the first half.

Over recent years there have been new discoveries, as neuroscientists continue to conduct research on how the mental and physical activities so integral to the arts are equally fundamental for brain function.

Charles Limb, brain scientist and musician at Johns Hopkins University, says: "The brain on arts is different from the everyday brain. Art is magical, but it is not magic. It is a neurological product and we can study it."

It is fascinating that through interactive activities designed to stimulate awareness, listening, coordination, language, and music you can increase your brain's capacity to learn. There are so many tools, books, videos, TV programs, apps that you can use to learn; we have entered the information age where knowledge is freely accessible to anyone.

It is obvious to state, but nonetheless important to recognize, that the benefits of lifelong learning not only enhance your life and the experiences you are creating, but also the community you live in.

During the time I was working in the corporate world, I learned that business, project teams and individuals learn through a cycle of observing, familiarizing, valuing, deciding, and acting while trying to navigate and find their way to business objectives and deadlines.

I adopted this method in learning about the inner wisdom that lay in me and in each of the clients I have coached. The results were remarkable; as I took them through a process of the lessons learned from past experiences, I was able to assist them in all five phases described above.

A member of parliament was referred to me recently for some coaching; here is an example of how I helped him by using this process to gain clarity on the issues he came to see me about:

✓ Observe – in our coaching session he would study lessons learned from past experiences. This helped him identify issues and obstacles long before they become a problem by making the indicators more recognizable.

✓ Familiarize – as I helped him familiarize himself with the deepest part of him, it helped him assimilate past experience in the context of the problem at hand. This reduced the time required to arrive at a decision or a course of action to follow.

✓ Value – taking him through this process helped him get clear on his highest values and aligned his goals and objectives accordingly. Living and working according to what he valued most helped him focus, remain energetic and positive.

✓ Decide – learning from past mistakes provides the necessary context, background and recommendations that facilitate the decision-making process.

✓ Act – being clear and looking at the components to well-defined lessons from his life helped him to act, he used them all as a set of guidelines.

A lesson learned is really not learned if it is not validated and made available to your conscious mind so you do not repeat mistakes of the past.

There are so many tools available to you to learn about you; choose the one that resonates to you and from which you get the most learning. The truth is there is an infinite amount of knowledge out there for you to learn, so what are you waiting for?

Love

"It matters not who you love, where you love, why you love, when you love or how you love, it matters only that you love."

John Lennon

Now that you have gone through all of the four subcomponents of the main second pillar, Love, let's dive deep and let's talk about it. Without love your life is meaningless.

The time has come for you to make the most important decision of your life, the one that will affect every other decision you make, which is the commitment to love and accept yourself.

This decision you are making right now directly affects the quality of your relationships, your work, your free time, your faith, and your future.

You may be struggling with making and living this decision, so let's explore why this is so difficult to do. There are many factors why loving yourself can be a difficult concept to grasp as you were taught different things about what love is.

You learned about love from your family of origin, the culture you were born into, and you were taught by society that your worth is found in the idols of your culture, technology, status, youth, sex, power, money, attractiveness, and romantic relationships.

If you base your self-worth on the external world, you'll never be capable of self-love. Your inner critic will flood you with thoughts of "I'm not enough, I don't have enough, and I don't do enough."

Feelings of lack are never-ending. Every time a goal is reached or you possess the next big thing, your ego will move the line.

You know that insufficient or lack of self-love can cause much disruption to anyone's life. And if you ask me, we are living in a world that is starved of love. It is not that love is not available but we have been starving ourselves from our basic need.

Chances are that it has been hard to escape from the constant bombardment of messages that made you believe how "not good enough" or unlovable you are. You hear them from your parents, friends, bosses, and media advertisements.

In fact, you have been hearing these messages from the time you were conceived and were born. It has been the case that ever since the time you were a child, you have been learning to compare yourself with others, that you need perfect looks, top grades, titles, money and status to be deemed worthy of love and respect. And so you use these forms of identification to define who you are. Should you fall short, you find it hard to love yourself.

Over the years this leaves a huge residue of lack of self-love, self-worthiness and you end up closing your heart to this beautiful universal energy of love.

A consequence of low self-love is a broken heart. Unfortunately, success, good relationship, attracting opportunities, money, great friends and lifestyle can be harder to achieve if the voice inside your head becomes overwhelming. You constantly judge yourself for being "wrong", "imperfect" or "not good enough."

You also apply labels such as a "failure", "loser" or "freak" on yourself. Admittedly, it is difficult to experience any ounce of joy when you are convinced of the debilitating stories that you tell yourself.

"Of all the judgements we pass in life, none is more important than the judgement we pass on ourselves."

Nathaniel Branden

Because you have been trapped in a negative mental state for so long, loving yourself is not something that comes easily. Even though you wish to break free from your inner critic, you face problems knowing where to start. You find yourself drowning again and again in a whirl of self-pity, self-rejection and self-blame.

Hence, it would seem that loving yourself has to be a practice until the day that it becomes natural, just like breathing. So it means that you may just need to start from understanding the basics of what it means to love yourself.

Before going on to that, let's look into the consequences of what happens when there is a lack or low level of love:

1. *You find it hard to believe in yourself.*

2. *You criticize yourself constantly and believe that you are unworthy.*

3. *You are excessively hard on yourself, but find it easy to be lenient toward others.*

4. *You have low expectations for yourself.*

5. *When you look in the mirror, all you notice are your flaws, imperfections and faults.*

6. *You neglect self-care – for instance, not caring about your eating habits, not putting up a neat appearance and so on.*

7. *You often operate out of a fear of rejection and have low self-confidence.*

8. *You cannot function well in social groups.*

9. *You downplay your gifts, talents and abilities.*

10. *You feel lonely over long periods of time.*

11. *You suffer from bouts of depression or sudden and inexplicable bouts of sorrow.*

12. *You constantly crave the approval of others.*

13. *You dull pain and feelings of unworthiness through addictive behavior such as smoking, sex and shopping.*

Most certainly, life can be more of a struggle especially if you are in the habit of deriding yourself. It is hard to function well when you are your greatest enemy. Invariably you will face problems in relationships, health, success, career and wealth. It is possible to remain stuck in negativity for years, without knowing how to help yourself out effectively.

Well, what you need to realize is that it is not possible to enjoy abundance of any form if you lack self-love. The vibration of abundance is love. Love has creative power. It creates everything that you see around you.

Often I am asked the secret to my success, both material and spiritual; my answer is that manifesting abundance can only begin with loving yourself. And so if you are hoping to enjoy some level of happiness or even to create a great life, you will need to learn how to love yourself. In fact, the more self-love you have, the greater your ability to manifest abundance.

> *"You yourself, as much as anybody in the entire universe deserve your love and attention."*
>
> **Buddha**

Self-love is about your being. It encompasses more than just doing. Hence, to truly love the self is more than a physical act of self-care, having material goods, using mental force to will yourself or having the day off to rest. It is also more than saying positive things to you. Self-love necessarily involves the mind-body-spirit. It incorporates an inside-out approach.

In my life I have come across many old myths; holding on to myths can prevent you from loving yourself more fully. If you believe that self-love is simply about having a long bath, a manicure, massage or having your hair done, then you are sadly mistaken.

Sure, these self-care activities make you feel good about yourself. Buying a branded handbag or expensive car may be able to give you a high; however, these are just externals. The satisfaction that you derive from them does not last long. The excitement dies out – fast!

Hence, it is possible to be engaged in years of self-care but still face difficulties with loving yourself. In fact, by keeping yourself endlessly occupied with forms that engage your senses, you may even miss the whole point about what it truly means to love yourself. And so you get an instant perk through these activities or material possessions but they do not transform you from the inside. The rush of energy fizzles out rather quickly.

You will eventually discover that you are the one that you seek. Answers to having a more successful life do not lie outside but from within. It is only when you search inside your heart that you will realize who you really are.

Your inner being shines with luminescence, touching and inspiring everyone around you. You become alive and very much awake, your light switch is always on.

I was in my twenties when I became desperate enough to seek out my first healer and therapist. I felt alone, stuck and unlovable. I was determined to change.

After years of working through my childhood issues, old thoughts, beliefs, and events, I felt alive again. It was like stripping several layers of paint from a piece of antique furniture. I found myself restored to my original beauty, I just needed to be nurtured and loved.

We are all interconnected, so when you love you, I also know you love me. Together through our love, we can heal ourselves, each other, and the world. Love is our purpose, our true calling. It begins with and within each of us.

Love is the most amazing thing in your life. It is what makes you human, what makes life worth living. Nothing else really matters. The size of your home, bank balance, the beauty of your spouse, the speed of your car – all these things pale into insignificance when you face the splendor of what it is that makes you tick.

Love does not make the world go around; it is not the highly commercialized circus you see on Valentine's Day, love simply makes the ride worthwhile. Love is much deeper and much more profound than sending someone a dozen roses at a hugely inflated price. It is much more than candlelit dinners and fancy chocolates.

You yearn for that deep connection with others, those moments of bliss, joy, completeness. You crave to have more of those delicious moments you may have had with a romantic partner. Such moments seem so rare and forlorn.

You remember the blissful moments when strangers have shared their love and made a difference. You remember the feeling of gratitude in the eyes of someone whom you have helped. You remember how great it feels to do something for someone without expecting anything in return.

You cry when you see happy stories on your TV screen of families reuniting. Such stories touch your heart and yet they are so rare, as you continue to get bombarded with so much doom and gloom by all the propaganda around you.

You remember the sheer joy of children playing and the love in their eyes. Your heart skips a beat, you get goose pimples and you get teary eyed when you witness an act of sheer love – pure, unadulterated and unconditional. Such moments literally take your breath away.

Love is much greater than what you feel romantically. It is what makes you sing, dance and makes you human.

You spend so much time waiting to be loved, hoping love will find you, searching, and yearning for that special love, feeling empty and lost without it. Wanting someone to give you love and fill you up. Unfortunately, that's not usually how life works. Loving yourself is mainly having self-respect, which is the only dependable way to create love in your own life to share with others.

When you expect love from an external source, and someone or something does not fulfill your void and fantasies, then you will feel worse than before. To be able to be loved, you must love and respect yourself as much as you do others.

Understanding the effects of loving yourself will only enhance your ability to love others. By doing so, you are enabling positive energy and allowing for great situations to occur in your life.

Never think that you're living your life for nothing. Every day, there are people coming in and out of the world, so spend it wisely and respect yourself. Sometimes you may feel as if your life relies on one person. You think: If I do this, he/she will like me. You tend to waste time avoiding certain people, and regret it later. You miss them, yearn for their love, and even waste birthday wishes on them. In order to love someone, you must love yourself.

Feeling worthy of love requires you to see yourself with fresh eyes of self-awareness, to let go of old beliefs, and to love yourself from within. You don't have to be different to be worthy. Your worth is in your true nature, a core of love and inner goodness. You are a beautiful light. You are love. You can bury your magnificence, but it's impossible to destroy.

Loving yourself isn't a onetime event. It's an endless, moment by moment, ongoing process. It begins with you, enfolding yourself in your own affection and appreciation.

Exercise for you

Here are some steps to discover your worth and enfold yourself in affection and appreciation.

1. *Begin your day with love (not technology). Remind yourself of your worthiness before getting out of bed. Breathe in love and breathe out love. Enfold yourself in light. Saturate your being in love.*

2. *Take time to meditate and journal. Spend time focusing inward daily. Begin with five minutes of meditation and five minutes of journaling each morning. Gradually increase this time.*

3. *Talk yourself happy. Use affirmations to train your mind to become more positive. Put a wrist band on your right wrist. When you're participating in self-abuse of any form, move the band to your left wrist.*

4. *Get emotionally honest. Let go of numbing your feelings. Shopping, eating and drinking are examples of avoiding*

discomfort, sadness, and pain. Mindfully breathe your way through your feelings and emotions.

5. Enjoy life-enhancing activities. Find exercise you like. Discover healthy foods that are good for you. Turn off technology for a day and spend time doing things that make you feel alive.

6. Become willing to surrender. Breathe, relax, and let go. You can never see the whole picture. You don't know what anything is for. Stop fighting against yourself by thinking and desiring that people and events in your life should be different. Your plan may be different from your soul's intentions.

7. Work on personal and spiritual development. Be willing to surrender and grow. Life is a journey. We are here to learn and love on a deeper level. Take penguin steps and life becomes difficult. One step at a time is enough to proceed forward.

8. Own your potential. Love yourself enough to believe in the limitless opportunities available to you. Take action and create a beautiful life for yourself.

9. Be patient with yourself. Let go of urgency and fear. Relax and transform striving into thriving. Trust in yourself, do good work, and the universe will reward you.

10. Live in appreciation. Train your mind to be grateful. Appreciate your talents, beauty, and brilliance. Love your imperfectly perfect self.

11. Do what honors and respects you. Don't participate in activities that bring you down. Don't allow toxic people

in your life. Love everyone, but be discerning on who you allow into your life.

12. *Accept uncertainty. Suffering comes from living in the pain of the past or the fear of the future. Put your attention on the present moment and be at peace.*

13. *Discover the power of fun. Self-love requires time to relax, play, and create face-to-face interaction with others. Our fast-paced world creates a goal-setting, competitive craziness that doesn't leave room for play. Dr. Stuart Brow says, "The opposite of play isn't work, it is depression."*

If any of the above did not work for you, seek professional help. Self-rejection and neglect is painful. You deserve to be happy. You have a right to be accepted and loved. If necessary, seek help from a friend, support group, counselor, coach, or alternative therapist. It's the best investment you can make.

The Love2Love workshop was created with one thing in mind and it has helped many who attended get inspired, empowered and feel uplifted on their own self-love journey. It would be my honor to see you there and help you too.

This workshop provides a wonderful starting point whether you are starting out on the self-love journey or already on the path. The tools and tips are practical and will help you move closer to having inner peace, loving yourself unconditionally and raise your vibrations to attract abundance into all areas of your life.

Most certainly, an increased ability to love yourself more fully can have tremendous positive impact on your life. Here are some of the possible benefits that you may derive by using this powerful yet simple method you are learning on your journey to self-love:

- ✓ The world becomes your oyster
- ✓ You become happier as a person because you are better able to accept your flaws, imperfections and uniqueness
- ✓ Your self-talk becomes more positive
- ✓ Your well-being improves
- ✓ You are able to practice forgiveness and compassion
- ✓ You enhance your ability to receive love because you know that you are deserving
- ✓ By being self-accepting, you also become more accepting of others
- ✓ Your relationships with your spouse, loved ones, friends, colleagues and clients improve tremendously
- ✓ From improved relationships, you enhance your ability to become successful
- ✓ Your energetic vibrations become more positive and so you enhance your ability to attract more positive outcomes
- ✓ You enhance your ability to reach maximum potential, because you are less inclined to put yourself down
- ✓ You are able to honor your dreams
- ✓ You are better able to align with your higher purpose, thus leading a more fulfilling life

Self-love is something that we can all experience, and continue to cultivate more deeply into our being.

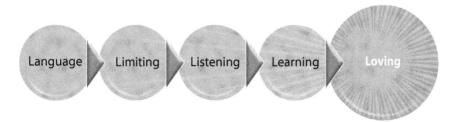

ACHIEVEMENTS

Congratulations for remaining focused and coming so far in your journey; now let's look at the next main pillar that helps you evolve to your greatest self – Achievements.

In this part of the process you will learn four subcomponents that support this pillar. As you acknowledge yourself and start loving yourself you start living in an abundant state; from this state know you can look at what truly it is you came here to do, what achievements you want to have.

For this, you must adopt the right attitudes, learn to be authentic, do the actions that are required for you to achieve the results you want to create in your future, and use the right affirmations to support you in this journey.

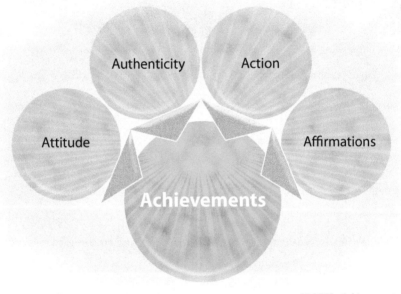

ALARM - *Achievements*

ATTITUDE

In this pillar we will explore how you too can change, accomplish your goals, and achieve balance in the eight key areas of your life. The reason why having the right attitude matters is that without the right attitude in life, you cannot move forward in the direction you want to take your life.

A PATH to WISDOM

As you develop a positive attitude to life, you start being more the love you are, you free yourself from all that you have read so far, you become authentic, start doing the actions, and daily you adjust your actions and goals so they remain aligned to your highest values.

One of the most important steps you can take toward achieving your greatest potential in life is to learn to monitor your attitude. It impacts you, your work performance, relationships and everyone around you.

Your attitude is a powerful sentiment. It affects every part of your life, self-image, relationships, business, and even your health.

To change something, you need to know it, so let's look at what attitude means. A simple definition of attitude is a person's feeling or emotion toward a fact or situation. It's a person's mental outlook on circumstances; one's temperament, mood, or viewpoint. People tend to think that there are only two kinds of attitudes – positive and negative – but really there are many.

Here are just a few: friendly or reserved, confident or insecure, cheerful or depressed, compassionate or callous, determined or indecisive, peaceful or destructive, appreciative or ungrateful. It's easy to see that all can be classified as either positive or negative and that they will truly identify who you are.

Attitude is a key component in defining your personality. Your attitudes affect how people see you, whether they like or dislike you, whether they want to be around you or avoid you. It affects their viewpoint about you, how they respond to you, whether you gain or lose influence with them.

Your attitude is reflected through the tone of your voice, the expression on your face, your body language and the courtesy or lack thereof extended to others.

Good and Bad Attitudes

Think of someone you know who always seems to have a good attitude. Who immediately comes to mind? How do you feel about this person? Is this someone you enjoy being around? Is this someone you would hire if you were an employer? Is this someone you would buy something from if he or she were selling something you needed?

Now think about someone who always seems to have a bad attitude. Who do you immediately think about? How do you feel about this person? Is this someone you enjoy being around? Does this person give you energy or draw energy from you? If you were having a party, would you invite this person? How likely would you be to embrace any idea that comes out of his or her mouth?

Your Attitude is a Choice

Your attitude is a choice and that choice is 100% within your control. Just know that the choice you make will influence every aspect of your life. Let me encourage you to begin looking at what's good in your life and not what's bad. If you are going through a difficult period, remember your attitude can make your life even worse or it can be the catalyst to turning your life around.

I generally start my workshops and seminars by asking a fundamental question: What attitude did you bring into this meeting? Often, this brings puzzled looks. In truth, people generally don't have a high level of attitude awareness. They'll know if they are hungry or if their feet hurt, but they usually don't have a good handle on their attitude.

That is a mistake because attitude is everything. It governs the way you perceive the world and the way the world perceives you.

We all have a choice. We can choose an inner dialogue of self-encouragement and self-motivation, or we can choose one of self-defeat and self-pity. It's a power we all have. Each of us encounters hard times, hurt feelings, heartache, and physical and emotional pain. The key is to realize it's not what happens to you that matters, it's how you choose to respond.

Your mind is a computer that can be programed. You can choose whether the software installed is productive or unproductive. Your inner dialogue is the software that programs your attitude, which determines how you present yourself to the world around you. You have control over the programing. Whatever you put into it is reflected in what comes out.

Many of us have behavior patterns today that were programed into our brain at a very tender age. The information that was recorded by our brain could have been completely inaccurate or cruel. The sad reality of life is that you will continue to hear negative information, but you don't have to program it into your brain.

The loudest and most influential voice you hear is your own inner voice, your self-critic. It can work for or against you, depending on the messages you allow. It can be optimistic or pessimistic. It can wear you down or cheer you on. You control the sender and the receiver, but only if you consciously take responsibility for and control over your inner conversation.

Habitual bad attitudes are often the product of past experiences and events. Common causes include low self-esteem, stress, fear, resentment, anger and an inability to handle change. It takes serious work to examine the roots of a harmful attitude, but the rewards of ridding ourselves of this heavy baggage can last a lifetime.

If You Are Going To Do Something, Do It With a Good Attitude

Think of the last time you were asked to do something by your spouse, employer or a friend but you really didn't want to do what was requested. How would you describe your attitude in this type of situation?

While I was writing this book, my mum asked me to do something for her. Because I was in the middle of writing a paragraph, my immediate response was negative. I then had a choice. I could be grumpy and do what she requested or I could do it with a good attitude.

Because I am personally working on doing everything with a positive attitude, I interrupted what I was doing, put a smile on my face, and happily helped her. It made the experience better for both of us.

The next time you have to do something you don't want to do, let me challenge you to do it with a great attitude and see how it makes you feel. You will stand out!

Challenge yourself to do everything you do with a positive attitude. Not only will this bring more joy and happiness into your life, but it will also build self-esteem and self-confidence.

Starting this very minute, stop worrying about the things you can't control and start attacking the things you can. This is a choice you control. Don't allow yourself to think differently.

When times get tough, be the person who stands out from the crowd with a positive attitude. If you are going through a difficult period right now, then be strong, be bold and read *It's a New Day.*

M. Scott Peck wrote the book *The Road Less Travelled.* In the first sentence he comments that life is hard, and once you accept that fact you are better able to move forward.

Everyone, regardless of the credentials on the wall, the title or the pay check, has struggles and disappointments and setbacks. That is just the way it is. There is no Camelot. There is no perfect world. Once you recognize that everyone struggles with the same fundamental issues, it becomes a little easier to move forward.

But if you assume a victim mentality and you aren't willing to try to improve yourself or your situation, you are doomed.

Attitude creates reality. For example, Mayo Clinic researchers have clearly documented that having a more positive, optimistic view of the situation provides health benefits for individuals with some forms of lung cancer. So how you view a situation can have enormous impact on how you live.

Some people see setbacks as absolute devastation whereas others view them as opportunities. The choice is really up to you.

AUTHENTICITY

In my personal journey I found that being authentic is like charity, it begins at home, with developing mindful practice within oneself in any singular moment of what one is "SIFT-ing" i.e., SENSING (hearing, seeing, feeling, tasting, smelling); IMAGING (mental pictures or memories); FEELING (emotions experiencing); and THINKING (what one is thinking or valuing) in that moment.

Authenticity is one of those fascinating subjects that in my spiritual journey I found many other spiritual seekers love to sink their teeth into. It is the second subcomponent of the third main pillar of TJS Evolutionary Method: Achievement.

Your ego mind feels threatened by being authentic, because the true energy of authenticity means the demise of ego-led behavior. If we logic it solely through the intellect, then we can rapidly lose the meaning behind it.

So here I feel like shining a little light on the subject by sharing a perspective on what being authentic really means to me, the process I went through to align my life to simply being me, and perhaps even dispelling a few myths in the process.

Being authentic is being genuine and original. It could also mean being true and trustworthy. Bottom line, any way you look at it comes across in a positive light. The question I have for you is why wouldn't you want to be authentic?

Authentic means from the source or origin. To be authentic is simply to be true to your true self. Authenticity is a simple way of being that rises spontaneously, without control, from the core.

Authenticity is what is left over when the mind steps out of the way and lets the soul shine through. Authenticity is when you are being you, from the core.

Being authentic in a spiritual sense means "as expressed directly from the source", through the soul. It is the raw, naked, unhindered expression of beingness of the soul. Authenticity is a quality of being. That's why we say "being authentic" not "doing authentic."

Yet we see people all the time that are being more fake than real. Take the sales people in the high street, the presenter/speaker who is performing instead of presenting, or a friend who pretends to like you until you've served your usefulness and they move on. How did that make you feel: not appreciated, used, ignored, and invisible?

You see authenticity in people from all walks of life. These are the people who are just really comfortable in their own skin and they feel real and natural. They say it "how it is", yet with compassion and awareness. These are the people you know that you trust in life, because they are real.

You can't "try" to be authentic. You can't train yourself or follow a technique to learn. You can, however, self-realize and allow your layers of baggage to fall away. In so doing, authenticity will arise more and more as a divine expression of your being.

Following and doing the actions of the TJS Evolutionary Method you have learned so far will help you to achieve this.

Authenticity is all about the moment. It's about now. It's about presence. It's not only seeing beyond the veil, but being beyond the veil and bringing that through to the experience of being human.

What gets in the way of being authentic?

- Childhood traumas
- Fear of what others think of you (judgment)
- Comparing yourself with others
- Being swept along by other people's energies
- Being trapped by others expectations – being "labelled"
- Non-acceptance of self and others
- The spiritual identity
- Lack of confidence

Was there ever a time when you were young and exhibited your true thoughts and feelings only to have someone cut them down? Sure there was, who hasn't experienced this? No wonder it's scary to be authentic. It's that age old fear of not being accepted, liked, or criticized if you do show the real you that has been lingering inside you just festering.

Recently I started to work with a client who was experiencing extreme difficulties in accepting and being himself. As we went deeper into his subconscious mind, he was able to access the exact moment in time when he decided to stop being authentic. It was at the age of seven, he was in a restaurant with his parents being lively kid and wanting to share his ideas, jokes, and laughs with his parents. His father took him out of the restaurant and gave him a beating.

This moment and many to follow were the exact seeds of why he could not be authentic. The fear of not being liked, wanted, accepted is what was keeping him from being his true self.

As I took him through a guided meditation to access his inner child, at first there was a resistance, but then he was able to reconnect to the little boy who was traumatized by these events. As I embraced him at the end, I asked him to decide if he was going to continue letting that fear dictate his future growth.

Immediately he knew the answer, that he could not go on like this anymore and it had to stop. If he wanted to move on and be successful, he couldn't let that childhood fear stop him from being who he was meant to be. Over the next few months as we continued to do more inner child work, he felt more connected, empowered, and started to love himself more, and in turn being more authentic.

The desire to be the real genuine you must be stronger than the possibility, and it is only a possibility, of not being accepted or liked. Eventually in my personal journey I got to a point in my life where I just don't give a hoot what anyone thinks or says about what I do.

It's your life, and therefore the only person you need to be true to is yourself; as you do so, you are true to anyone else around you. As I said above, authenticity starts at home – with you!

For me and others like me that have reached a point where being authentic is a default way of being, accept that others don't have to like it. We know that's how that person is going to show up in the world and you've got to respect someone who can stand in their own power. It's what gives that person character. No matter how difficult it may be, when someone makes a stand, it's respected.

In your journey to being authentic, one key important thing to remember is to accept your light and darkness, your good and your bad, your fear and your trust.

It may be that you can't be fully authentic because a distortion is coming through. You might feel an authentic impulse that becomes distorted by a filter, in which case you have the option to be real at least. Being as real as you can possibly be, distortion is a powerful precursor to authenticity. This means you are able to see how you are not being authentic and peel away those layers – leading to authenticity.

It's acceptance of all your inner darkness – each of us has it – and not being afraid of what others may think of you. It's not placating others at the expense of being true to yourself. It's not showing others your likable traits in order that they accept you, because of fear of being rejected.

It's having the courage to be true to yourself. Do you have the guts to do that, to be your full-out genuine self? What would that do for you?

The truth is you are already a unique human being, therefore you get to be you. No pretending to be someone else. It's all you. There is no script to follow. You make it up as you go along. How is that for fun?

You start being genuine, that means you are able to express your inner self and be the loving, kind-hearted, generous person that your heart longs to be. Imagine being your true self – how would that feel? Would that give you inner peace and contentment? Think of it as God saying to you: "I love you just the way you are. Don't change a thing."

Now, take a deep breath and say those words to yourself. Exhale. Only you have the power to be authentic. I'm leaving it all up to you. You decide what you're going to do.

During the days when I was training to be a Transformational Life Coach at the Animas Institute of Coaching, in one of the training days the founder Nick Bolton spoke about the importance of Transactional Analysis when coaching clients. You have already read about it in previous chapters, although knowing this process at a deeper level and how to use it with yourself and others helps you in your journey to be and remain authentic.

Working with a thousand or more clients and during my own personal healing journey, I learned so much about the different Ego States (E.S) that Dr. Eric Berne talks about and how you can spot them when talking to people.

Once I was able to distinguish them in each of the clients I was working with, I was able to help them deepen their awareness, first of self, then of others and "where they are coming from" at any moment. Whether just musing or interacting with others, I was able to focus on my clients' "self-talk" and notice the comfort level of each.

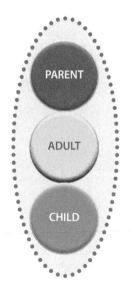

Parent ego-state
Behaviours, thoughts and feelings copied from our parents and parental figures, (typically modelled behaviour by observing adults from ages of 6-12).

Adult ego-state
Behaviours, thoughts and feelings which are in direct response to the here and now.

Child ego-state
Behaviours, thoughts and feelings replayed from our childhood (imprinted during the first 6 years of life).

I use the three states to process interactions and help clients respond appropriately to both their internal thoughts and their dialog with others.

This helped them to have awareness and compassion for both self and others and to respond congruently to what is being experienced by each at the moment.

When you learn and practice mindfulness in this way, it can become integrated into your processing and become a part of you, not in a navel-gazing fashion, but in awareness and compassion toward yourself and others as a result of your deeper understanding of the thoughts, emotions, and behaviors of self and others.

Knowing the Ego States can help you see the difference in what individuals are comfortable in sharing. You have the option of changing or breaking off the dialog using the Adult E.S.

It is being authentic to confront another in a direct, noncritical way and set appropriate limits on behaviors that may violate your sense of personal integrity or physical or emotional safety.

It's the "job" of the Nurturing Parent/Adult/and Free Child of Ego States to non-aggressively assert yourself so you can set your "default mode" to feeling contented and safe.

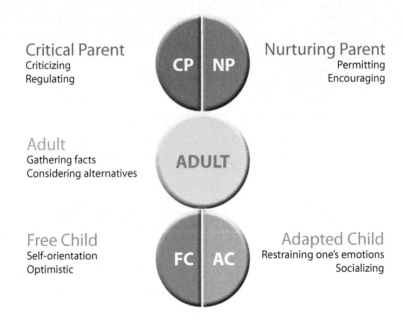

Critical Parent
Criticizing
Regulating

CP **NP**

Nurturing Parent
Permitting
Encouraging

Adult
Gathering facts
Considering alternatives

ADULT

Free Child
Self-orientation
Optimistic

FC **AC**

Adapted Child
Restraining one's emotions
Socializing

Sharing time with others, the prior events tend to happen in varying degrees with one another, though there are those extremes that you may want to be aware of.

However, there is another point that you are reaching here for the moment: being authentic to how you were created. Sometimes, when you just stop and think about what that might be or entail, you may not be entirely sure what it is.

After all, you have spent most of your life creating a specific life that was encompassed around the expectations of those around you. Such as creating a family, a fulfilling career or job obligations, fulfilling specific social roles or a "status" that it may have been assumed you would take on – and the list can go on, from church to politics to volunteering.

Sometimes it takes assumptions according to the dynamics of your environment, such as exposure to or lack of education, finances or social expectations. All of which, looking beyond the assumptions and looking within toward your own desires, drives, abilities to be developed or that have come more naturally – anything is achievable beyond whatever surrounding circumstances you may be in or have observed.

The question is, with all the roles you chose to take on regardless of the motivation for doing so, whether it was expected, you wanted to, you thought you had to, etc., have you taken the time to stop and ask yourself: Is this expressing who I really am, my abilities and what I truly wish to do with my life to express myself and how I want to share my time?

It is never too late to ask yourself this question, nor need you ask this question only once. The only experience of loss or lack of fulfillment that you may feel is to have never asked yourself the question at all and then acted upon it with kindness to yourself.

Exercises for you

1. *Write down what it means to be true to yourself.*
2. *What does it mean to be you?*
3. *What stops you from being authentic?*
4. *What path do you want to take yourself to be authentic?*

So now you have asked and decided that you want to be more authentic to yourself. Now what?

Now you start making decisions. Decide what events in your life you do enjoy and feel that you are expressing your true abilities and talents by doing them, then you know this is what you want to keep doing.

Stop doing what isn't a true expression of you or stop doing it in a way that doesn't express the depth of your personality and your genuineness. In other words, don't take on a task just because someone else thinks you should do it or tells you would be good at it.

Do it because you are willing to express your abilities, gifts and time in that area with an earnest effort that comes from within you. That is being true to yourself and honest to who you really are. In doing so, you will develop and grow in areas that you may have desired and have not yet explored until now.

Or you will finally let go of the attitude that you have to be the "I will do it to make do" personality and really live your life to a fuller potential. When you do this, others then begin to appreciate more what you have to offer as well. The reason is that you have now become more authentic and it will be obvious that your efforts are not forced; you will be expressing joy freely and perhaps even passionately.

For an added note, a life coach, healer, or clairvoyant can bring added clarity to matters or issues and may aid in a direction. However, my perspective on this is that they are not your sole answer or the one who is your voice. You are that, they are just tools you can use.

You are in your body, you are thinking your thoughts and feeling your emotions and you are in control of them, no one else is, so you are the one who will have to share them.

To be true to yourself in this manner is doing just that – speaking your own mind, your own thoughts no matter what others' opinions of you might be. You have a right to change your thoughts or your beliefs.

Once voiced, once you have heard your own words aloud, you have better clarity. Being authentic is not pretending to be one type of personality just because it is who you would "like" to be, but being who you really are.

This does not mean that if there are aspects you would like to change within yourself that you cannot. I made this mistake when I was finding it difficult to accept me for all that I was. You proceed to do so, just don't lie to yourself if you are not there yet, and as a result you will get there sooner.

In other words, if you are working at becoming more joyful and friendly with others, the concept "fake it 'til you make it" doesn't work. The reason is, you will be lying to yourself and, in turn, lying to others and never achieving your desired goal.

However, by first letting go of any thoughts that you cannot be happy or friendly with others is a start. Or letting go of any anger issues you have been holding on to that said "I have to distance myself from people and not get close" – then you can allow yourself to replace that with feelings of peace and joy. Thereby, you will be automatically friendlier with others, feel naturally joyful from within (not forcing it) and this is being true or authentic to you.

Of course, it's common that when people realize they are "people pleasing", "trapped by expectations" or "washed through with other people's energy", the spiritual identity can then swing in completely the opposite direction, in a valiant effort to rebalance and make up for lost time.

I have seen people pleasers become incredibly selfish. I have witnessed people who have been brainwashed or hurt in some way reject just about anything to do with authority. People liberated from being trapped by others' expectations also run the risk of becoming thwarted by a false sense of self-empowerment.

Beware of overcompensating with stubbornness! It's understandable, but not authentic. It can be useful to swing the other way for a short while, to feel the polarity of the distortion. It can help to shake off the distorted behaviors.

Anything that is not forced, that feels natural and doesn't create a sense of internal upset, worry, anxiety, stress, discomfort, anger and negative emotions is an indication that you are being authentic and/or true to yourself. Learn to trust this and you will live a more fulfilling life each and every day.

The wonderful thing is that authenticity is your natural state of being. It is boundless. It's the return to who you truly are. Your soul will, one way or another, always urge you back to your true and authentic origins. If you can allow anything that is not you simply to fall away, you can be who you are divinely given to be.

Once you realize this, you need not wait a moment longer.

- See more at: **http://www.apathtowisdom.com/**

ACTION

For sure, life could be more fulfilling. You could be saving more money, putting more into that course, or that job, or that relationship, and maybe next year you'll knuckle down and see about changing direction to something you really want to do.

But that voice in your head tells you that's not right now. Let's just enjoy the here and now. Life's too short to get too worried. So the path you want to take to achieve what you want requires you to take action. Action is the third subcomponent that supports the main third pillar – Achievement. Without taking action, your life stagnates and your goals become words written on a sandy beach that disappear with a single wave.

The trouble with drifting is that it is directionless. Floating along with the tide means that you don't use your arms and your legs or your head or your heart. It takes no effort. The current does all the work while you just need to lie back and watch the clouds drifting overhead.

Many of the clients I help say that behaving in such a way helps them remain in the space they call "comfortable zone." My question to them is: If it is comfortable zone why do you need a coach to get you out of there?

I call it a "familiar" zone, a place in which you know how to react, feel, sense, and think in any given moment.

Let me ask you a question: What do you plan to do with what's left of the rest of your life?

You may be thinking about getting around to something next year. Is this when you'll finally be ready to learn a foreign language, tie the knot, build yourself a boat and steer your way to your goal?

But you know what? For some people every year is the same. I hear it with members of my family, friends, clients, when I am out and about with members of the general public; every year someone says: "Well maybe when I have more time I'll do such and such." Or "When the kids have left school and left home, I'll do this." Or maybe even "When I retire, I'll have more time."

Soon you will realize that life is slipping past, so don't wait any longer, take action. Now is your moment. Right now! This minute! The words you're reading right here on this page mark each and every second of your precious life floating past.

Take action now to find your true purpose in life. Learn about your own body ALARM that keeps you living your life on snooze. Discover what it is that will fill you with excitement and inspiration. Live every second of your life. You deserve to feel the joy of living.

Get yourself into a boat, take the paddle, and row with the current to where you want to be, where you want to go, where you know you will find clarity, peace, balance, happiness and fulfillment.

Don't wait until next year, or when you retire, or when the time feels right. Think about what it is you want in life and where you want to be.

And take the first step into that future. The time is now. Take action on everything you have identified so far, take that list, prioritize your goals to your highest values and start doing it right now!

AFFIRMATIONS

To help you fully embody the wisdom learned so far, achieve the goals you may have set yourself in this process potential, and help you manage the billions of thoughts and beliefs that you may have created since you were born, the fourth subcomponent of the third pillar – Affirmation – plays an essential part to complete this process.

You may be familiar with Louise Hay's work. She has been another inspired teacher in my life; her book *You can Heal your Life* is full of ideas and strategies that have worked for me and for millions of people worldwide. This practical self-help guide helped me change the way I think forever!

As she would say: "Today I breathe, go within, and ask, 'What is it I need to know?'"

Her work helped me in my self-healing journey and profoundly altered my awareness of the impact that the mind has on our health and well-being.

In this inspirational work, she offers profound insight into the relationship between the mind and the body. TJS Evolutionary Method that you are learning adds another layer and dimension to explore the way that limiting thoughts and ideas control and constrict you. If you have answered the questions and done the exercises, you now have a powerful key to understanding the roots of your physical diseases and discomforts.

Louise inspired me very much to use affirmations on a daily basis. Yes, for sure, when you start this process they can feel fake, untrue, unreal, but your brain has the ability to adapt, learn, and create new neuron pathways. Memory is created by simply repeating the same information over and over, it is how you learned everything you know now.

I adopted one of her affirmations: "Trust life to hear and respond to your positive words." I said this affirmation and few others that I wrote back in 2009 every day for a year and my whole world for sure did change for the better.

So let's look at what affirmations are, how they work, and how to write your personal affirmations.

Affirmations are statements that are repeated either consciously or subconsciously. They can be negative or positive. An example of a positive affirmation could be "I know I can do this" and an example of a negative affirmation could be "Why can't I ever get a break?"

Affirmation is nothing but a blend of visual and verbal techniques of an ideal condition of mind. Human beings can achieve any goal through strong and powerful affirmations! A strong affirmation is much more powerful compared to a weak affirmation. Affirmation is simply a statement made by a person, about anything or about a condition of a being. You can make yourself healthy in mind, spirit and body through powerful affirmations.

How do affirmations work?

Affirmations program the mind the same way a script programs a computer. We all become what we think, and one way of achieving what is possible for you is by using the power of "I am" – and you are the big "I am." You may have a wish to stop being poor, unsuccessful, unlucky, single or unhealthy. It's not helpful to express your wishes in a way of what you don't want.

Repetitive words give the mind something to focus on and it automatically triggers the subconscious mind to start looking for ways to make those repetitive words reality. It's more helpful to express your desires; change to using the power of "I am": "I am superbly wealthy", "I am happier", "I am attractive" and you will feel better. At least try to say one of these affirmations now and notice whatever feelings or thoughts come up. If you really want to be persistently happy, it will happen when your mind gets comfortable with the idea that you are happy and you always have been. Remember, today is practice for tomorrow.

A good and strong affirmation is always in present tense like "I am a happy person now." Using present tense in affirmations is much more helpful than using future tense. Affirmation is not supposed to work against you so it should always be encouraging. Look how pleasant it is saying that I am happy rather than saying I am not sad.

Affirmation should not consist of long lines, it should be short and concise. A very descriptive affirmation can work against you rather than making a positive and constructive mindset. Creating short affirmations is great as they can be repeated again and again with full ease. It can be used as a song that can be repeated time and time again.

You need to repeat your affirmations if you want them to be effective. Repetition always pressures positively the subconscious of beings and helps them out greatly in acting out their affirmation. The creator of the affirmations should be extremely familiar with the words they are using as this is necessary in actualizing the affirmations.

You can create affirmations in simple words that you think are familiar to you. Only creating an affirmation and repeating it over and over cannot be effective. The key point is to live one's affirmation and to be open-minded to practically do the things that would aid the affirmation become a truth. You can actualize the affirmation only if you are feeling it and applying it to your life.

Affirmation does not only make a being better, it can also boost another person's worth. If you are affirming your fellow's existence, you are indirectly aiding them to improve their value.

Write Your Own Affirmations

Affirmations are everywhere, and they have the strong ability to lift your spirits to get through hard times. This is because we're all highly suggestible, even if we think we're not!

Affirmations help us to keep a positive attitude about life. It's only natural that we'll get more out of these positive sayings if we formulate them ourselves. Writing our own affirmations makes them personal to us, which can then help us to get through our own individual situations.

When you start writing your own affirmations, keep these tips in mind:

1. Make them personal. When you write affirmations, it's important to remember to use "I" in them. They are personal to you after all.

   Example: "I am having an exceptional day today!"

2. Use the present tense. Affirmations are built in order to change our feelings now, which is why you want to stay positive and strong in this moment. When you use the past

A PATH to WISDOM

tense, you get nostalgic. When you use the future tense, you get hopeful. The present tense helps you feel the difference right now.

Example: "I am feeling relaxed."

3. **Be down to earth.** This just means to use your own style and try not to make your affirmations too formal or wishy-washy. You want to capture your own voice.

    Bad Example: "Presently I feel the urge to enjoy my existence."

    Good Example: "I enjoy my life."

4. **Be short.** Affirmations are meant to be short, simple and sweet. Stay on target and make your affirmation a one-liner. If it's too wordy, try breaking it up into a few affirmations. The trick is to stick with one simple idea at a time.

    Example: "I am in perfect health."

5. **Make it positive.** Affirmations are positive statements, so avoid negative words like "not." You're using affirmations to make a life improvement and positive statements motivate you to make this improvement.

    Example: "I am at peace with my mind."

6. **Make it believable.** You don't want your affirmation to sound like something out of this world. If it's not believable, you won't take it seriously and your subconscious will just dismiss it.

    Example: "I am choosing to be happy today."

Believe in the Power of Affirmations

When you say your affirmations, believe them to be true. Affirmations are truly powerful sets of words as long as you believe what you're telling yourself. Affirmations alone have been known to help people cure addictions. Women even use them during childbirth to help them stay calm and collected during natural delivery.

First, set your eyes on your goal and then write your affirmations to get yourself there.

Write Them Down

Practice always makes perfect. Write down the affirmations you're feeling. Then go over the list above and make sure that your affirmations follow the rules. Once they do, start using your affirmations and feel the difference. Say your affirmations to yourself daily. Take deep breaths and keep your eyes on your goal.

Also if need be, tweak your affirmations. These positive sayings aren't written in stone, so as you change, your affirmations can change too.

It's best to keep your affirmations in a place where you can see them. You can simply keep a list in your pocket or you can post them around the house. Paste them on the bathroom mirror, on your computer, or wherever you know you'll see them each day. I have them recorded on my cell phone and listen to them when I am on the bus home, or taking the subway.

Affirmations can make all the difference in reaching your goals. Give them a try and enjoy the benefits these positive statements can make in your life.

Achieve

How would you like to increase the odds of achieving your goals in the eight areas of your life? Whether you desire to reconnect yourself to your spirit, lose weight, create financial independence, build a healthy relationship, or raise responsible children, the formula for achieving any goal is the same. You have so far learned all of the four subcomponents that you need to achieve the outcomes you wish to have for yourself.

Here are 12 recommended steps that I have used myself and helped thousands of clients increase the odds of achieving their goals:

1. Know your Values.

   Once you are clear about your values, making your choices and decisions becomes easy. It is an essential step to discovering your true purpose and aligning your life to it. What helped me most in this process is Dr. John Demartini's *Inspired Destiny*, and learning The Demartini Value Determination Process, I have helped and inspired many to do the same. Make a list of your highest values and know which three are your strongest values, and which one is your top priority.

2. Identify, clarify, and acknowledge what's important to you!

   The only goals you will succeed in reaching are those that are truly important to you and are aligned to your highest values. When you honor what is most important to you, then you want to dedicate your life to being, doing, and having it. If a goal is not meaningful or significant to you, you will quit when faced with obstacles. Take an afternoon off and make a list of the things that are truly essential in your life, those that you highly value. Then highlight the most important points on that list and set your goals.

3. Learn from someone who is on a similar path or from those who have already achieved *"your"* goals.

   Once you are clear on what you truly want to achieve, your next step is to learn what you need to know. The best source of knowledge will come from those who have already reached goals similar to yours. Identify people you respect and admire, who have achieved the goals you desire, and learn as much as you can from them. Bond, form true genuine friendships, and ensure you nurture them for the rest of your life.

4. Be clear about the person you need to become.

   Far too often, people focus on what they need to do to achieve their goals and fail to consider who they must become. No one likes needy people, why would you want to have goals that start from need? To accomplish something you have never accomplished before, you must be willing to do what you've never done before; go where you've never been before; become someone you've never been before. As you learn from those who have achieved *"your"* goals, pay as much attention to their personal attributes and characteristics as you do to what they did to realize their goals.

5. **Start planning.**
    After working for many years in the corporate world, learning from and studying those who have been successful in reaching similar goals, trust me on this: your next step is to put together your plan. You need to outline clearly what you need to do and when, step by step, and then reduce those steps into daily activities. Knowing exactly what you need to do every day is critical to achieving any worthwhile goal.

6. **Pay the Price.**
    If you are willing to pay the price required to achieve your goal, you will succeed. After you complete your plan, be honest with yourself and determine if your goal is important enough to you that you will discipline yourself to do what's required each day to achieve your goal. One of the biggest reasons people fail to reach their goals is that they are not willing to do what's required over a sustained period of time. How about you?

7. **Give yourself the time required.**
    When I started to write this book, my book coach Mindy Gibbins-Klein actually made me block out the time in my diary, it helped me focus. Your next step is to block out the time necessary each day to work your plan. If you are like most people (and that includes me), you will need to give something up that's less important so you have the time to achieve what's more important. Blocking out time each day to work your plan is vital. Success comes from consistent daily action!

8. **Action.**
    Without taking action you are not going to start or change anything in your life. Once you have learned what you need to know, divided your plan into daily activities, and blocked out time each day to do the assigned tasks, it's time to Work Your Plan. Start tomorrow! When the time you've blocked out arrives, push yourself to do what you know you should do without any further delay. It's time for action. You could continue to study dozens of books, listen to CDs, and interview

successful people (all helpful), but the greatest, most practical knowledge comes from implementing what you've learned.

9. Decide.

When you make a conscious decision about doing something, the odds of achieving your goals improve dramatically when you follow a logical process of making your decisions, both big and small. With each decision you make, consider all your options; write down the pros and cons of each option. From there, the right decision is usually obvious.

10. No More Excuses.

I know it is tempting to be lazy; however, research shows that the number one reason people fail to achieve their goals is they allow themselves to make excuses for not doing what they know they should do. One of the most crucial keys to success is doing what you know you should do, every day, even when you don't feel like doing it. This means never allowing yourself to justify not doing what you know you should do. Make a commitment that you will not make excuses under any circumstances!

11. Go Platinum.

The No.1 key to my success over the many years that I have worked is that I have always strived (and I continue to do so) for excellence, being true, and commit to whatever I do. I self-reflect daily on everything I've done and consider how I could do it better. As you work your plan each day, evaluate everything you are doing and consider how you can refine what you are doing so that your results improve. The compounding effect of small daily improvements is powerful. The best of the best are those who strive for constant and never-ending improvement.

12. Love what you do, do what you love.

As you align your life to your highest values, you start focusing your energy toward the goals that truly matter to you, you increase your confidence, self-worthiness, and you start experiencing tremendous amounts of joy in all that you do. You start doing, living, and loving.

Take the time right now to study and use each of the above tips and the corresponding lesson highlighted in many of them and apply them to your life, your goals, and your day-to-day living. You will significantly increase your odds of achieving the goals you have set up for yourself.

The reason many people fail to achieve their goals is that they are unwilling to do what is necessary over the required period of time. If you're like most people (and that includes me), you will go through periods of discouragement and disappointment. That's normal.

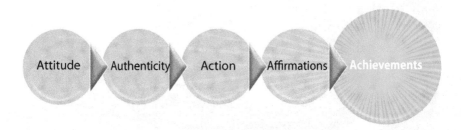

RESULTS

The fourth pillar of my methodology focuses on how to help you create lasting Results to support you in your evolution as a human being and the future you want to have for yourself. Its building subcomponents are the reasons you may be coming up with to keep you in the space you are right now, as well as the perceived resistance that prevents you from creating the results you want.

It also looks at the importance of repetition and rewarding yourself in this process.

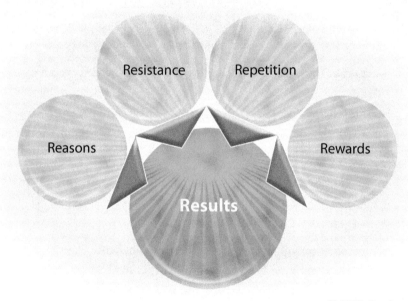

ALARM - *Result*

To best illustrate the fourth pillar, right now decide a specific result you may want to create in your life – for example, you are struggling to make money.

You may feel no matter what you do or don't do, money is simply hard to make.

Most of the clients that I coach, and people I know in my life, experience some issues around lack of money. They go through the cycle of telling me all the reasons, the resistance they see on why it may be difficult for them to, let's say, create $10k a month income; they keep repeating the same affirmations over and over; they get discouraged by not receiving the rewards they wish to have, and remain stuck in the same situation as they do not experience the expected results they wish to have.

REASONS

This part of the method is about the human faculty of reason or rationality. So if you are worried about money, or have been stuck in a financial rut for some time, you may believe that it is not possible to change your situation. You are feeling disempowered, and come up with a lot of reasons why you are so frustrated and feel helpless in not being to change the situation you are in. You are in agony, as you cannot find a way out of your problems.

Let's take the example of being in a situation whereby you are barely making ends meet. Perhaps you see that the problem lies in the job you do, or it is because you have just started on a new entrepreneurial venture which has yet to take off. Whatever it is, you are not able to afford the things you would like to have.

Over time, you start to feel worse and worse. You try to think positively or put in more hours at work, but it is of no use. You cannot seem to manifest a better outcome for yourself.

Your emotions go into disruption. You experience massive energy leakage. You may even become aware that it is some of your childhood patterns that are holding you back but you have no idea what to do or where to start. Eventually, you may become convinced that you will never be able to deserve more.

The thing is that the longer you stay stuck, the deeper you sink in the mud. With this, you become aligned with poverty consciousness. All that you think, see or do is borne out of lack. Now, unless you make the commitment to get help, you can be stuck for a very long time.

As I have found out myself, this is clearly not necessary. I often think about how things would have been a lot better if I had started inner work at an earlier age. I wouldn't have spent years feeling lousy and sorry for myself.

A PATH to WISDOM

The good news is that once you make that commitment, things can shift. It is possible to make changes faster (especially if you work with a trained professional) too, as compared to just putting in physical action.

I often get asked the question: "How do you become a money magnet?" not only by many people I helped to overcome money challenges, but also by family members, friends, and strangers that I meet when I fly, when I socialize, or even when I go to parties I get invited to.

I am asked: "So how do you reclaim your power to manifest prosperity quickly when you are feeling a sense of despondency, hopelessness and powerlessness? How do you heal yourself from the past that has kept you hostage for eons? How do you overcome your resistances to doing things differently, in order to attract prosperity?"

Having overcome this challenge myself by going through the TJS Evolutionary Method you are learning, the answer lies with making changes at the mind, body, and the energetic level that draws on one of the sacred truths that I often remind my clients about – that the point of power is always in the present moment. As you continue to increase your self-worth, you will increase your net worth.

What about the reasons you give yourself when your body experiences any illness? What do you use to keep justifying your current state – are they medical reasons, work stress related, or perhaps personal ones?

Over the years I learned many disciplines, and my approach to the way I look at my life has changed. I no longer use reasons to keep me in the state I am, I focus on the result that I want to achieve. If perfect health is my result, through the power of visualization and communication with my body I reprogram my own DNA to help me in my healing process. You too can do this by using the tools you have learned so far. Your body has an innate wisdom to help you heal.

Continuing telling yourself or others the reasons why you experience what you may experience has a knock-on effect on your healing process; you are concentrating on the illness and not health.

Let's look deeper at what reason is. According to scientists, philosophers and Wikipedia, it is the capacity for consciously making sense of things, applying logic, for establishing and verifying facts, and changing or justifying practices, institutions and beliefs based on new or existing information.

Reason is closely associated with such characteristically human activities as philosophy, science, language, mathematics, and art, and is normally considered to be a definitive characteristic of human nature. The concept of reason is sometimes referred to as rationality and sometimes as discursive reason, in opposition to intuitive reason.

Reason or "reasoning" is associated with thinking, cognition, and intellect. Reason, like habit or intuition, is one of the ways by which thinking comes from one idea to a related idea.

For example, it is the means by which rational beings understand themselves to think about cause and effect, truth and falsehood, and what is good or bad. It is also closely identified with the ability to self-consciously change beliefs, attitudes, traditions, and institutions, and therefore with the capacity for freedom and self-determination.

In contrast to reason as an abstract noun, a reason is a consideration which explains or justifies some event, phenomenon or behavior.

The ways in which human beings reason through argument are the subject of inquiries in the field of logic.

Throughout the centuries, psychologists and cognitive scientists have attempted to study and explain how people reason, e.g. which cognitive and neural processes are engaged, and how cultural factors affect the inferences that people draw. The field of automated reasoning studies how reasoning may or may not be modeled computationally.

The proposal that reason gives humanity a special position in nature has been argued to be a defining characteristic of western philosophy and later western modern science, starting with classical Greece.

Philosophy can be described as a way of life based upon reason, and in the other direction reason has been one of the major subjects of philosophical discussion since ancient times. Reason is often said to be reflexive, or "self-correcting", and the critique of reason has been a persistent theme in philosophy. It has been defined in different ways, at different times, by different thinkers.

For many classical philosophers, nature was understood teleologically, meaning that every type of thing had a definitive purpose which fit within a natural order that was itself understood to have aims. Perhaps starting with Pythagoras or Heraclitus, the cosmos is even said to have reason.

Reason, by this account, is not just one characteristic that humans happen to have, and that influences happiness amongst other characteristics. Reason was considered of higher stature than other characteristics of human nature, such as sociability, because it is something humans share with nature itself, linking an apparently immortal part of the human mind with the divine order of the cosmos itself.

In my own path I went ahead and researched what scientists, psychologists and great philosophers had to say about it. Within the human mind or soul (psyche), reason was described by Plato as being the natural monarch which should rule over the other parts, such as spiritedness (thumos) and the emotions.

Aristotle, Plato's student, defined human beings as rational animals, emphasizing reason as a characteristic of human nature. He defined the highest human happiness or well-being (eudaimonia) as a life which is lived consistently, excellently and completely in accordance with reason.

The early modern era was marked by a number of significant changes in the understanding of reason, starting in Europe. One of the most important of these changes involved a change in the metaphysical understanding of human beings.

Scientists and philosophers began to question the teleological understanding of the world. Nature was no longer assumed to be human-like, with its own aims or reason, and human nature was no longer assumed to work according to anything other than the same "laws of nature" which affect inanimate things. This new understanding eventually displaced the previous world view that derived from a spiritual understanding of the universe.

Accordingly, in the 17th century, René Descartes explicitly rejected the traditional notion of humans as "rational animals", suggesting instead that they are nothing more than "thinking things" along the lines of other "things" in nature.

Any ground of knowledge outside that understanding was, therefore, subject to doubt. In his search for a foundation of all possible knowledge, Descartes deliberately decided to throw into doubt all knowledge – except that of the mind itself in the process of thinking.

This eventually became known as epistemological or "subject-centered" reason, because it is based on the knowing subject, who perceives the rest of the world and itself as a set of objects to be studied and successfully mastered by applying the knowledge accumulated through such study.

Breaking with tradition and many thinkers after him, Descartes explicitly did not divide the incorporeal soul into parts, such as reason and intellect, describing them as one indivisible incorporeal entity.

A contemporary of Descartes, Thomas Hobbes, described reason as a broader version of "addition and subtraction" which is not limited to numbers.

This understanding of reason is sometimes termed "calculative" reason. Similar to Descartes, Hobbes asserted that "No discourse whatsoever can end in absolute knowledge of fact, past, or to come" but that "sense and memory" is absolute knowledge.

In the late 17th century, through the 18th century, John Locke and David Hume developed Descartes' line of thought still further. Hume took it in an especially skeptical direction, proposing that there could be no possibility of deducing relationships of cause and effect, and therefore no knowledge is based on reasoning alone, even if it seems otherwise.

Hume famously remarked: "We speak not strictly and philosophically when we talk of the combat of passion and of reason. Reason is, and ought only to be the slave of the passions, and can never pretend to any other office than to serve and obey them."

Interestingly, Hume also took his definition of reason to unorthodox extremes by arguing, unlike his predecessors, that human reason is not qualitatively different from either simply conceiving individual ideas, or from judgments associating two ideas and that "reason is nothing but a wonderful and unintelligible instinct in our souls, which carries us along a certain train of ideas, and endows them with particular qualities, according to their particular situations and relations."

It followed from this that animals have reason, only much less complex than human reason.

In the 18th century, Immanuel Kant attempted to show that Hume was wrong by demonstrating that a "transcendental" self, or "I", was a necessary condition of all experience. Therefore, suggested Kant, on the basis of such a self, it is in fact possible to reason both about the conditions and limits of human knowledge. And so long as these limits are respected, reason can be the vehicle of morality, justice and understanding.

Exercise for you:

1. *Stop for a moment, close your eyes, take few deep breaths, relax and focus on what reason is to you, how you use it, and how it serves you.*

2. *Make a list of reasons that stop you from living your best life.*

3. *Now make another list of what reasons you need to create the future and the life you want.*

4. *Incorporate your reason why you do what you do into your own mission statement.*

RESISTANCE

> *"If we don't change, we don't grow. If we don't grow, we aren't really living."*
>
> **Gail Sheehy**

To acknowledge, love, and achieve the results you want to have in your life, the second supporting subcomponent of the fourth pillar Results is Resistance.

Even by reading this book you may already resist doing the work, or the changes required for you to shift to new states of awareness.

It is so easy to remain stuck in the familiar zone. It is what your ego, brain, and your subconscious programing tell you to do without you even having to do anything; there is no resistance to be in this unresourceful state.

To help me overcome this, I turned east for answers and I started to meditate. I have always been fascinated by various spiritual teachers, healers, and their ability to overcome one of the biggest built-in resistive tools that we have in our mind, body and heart.

The sacred truth can sound abstract especially if you are new to meditation, spiritual practices or universal teachings. Hence, I recommend that you take the time to ponder over it. Realizing the depth of its meaning can help expedite your healing and boost your abundance quotient exponentially.

Living in the present moment means that you give your presence fully in the now. Your consciousness rests in this very moment. You are centered, fully alive and completely alert (that involves your entire holistic being) to what is going on.

Thus, your mind is neither trapped in the past nor caught in the future. You are not griping about how your ex-lover left you with a bunch of debts 10 years ago or how your parents failed to affirm your sense of worthiness when you were a child. You are also not thinking about what your weekend plans are when it is the beginning of the week or worrying about your retirement plans in the future.

You are in full attention to the moment. You are in acceptance of what-is, neither resisting nor struggling against the now. You are in full acceptance of your current situation and you perceive it as an opportunity to heal your wounded child or free yourself of old patterns in order to step into the new. You no longer give power away with a mind that is distracted away from the present.

Your mind is in its fullest power when it is fully centered in the here and now.

Only the present moment is real. The present moment is the entry point where your mind perceives a past and conceives a future. It is from the present moment that the past and the future exist in your mind.

However, the past and the future are not real. They are merely psychological concepts that your mind has created. By being stuck in the past or in the future – instead of being present in the now – you become trapped in an illusion.

I was called ignorant and arrogant, and from experience I can tell you they are any entrepreneur's indispensable allies. If you are an entrepreneur, then you must be clueless enough to have no idea how difficult your enterprise is going to be – and cocky enough to believe you can pull it off anyway.

So to achieve this state of mind you can let go of what you are resisting; one way to do it is by staying stupid, by not allowing yourself to think.

As a child you had no trouble believing the unbelievable, nor does the genius or the madman. It's only you and I, with our big brains and our tiny hearts, who doubt and overthink and hesitate.

Let go of the resistance that you know is preventing you from not living your life exactly as you want, with the love and friendships you want, the abundance you want, and the happiness you are seeking.

Essentially, resistance is any thought, belief or behavior, either conscious or unconscious, that stands contrary to your desire. On the surface, you can be doing positive affirmations, creative visualizations and imagining your success. But in the end, you get what you expect every single time.

Sometimes it can be as simple as not believing that you can have what you want. That way of thinking places limitations on what is possible for you. You are restricting what could be with what you think will be. And you end up getting what you expect.

Your consciousness is a powerful tool. If you don't believe you can have the thing you desire, it shows up as resistance, despite all the things you are doing to achieve your goals. You too can change your attitude and start to live in the possibility rather than the probability.

The reason anything is not happening in your life is that in one way or another you are not yet lined up with it. When I coach clients and go deeper into their subconscious awareness, they tell me: "I don't think it's possible, don't think I am worthy of it, don't think I can have it, I am not lucky like others, I need to do something else before I can have what I want, I need to work hard" etc.

Here are 13 helpful ways to help you let go of your resistance to change and assist you in continuing to build this very necessary skill:

1. Be Honest.
    Be clear on how you participate in the reality you continue to experience. Ask yourself: What limiting thought, belief or pattern of behavior am I currently holding on to that is standing in the way of my desire? What story do I keep telling myself or others that affirms the current position I'm in?

2. Be Aware.
    What part of the equation am I participating in that continues to get me the same results? Because the truth is, you are always living your unconscious expectation. Becoming aware of your "status quo" will give you the first clue on where your work lies.

3. Be Responsible.
    Take 100% responsibility for being the powerful creator that you are.

4. Stay out of self-judgment.
    Just like in the acorn lives the potential of the oak tree, that which you are seeking is already within you. This is a big one, and just generally a really awesome gift to give ourselves, regardless of what we're talking about. That said, creating change requires looking at our "stuff." It is necessary to do so with as little judgment as possible, while still being brutally honest. Getting caught up in "I should've..." or "Why didn't I..." simply stops any forward momentum we had going.

5. Look Within.
    None of this is a race to the finish line. Instead, use the resistance to point you to areas that need "clearing." Use it

as an opportunity to become more authentically who you already are. Nothing is outside of yourself.

6. **Be Open.**
    Everything comes to you along your own path, as you are ready. So, prepare yourself and be open to receive. Do what you can do something about. Let go of what you have no control over. Sometimes becoming aware of your repetitive patterns is all that is required. But other times, we need to take additional action.

7. **Be Stubborn.**
    Once you commit to action, the worst thing you can do is to stop. You don't have to be a hero to be stubborn. You can just be a pain in the butt. When you're stubborn, there's no quit in you. You're mean, you're mulish, and you're ornery. You're in till the finish. Sink your junkyard-dog teeth into Resistance's ass and do not let go, no matter how hard he kicks.

8. **Blind Faith.**
    Is there a spiritual element to creativity? Oh, yes. Your mightiest ally is belief in something you cannot see, hear, touch, taste, or feel. Resistance wants to rattle that faith. Resistance wants to destroy it.

9. **Go Behind.**
    In my Fear2Freedom workshop, I speak of what's the seed of fear and how you can make your fear your best friend. If you are in a place of resistance about something, look for the fear behind it and find a way to dissipate it.

10. **Meditate.**
    Meditation is one way, but so is arming yourself with knowledge, telling yourself a different story (i.e. stop scaring yourself), making phone calls, getting into action, etc.

11. **Focus on something else.**
    When you're thinking about the thing you want, and why you want it so badly, resistance (belief, frustrations, thought, feeling or unconscious beliefs) is usually present at the same time. When you distract yourself entirely, and think about

something else that pleases you, you're in a much more relaxed place of allowing. And the universe can bring it to you with the least amount of resistance. This is why people who fall in love finally drop the extra weight they've been carrying, or get the promotion they've been wanting. They are in a place where they're open to receiving.

12. Be Passionate.
Picasso painted with passion, Mozart composed with it. A child plays with it all day long. You may think that you've lost your passion, or that you can't identify it, or that you have so much of it, it threatens to overwhelm you. None of these is true. Fear saps passion. When we conquer our fears, we discover a boundless, bottomless, inexhaustible well of passion.

13. Be Clear.
It is difficult to begin to create change when what you want to change is vague or ill-defined. Clarity of mind means clarity of passion; this is why a great and clear mind loves ardently and sees distinctly.

The goal here is for you to look within and explore your own behaviors. It would be pointless to expend time and energy justifying the behaviors you want to change during this process.

Remember, things are delivered to you on your path, most of the time pretty effortlessly. But you have to get out of the way and feel worthy of receiving them. That is your work, this is the work involved in releasing resistance.

The rest of the work is to surrender to your now. Bask in the glory that is your moment. Savor the experiences that continue to add to your life. And seek joy!

In other words, as you let go of the expectation that you're supposed to be anywhere other than where you already are, right now, you let go the resistance.

Things will change soon enough and they will find you along your path, as you are ready. But until then, enjoy here, now. And prepare yourself to receive.

REPETITION

This is the third subcomponent of the fourth main pillar – Results – that you need to build into your day-to-day routine to achieve the transformational results you are seeking, whether professional or personal.

Your mental mind likes to repeat a debilitating story about how horrible your situation is, how someone else should be blamed about your predicament and how the universe has been so unfair to you. Once you are trapped in this illusion, you imprison yourself, and it becomes a "safe" place to be as the fear of getting out is much greater than the fear of staying in.

The stories paralyze you into inaction, you lose your zest for life, and before you know it your life is like a rollercoaster that is out of control.

Realize this: by giving power away to the past, you become frozen in the present moment, and by giving your power to the future, you become trapped in it.

I came across Will, a personal trainer, who at the time was working at my local gym, LA Fitness Piccadilly. This was my transition time when I changed my career from IT into starting my coaching and healing practice, and his too as prior to that he used to work for Hilton and deep down he wanted to be free.

When we first started to work together, in his initial consultation he told me a lot about his life and the many obstacles he was facing in his personal, professional, health, relationship, spiritual, and money matters.

My first observation about him was that despite his looks and easy-going personality, deep down he did not love himself, he was insecure, and for sure was not living in the moment. He kept doing what he was doing, seeing the same people, doing the same things. He realized doing the same things would only get him the same results.

As he started his healing-coaching journey with me, he started to see how his moments became congested with thoughts that were emotionally corrupted with anger, blame, frustration and pain. As a result, he was not able to think, feel or love freely and completely. If there was an important decision that he needed to make, he could well end up making one that was not in his highest good or in the best interest of all parties concerned.

As time went on, I helped him see and peel away the many layers that I have been talking about so far in this book; there was a lot of repetition happening in all areas of his life as well as from within that needed to be changed.

Let me share with you an extract from the blog he wrote about his personal journey with me:

"If you had met me just a few years ago, you would have observed a very different person: a quiet, shy, reserved and nervous individual, unsure about himself, his opinions, his wants or his desires. Full of self-doubt, insecurities and fears, he struggled to be authentic around other people.

Looking back on that first session, I remember how uncomfortable I felt. I felt prodded, nudged and gently wrestled into opening up and talking about myself, my feelings and my emotions. As a British passive/aggressive introvert, it was my idea of hell. My ego kicked in with a vengeance: Who was this man asking so many questions? Who did he think he was? How dare he make me feel so uncomfortable? Part of me doubted and distrusted, another part of me was intrigued. But I knew deep down that I was exactly where I was supposed to be.

The concepts of energy, of manifestation, of the Law of Attraction etc. were all new to me. Years and years of belief in the physical world as the only reality held me back, and it would take me many months before I could fully release my doubts and trust what Tony was talking about.

At the same time, I still held on tightly to my old destructive habits, my old thought patterns, my old conditioning. For over a year, I went through many ups and downs: one day feeling elated and on top of the world, the next back to the grey gloom and doom. I caught a glimpse of the happiness and self-love Tony talked about, and then found myself doubting I had ever experienced it.

In hindsight, these cycles matched the times when I listened and nurtured my inner voice, my truth, and the times when I blocked it out, doubted myself, and forgot my heart. Time after time, I returned to see Tony, and at every single session, I opened up a tiny bit more, learned a bit more about myself, and felt a bit more hopeful.

The fog slowly started to lift and I saw my life with a whole new perspective. I was able to see how for years I had avoided looking deeper into myself, always scared of what was inside. I was able to see how I had blamed my lack of love on everyone else but myself: my family, my friends, my clients. And I was able to see how much better my life was when I trusted and followed my intuition.

And as my inner world changed, so did my outer world. I stopped my old destructive habits, and began to nurture the parts of my life that needed me. My business began to take off, I attracted new wonderful friends, and reconnected with my twin, my brothers and my parents. My life slowly began to fall into place.

The job of a good coach is to allow you to come to your own conclusions, make your own decisions, and choose what is right for yourself. And that is exactly what Tony did. His greatest skill has been to help me believe and trust my instincts to achieve my potential. We are all born great, with unique gifts, talents and personalities – however, many of us suppress our true selves and forget our dreams and desires. Drawing on his learnings from many avenues, including his own life story, Tony empowered me to push my boundaries, transform my mind and release my inner self."

Will Pike, Fitness Professional

As you can see from Will's example of his personal transformational journey, when you give the moment power, the past just drops away. You are able to heal this very instant. You let go of the burdens that you have been carrying and the nightmares that have haunted you in your sleep. You give permission for your wounds to close and heal this very moment.

Giving this moment full power also means that the future no longer binds you in knots when you have no idea how to reach your goals. Your attention is focused on the now, on what you can do. The quality of your attention to the present moment is full. You are engaged in your art, the act of doing something that you love. In the present moment, you become one with the act of doing in a synchronistic dance of creation that is powerful, magical and expansive. Your capacity to experience abundance is greatly enhanced.

Power fuses you when you are free. No longer burdened, you are free to craft out a life that you desire. Aligned with inner power, you are free to be the best that you can be. You are able to forge a purpose-driven path that will result in prosperity, as you operate from an abundance paradigm.

Learning to change your habits, identifying your barriers and transforming them into a full and abundant life does not come with a single action. It requires you to do a lot of repetition.

Repetition is the mother of learning and is an essential key to the physical development of a child's brain that includes you too; you may have grown up, but your brain learns the same way, through repetition.

For the reason why repetition is so important I turned to science to see what it had to say about it.

When you create a memory, a pathway is created between your brain cells. It is like clearing a path through a dense forest. The first time you do it, you have to fight your way through the undergrowth. If you don't travel that path again, very quickly it will become overgrown and you may not even realize that you have been down that path. If, however, you travel along the path before it begins to grow over, you will find it easier than your first journey along that way.

Successive journeys down the path mean that eventually your track will turn into a footpath, which will turn into a lane, which will turn into a road and into a freeway, and so on.

It is the same with your memory: the more times you repeat patterns of thought, for example when learning new information, the more likely you will be able to recall that information.

So repetition is a key part of learning. If you look at your brain's natural rhythms you will find the optimum plan for reviewing (repeating) information to get it into your long-term memory.

The question I always ask my clients who give up halfway through is: Why do you have this expectation of instant results and gratification?

The truth is, everything you know about yourself is due to repetition. All you need to do to remind yourself of this is to look at a toddler: the way he/she is trying to learn to walk, talk, and get used to the new environment he/she was born into is through repetition.

The more something is repeated, the more likely you are to remember it. Having ordinary routines and rituals, such as morning wake up routine, if you are a parent, having bedtime stories routine, cooking Sunday dinners for close friends, or making birthday cakes, even the daily chores you do are all the result of repetition.

Researchers found that life's little routines add up to a big security blanket, especially in times of stress.

One way of developing a skill is to make it a stored routine in your system. To make this happen, the most important first step is to bring the skill to a conscious level where you are deliberately thinking about the activity (not necessarily the skill).

In other words, you know what skill you're lacking in and focus on doing activities that will help you build this skill. This can be termed as learning by repetition.

As a skill is practiced or rehearsed over days and weeks, the activity becomes easier and easier while naturally forcing the skill to a subconscious level where it becomes permanently stored for recall and habitual use at any time.

Once the skill improves, you no longer need to think consciously about your participation in the skill-building activity. Likewise, once a new activity becomes really easy, it is evident that new skills have been built.

To create enough closely associated repetitions that drive a newly strengthened skill into a subconscious, automatic mode, the skill training should be delivered over multiple days each week and over at least a three-month period. The problem I have seen over and over is that many give up halfway and stop committing.

For example, in learning how to ride a bike, the more attempts a child makes, the more the brain reinforces the particular skills necessary to stay balanced and in motion. After some time, the child doesn't have to stop and think about each part of the procedure to stay upright, balanced, and in motion, or how to stop without falling off. Every time the child rides, the skill is reinforced. Even years later, with no additional riding experience, it is possible for a person to get on a bike and ride because it was so firmly encoded in the brain. This is the power of learning by repetition.

The various fears you may have is problem number one that stops you from remaining focused and repeating the tasks that you need to do to create the results you want in your life. Babies don't have this fear, hence why they learn faster than adults: they keep doing the same thing until they learn.

Repetition is the most basic technique for learning and plays an important role in learning as repeated exposure to information can help us to learn it better.

REWARDS

Reward is the fourth subcomponent of the Results pillar. You are so used to rewarding others for good behavior, but when it comes to yourself you are too afraid to do it. So far, reading this book and doing the exercises you have gone through a deep inner exploration.

Before you go any further, stop and do something to reward you: massage, a trip to the movies, and going shopping for some new clothing items are ideas. You can also give yourself a hug, take yourself out, or you may want to go and have a spa day – whatever it is, just do it.

You get the best results and most benefits when rewarding desired behavior consistently until it becomes part of your normal routine.

This does not mean you have to reward yourself immediately every single time you do the right thing; however, you should reward yourself frequently for changing bad behaviors into good ones. Using treats as a reward sends a confusing message to your brain and encourages the bad behavior that got you where you where you're at in the first place.

Start by knowing your short-term and long-term behavioral goal changes. For instance, what I do for any long-term goal is I put a dollar for every day I do the right thing into a jar to purchase a special gift for myself at 30-day intervals or when I reach my fitness goal. You may want to buy perfume or piece of clothing so it reminds you of your good behavior.

Another idea that involves no money is to make someone else happy by doing an act of kindness or volunteering. Doing something for someone else will make both them and you feel good! Go on, I challenge you for 30 days to try it and see how you feel at the end of this process.

If you are a foodie like me, I use food as a reward for any key milestones I achieve. Either I take myself out to a fancy restaurant, or I will go to Borough Market and buy some fresh organic fish, vegetables, and a selection of cheeses to cook at home and invite a friend over.

I have found that a monthly massage has become a habitual celebration of me becoming healthier. This gives me the incentive to actually be patient and give my body a treat, which I've grown to love.

I also reward myself with mini road trips, and overall random things. I lost one pound last week and I went to a barber to have a shave instead of doing it at home. I also got a nice wallet that I found on sale. I don't make rewards too complicated, just kind of simple, because the simple things are the most satisfactory.

I do have major goals for big milestones; when I sell, reach and empower one million readers with my book, I'm getting myself a brand new TV. I've wanted one for forever, because the one I have is 20 years old. And when I reach 10 million readers I am taking myself and a lucky friend on a two-week vacation in Bora Bora.

When you have taken a positive step to self-improvement, or when you have accomplished a goal or a milestone toward a long-term goal, you deserve to feel proud of yourself, celebrate and give yourself a treat or reward.

It is always a challenge in making life-changing decisions as it requires you to step out of your comfort zone. One such important decision is a change in lifestyle and making it healthier.

This requires a lot of discipline, perseverance and persistence in altering your diet, exercise at the gym, quitting smoking, reducing alcohol intake, and so on. Yet, such a decision has strong impact on your life in a positive way, especially in the long run.

Is making such a decision and meeting the goal impossible? It will be difficult, but it is not impossible. Many people have done it. Among the people who have made it, some experience a relapse.

Relapse can be avoided by rewarding yourself every time you accomplish a milestone toward a desired healthy lifestyle change.

For instance, if you are on a weight-loss program, when you have met a mini-goal, reward yourself. That will make your weight-loss journey more pleasant. If you don't celebrate and reward yourself for small success, you will feel your long-term weight-loss goal seems so far away.

You may feel despair or be tempted to give up. Having little stops to celebrate along the way makes that journey less difficult and your goal more likely to accomplish.

Below are my "personal rewards favorites" which I use to reward myself occasionally for my hard work, discipline and perseverance for achieving my target or goal in life. You can create your own personal ones to motivate yourself too.

Here is how: Make a list of things you enjoy. For each little success, reward yourself with choices from your basket. Each person's satisfaction varies. Consider what would really please you. For a change, put yourself first. Indulge. Spoil yourself. You have conquered yourself. You deserve it.

Affordable or Free Rewards

1. Take a membership to a movie house. It costs less than $20 a month and you can go as many times as you want; once a week, indulge yourself in watching a favorite movie or drama series.

2. Once a week, relax in bubble bath in your own sweet time. For example, once a month I go to Selfridges and treat myself to some bath products.

3. Indulge in reading something that inspires you.

4. Spend an afternoon at your favorite museum or gallery.

5. Connect with nature daily by taking a walk in a beautiful park.

6. Cook something delicious.

7. Light some candles and listen to some really uplifting music.

8. Savor a celebratory glass of wine with a special dinner.

9. Daily reward your body by taking a nap.

10. Take a day off from any goaled activities.

11. Get a new haircut.

12. Find new places to have coffee with good friends or a potential date.

Moderately Expensive Rewards

13. Once a month, travel – go to the coast or to the mountains.

14. Get a massage, manicure, pedicure or facial.

15. Have lunch at your favorite restaurant with your loved ones.

16. Have your favorite cocktail at your favorite bar.

17. Go shopping and buy something really special for yourself.

18. Attend a live concert of your favorite singers.

19. Watch an orchestra performance.

20. Splurge on a bottle of expensive wine or champagne with your loved one.

Luxurious Rewards

21. Go for a spa treatment.

22. Buy and wear something beautiful for an expensive dinner date.

23. Go to see your favorite show.

24. Buy yourself a nice handbag, jewelry, watch, devote the entire day to a shopping spree.

25. Go on a cruise to nowhere.

26. Sign up for an expensive vacation package staying in a luxurious hotel by a lake or at the coast.

27. Book a first-class ticket to your favorite destination, etc.

Keep it short and sweet. After you reward yourself, go back and continue your marathon run toward your goal immediately, and before you know it see the results of your efforts, actions, and the time you invested.

Results

The fourth main pillar of the TJS Evolutionary Method you have been learning is Results. This is what you truly live for; the results you wish to create, and the purposes you wish to fulfill are closely related with each other.

You learned the four main building blocks to help you stay focused in the results that create the future you want to live.

If you really think you deserve good things, then know this: your thoughts create results, so if you want to shift to new paradigms and learn to overcome challenges and obstacles you may be facing easily, you must change the way you think.

You do deserve a great life, and nothing but a great life. However, if you think you don't deserve something or that you'll always be stuck in an unhappy relationship or dead-end job forever, or that life will always be hard, then you'll prove to be right about these thoughts.

You'll keep yourself stuck if you focus on where you are now because you then perpetuate this exact set of circumstances over and over again.

Because the Law of Attraction states that you attract and manifest the things you think about, it pays to focus on what you want, not on what you don't want.

If you obsess about the problems you have now, you'll stay stuck in these problems. But if you concentrate on where you want to go from here, you'll start to move forward again and attract helpful events, in an ever-increasing measure, that will help you gain momentum.

Several well-known authors, speakers and teachers of the Law of Attraction were featured in the smash hit film *The Secret*. In it, they teach that everything coming into our lives is being attracted to us, through us, by virtue of the images we hold in our minds. This means when you think positive thoughts and focus on them intently, then like a magnet you will attract these good things into your life.

This can mean promising things if you remain aware of what you're thinking about; the problem here is that your reality is created mostly by your subconscious mind that you might not even be aware of.

You can turn your specific and hopeful wishes for health, money and great relationships into strong magnetic intentions by focusing your thoughts on these desires, and on nothing but these things.

Quantum physicists and metaphysicists tell us that our thoughts become form, so you literally bring the predominant events in your mind into your physical experience.

Not everything you think about happens, I don't mean that. But I am suggesting that what you think about most, over and over again, with the greatest amount of personal energy and attention, will indeed grow and come into your life.

For example, if you focus primarily on the feeling of happiness, you literally experience an expanse of happiness in the moment and you also attract future moments of happiness too.

One of my favorite affirmations that I adopted in early childhood was: "If They Can Do It, I Can Do It." Little did I know then how powerful this statement was and how it changed the way I think about life forever.

There are numerous examples of successful people who tell us how single-minded they became while focusing on a dream or ambition. A fun and inspiring modern-day sports example is Michael Jordan. Michael has spoken about his total mental fixation on becoming the best basketball player he could possibly be. His success started as a thought that he kept coming back to. He pictured himself being the very best before he became the very best; and we've all seen the results of such mental astuteness. Jordan is hailed to be the greatest athlete to have ever played the game.

It might be hard to relate to someone as famous as Michael Jordan, and perhaps your ambitions aren't the same as his, but you do have the same, equal access to the Law of Attraction as he does, or anyone does.

All of us are working with the Law of Attraction at all times. Successful people simply send out clear messages which they continually give thought energy to, and then participate with the many opportunities that arise as a result. And opportunities will present themselves to you too. They must because it's the law.

Don't worry about how everything is going to come about to help you. Just trust that things will. Favorable "chance" events will occur to support the thoughts that are foremost in your mind – and they are not luck or happenstance. These circumstances are designed for you, by you, and come about because your thinking has attracted them.

When I was transitioning out of my IT career and focusing intently on becoming a professional coach and a healer, suddenly and out of the blue many people showed up in my life to point me in the right direction. All of them had useful tips for how to grow my business, what courses I should take, and they shared ideas that I'd never heard of before.

You see, I received the much needed information only after I started thinking about filling my coaching and healing practice with local clients, and later on as I focused and visualized the places I wanted to travel, I started attracting international clients and opportunities. It was then that I found a multitude of people and networking opportunities available to me.

So far you have learned quite a lot about you, and you may have set some personal goals; I now invite you to focus, align your thoughts and visualize the results you want.

Not everything you think about shows up in the exact form you imagined, but the very essence of the things you think about most often and with the greatest amount of intensity will indeed appear.

Once I was coaching Selma, a busy professional who had had enough of toxic relationships that were going nowhere. Selma's sob stories of failed relationships spanned more than a decade. Finally, she decided things were going to change and came to see me for some coaching.

She knew she had to undo the thought pattern that was keeping her stuck, which was this: "I have to do everything myself because nobody really wants to help me."

I then took her through a process to imagine how good it would be to have a relationship with someone who had her best interests at heart and with whom she could be totally herself.

As she did so, she pictured all the elements she wanted in her ideal relationship and daydreamed about the details. She even created a long list of the qualities and characteristics she desired in this person so her eyes could see it on paper.

She then firmly decided she would settle for nothing less than what she'd envisioned, totally trusting and acting as if she knew for certain he was on the way.

Six months down the line he did appear; she started to talk to me about Adrian, how he reports an experience that complements her own. Just weeks before they met, he declared: "I'm not going to worry about meeting someone anymore. I'm going to be happy no matter what, and trust she'll show up when she's supposed to."

The irony is that Selma and her now husband have mutual friends who could have introduced them five years earlier than they actually did. She realized that only after her thoughts were aligned did she attract him, and it was the same for Adrian; it was only when his thoughts were aligned that they attracted one another.

You can do this with the smaller day-to-day things too. Each morning before you roll out of bed, you can practice visualizing and setting good intentions for the day.

Picture your day flowing smoothly, or unfolding any way you choose. See yourself calmly and easily getting everything done without stress, and with plenty of time and energy left to spare. See yourself smiling, relaxing and having fun with whatever occurs that day. Try it. None of this stuff will hurt you; you have nothing to lose and only good things to gain.

Trust me on this, I have done it many times, if you can see it in your mind, you can have it in your life. Formulate and stamp indelibly on your mind a mental picture of yourself as succeeding. Hold this picture tenaciously and never permit it to fade.

Your mind will seek to develop this picture, it is what the mind is chemically designed to do: find solutions to the problems you create.

Tips: If you want your life to change, you need to shift your focus and change your thinking. Imagine yourself enjoying the things you desire as if you already have them. You will then attract into your life the pictures you hold foremost in your mind. And be patient.

You live in the world of time and space. You can create some things instantly, like a good mood, and other things will take longer than you want them to and think they should. Little by little, you'll become more comfortable working with your thoughts, especially when you understand that most thoughts don't have instant manifesting power.

There's a buffer between your thoughts and their manifestation which gives you time to make improvements or corrections as you go, and to become clearer about what you really want.

Question: What super exciting goal, dream or idea will you focus on now? What results do you wish to create?

TJS Evolutionary Results Planning Method

I have learned that doing an activity that is not aligned to your highest values and purpose in life will drain your energy and suck the life out of you. So use this method to change that – let's start by asking five basic questions:

1. *What's your highest value?*

2. *What outcomes do you wish to create?*

3. *What's your mission and purpose in life?*

4. *What's your plan?*

5. *What's on your way?*

To help you in this process you need to ask five questions and take five actions, each day, until you achieve your goals.

Step one

Identify your top values, capture your thoughts, the outcomes you want, things you need to do and you need in your life, in one place, and have categories, otherwise it remains in your head. Have one place to capture it.

Step two

Create a list of all the outcomes you wish to create by answering those five most important questions:

1. *What are my top values? (money, business, career, love, relationship, etc.)*

2. *What do I really want? (results is my outcome, what is my result, measureable)*

3. *Why do I want it? (purpose: Why is it so important to me? Why are we doing it, why for me, why for the team?)*

4. *What obstacles are in my way?*

5. *What do I need to do to achieve this? (massive action plan)*

Step three

To manifest your purpose you have five actions to perform:

1. Be clear, committed and consistent.
2. Resolve your musts.
3. Minimum/maximum time.
4. Leverage.
5. Review.

Step four

Create your plan by looking at your list and put a star on actions of 20% of the list that have "I have outcome, I have a purpose."

Then ask yourself which 20% will make the biggest difference and support your top values; this will help you create your must items, that's why having a written list will help you get clear.

Take your item list and group them; below is a sample table, you may create your own table. Star the things/actions that are musts, establish real time minimum to maximum, and finally leverage (I know the outcome, I know the purpose).

Put a star on actions of 20% list "I have outcome, I have a purpose", which 20% will make the biggest difference, my must items, that's why I make my list, I do Results (juice) Purpose

My items (group them)	Mark with a star the things/actions that are musts	Establish real time minimum to maximum	Leverage (I know the outcome, I know the purpose)

Step five

Book your task of your must do goals in your diary, assign at least one hour each day, and create your personal affirmations: "I can have anything I set my mind to." "I am wise and I apply my wisdom," etc.

Concentrate on where you're going and what you want to experience! Keep your mind trained on your new direction going forward! Make a list of what you really want and keep giving these desires your positive thought energy.

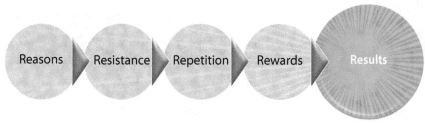

MIRACLES

In this final pillar of the **TJS Evolutionary Method** you bring together everything you have learned so far, and by giving the right meaning, living mindfully, introducing daily meditation practice, and having the right mindset, you too can create miracles and manifest the life you want.

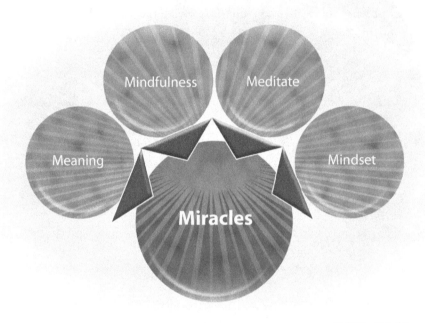

ALARM - *Miracles*

So, without any further ado, let's start with the first subcomponent and see why meaning matters.

MEANING

> *"Nothing has meaning except the*
> *meaning we give it."*
>
> **Anthony Robbins**

The reason why meaning matters for you to create the miracles you desire is that without having a meaning, nothing really matters. To put it another way, meaning drives the purpose of everything you do. Without that meaning, without purpose, why does it matter what you do?

If nothing – and by inference no one – matters, then the consequences of your actions are irrelevant beyond how they affect you. Of course, such a path quickly leads one to an extremely selfish existence – but so what?

Your lifestyle is environmentally unsustainable? So what – it doesn't matter. Your actions directly or indirectly hurt people? So what – they don't matter. Live life for number one and forget the rest.

But is that so far from reality for many people today? Perhaps one of the biggest challenges we face is that so many people wander through life without any real meaning – reflected in the social apathy that sadly is so familiar in the UK and, presumably, elsewhere.

Perhaps the majority haven't consciously decided to follow the above extreme example, but it's not so far from the truth of how an insular, purposeless life will work out. Even "enlightened self-interest" is, by definition, only slightly less selfish and still revolves around "me."

So how do you help put meaning back into yourself and the society so that people and actions start to matter again? How do you persuade individuals to put others before self – or at least on an even footing? How do you make the story relevant to the single mother and the out-of-work craftsman struggling to put food on the table for their families?

Agreeably, I believe there is hope. I believe most people do care about society more broadly, whether driven by their religion, cultural values, community values or what we might call innate humanity, and do want to live good, meaningful lives that matter.

It is a rare individual who is not inspired in any way by one of society's great purpose-driven achievers – be they philanthropist, politician or Olympian – and who dreams of doing "more." Our role is to give people the tools to help them.

I have mentioned more than once that nothing has any meaning except the meaning you give it, and I thought I would address that here and now.

The first thing that you have to understand is there is a difference between a meaning, a purpose, and a point. Secondly, it helps to realize that the mind, or a dictionary (which is created by the mind of the people to help society globally define something) is the only thing that gives something a meaning.

But as the dictionary will show you, there are many meanings to a single word. Same way the meaning is shaped by you, your intention, and the usage of the word, and in many situations, there are apparent dichotomies in the meaning of the word.

For example, the word "set" has the most meanings of any word in the dictionary, with a total of 464 definitions. The point is, one word, one situation can and often will have many meanings, all of which have been given by society. It is worth noting that society is governed by the mind of society – a global mind, but a mind none the less.

So it seems that we as human beings have a hard-wired "meaning-making" mechanism that judges almost everything conducive to your survival, or inimical to your survival – for you or against you. One of the first words that children learn, and then repeat incessantly, is "why." You need to understand what is happening and why so you can better judge the effect it might have on your life.

The need to discover an event's probable impact on you leads you to look for the meaning in events that have no inherent meaning. Any event in your life could have a multitude of meanings and you can't ever draw any conclusions, for sure, from any event. Meaning exists only in the mind, not in the world.

For example, if parents get angry when their children don't meet their expectations, most children will assign such behavior the meaning that they aren't good enough.

In reality, however, the fact that parents are angry at their child tells you nothing for certain about their child. As a result, you can't know anything for certain about a child from the fact that his parents frequently got angry at him. In other words, the events involving the parents and children have no inherent meaning.

We create two different types of meaning we give to events.

The first type is the meaning we give to a pattern of events, such as mom and dad being busy a lot of the time (leading to: I'm not important) or mom and dad arguing a lot and getting divorced (leading to: relationships don't work). These meanings become beliefs, which are generalized statements about ourselves, people and life that stay with us forever unless we find some way to eliminate the belief. Such beliefs are often variations of "I am …" or "People are …" or "Life is …." Beliefs are statements about reality that we feel are "the truth", thereby determining our behavior.

The second type is the meaning we give to specific events, both external (events in the world) or internal (such as thoughts, feelings, memories, physical sensations, etc.)

These meanings last only as long as our focus on an event lasts. Like beliefs, such meanings are created unconsciously and automatically. The meaning we give this type of event determines how it "occurs" for us. Most of us most of the time never distinguish between actual events and how the events occur to us. We think the latter is real and therefore we deal with the "occurring" as if it is the actual reality.

In other words, if a friend walks into a room and doesn't speak to me, and this event occurs to me as my friend doesn't like me, it seems to me as if the reality is my friend doesn't like me.

At which point we deal with this person as if he really doesn't like me, when all I know for sure is that when he walked into the room he did not talk to me. In other words, because we usually don't distinguish between an event and the meaning we give the event, we deal with the meaning as if it is what actually happened.

Ultimately, both types of meanings (beliefs and our occurring) get substituted for reality in our mind and we don't deal with what really is. In other words, we think our beliefs and occurrings are "the truth."

Getting rid of these meanings

When you eliminate beliefs, you create new possibilities in your life because "your reality" has changed. The filters through which you view reality are gone. Barriers to action, such as procrastination and anxiety, have been permanently eliminated.

When you dissolve the meaning/occurring you give events moment by moment, you are better able to deal with the situation (if it needs dealing with) because you are clear on the difference between the event to be dealt with and the meaning that exists only in your mind.

So you are able to see more possibilities for solving a problem. Moreover, because meaningless events cannot cause feelings, most of our negative emotions, such as anxiety and anger, come from the meaning you give events. By dissolving the meaning, you simultaneously dissolve the negative feelings.

Dissolve beliefs and occurring by making a distinction

As I pointed out in earlier chapters, we think our beliefs and the meaning we give events moment by moment are true because of a distinction we failed to make earlier, namely between the event(s) and the meaning we assign the event(s).

Therefore, the way to eliminate or dissolve beliefs and current meanings is to make the distinction we did not make earlier. When we are able to make that distinction, the belief and the current meaning/occurring disappear.

When people are told they can eliminate beliefs, some respond: "But won't that force me to do things that might be dangerous, for example, if I eliminate the belief life is dangerous, won't that make me oblivious to some real dangers?" The answer is no. Eliminating beliefs does not make you do anything. It only offers new possibilities from which you can choose freely.

A similar thing happens when I tell people that they can learn to stop giving meaning to events. One person asked: "Won't that lead to people becoming sociopaths?" What he meant was: If you have no feelings, won't you stop caring about other people? Won't you lose all sense of morality? Again, the answer is no.

Not giving an arbitrary meaning to moment-to-moment events does not affect your values at all. You can still value human life and have a desire to alleviate the suffering of others.

In addition, you do not need meaning to get you to take action. If you lose your job, you don't need to assume it means you will not be able to pay your bills and you will lose your home and you will never get another job, etc. in order to start looking for a new job. In fact, you will be better able to create strategies for finding a new job if you are not overwhelmed with the fear that would result from such occurrings.

How can you decide what to do without any meaning?

But if nature built a meaning-making mechanism into you because you need to know if what you encounter in reality is conducive to or threatens your survival, how will you be able to survive if you stop making meaning?

There is a significant difference between making reasonable assumptions that you know are assumptions and that you continually check for accuracy, and unknowingly giving meaning to an event and then thinking that the way the event occurred to you is what actually happened. You can never be better off by being blind to what actually is.

Automatic meaning-making might be useful in a world where real danger lurks beneath every bush, where a saber-tooth tiger might jump out at you at any moment. In such a world, you need to give meaning to events automatically and respond without conscious thought. You are better being safe than sorry and assuming the worst will probably save your life at some point.

But you no longer live in a world where you need automatic, unconscious meaning. In virtually every situation you have the time to think carefully about events and consciously determine their most likely meaning – all the while realizing that your consciously-created meanings are provisional and need to be checked for usefulness from time to time. You know they are your best guesses at that time and do not mistake them for the truth.

In today's modern world, thinking your beliefs and occurrings are "the truth" can never be useful. So eliminate your limiting beliefs and learn how to stop automatically giving meaning to current events. You'll be surprised at how much happier and more successful you will become.

As you give something a meaning, that is exactly what it becomes for you. The mind and you (your participation/engagement with the thoughts) will decide what something is, and the thing begins to metamorphosize into whatever it is you believe it to be.

This holds true whether we call it a "bad thing" or a "good thing," It works for you and against you, but it is the exact same happening.

How does knowing and realizing this fact help you to evolve into your spiritual maturity? Once you begin to see that you are the one giving something a meaning, and if that meaning is not working for you, you can change your meaning.

Another way of looking at it is to realize the game, see what the mind is doing and not buy into any of it, just let the situation unfold and not give it any label or meaning other than "This is the situation that I am in right now, and I also know that the Now is constantly changing."

The mind is divine and it is a beast, all at the same time. See that, and begin to work with it. Begin to understand it, stop buying into it, stop believing everything the mind says as being true, and begin to live from the authentic you, and be the authentic you that uses the mind for what it was designed to be used for.

Stop the labeling, or at least recognize that you are the one labeling, realize you are choosing your own labels for things, and go on about your business. Recognize that you are the one giving meaningless meanings to things and situations, and watch how life always supports life.

The root of the problem lies in the fact that despite living in an ever more connected global society, business has become ever more immune from the broader impact of its activities, and individuals have become ever more disconnected from their impact as both investor and consumer.

The first goal must therefore be to burst these non-information bubbles and help inform society of the true impact of its actions. Reconnect business activity with its impact upon society and the environment. Inform the individual similarly. Much has already been done in this regard, but there is still a long way to go.

The second goal must be to create the tools that translate improved understanding into action. Business needs help to understand, reduce/mitigate and price the true cost of its activities. Individuals need to be offered the products by which they can actively choose to make a difference.

If we can deliver on these goals, just maybe we can help society find some meaning – and that matters.

Exercise: Taking Control

The truth is you can choose to look at things and give them meaning in whatever way you please!
So you can ask these two questions to question everything, to experience, and change the meaning.

1. *Did something happen in your life that you've given a disempowering meaning to?*

2. *How can you look at it differently to turn it into a positive?*

I realize this may be a large request but I encourage you to take this approach and do the exercise anyway. It might just be the key to being significantly happier every day.

MINDFULNESS

To be mindful is a special way of paying attention that can help with how you cope with everyday life obstacles, or bounce back from tough times, and there are great benefits for your physical and mental health.

What mindfulness truly means is to really pay attention to your thoughts, feelings, emotions and the way you live your life on daily basis. It is about not getting caught up in the past or worrying about the future, it is about focusing on the present; it is about simply being present.

Mindfulness is about training yourself to pay attention in a specific way. When a person is mindful, they are focused on the present moment, they do not worry about anything that went on in the past or that might be coming up in the future.

A mindful person is concentrating purposefully on what's happening around them and to them, they are not being judgmental about anything they notice, they know that the way they think and feel impacts everyone around them.

We spend so much time thinking over stuff that happens, or worrying about things that may be happening in future, that often we actually forget to appreciate or enjoy the moment. Mindfulness is a way of bringing us back to experience life as it happens.

When you're mindful, it gives you a clear head, slows down your thoughts, slows down your nervous system, gives your body time to heal, lets you relax, it helps you cope with stress, helps you be more aware of yourself, your body and the environment.

Mindfulness is something that everyone can develop, and it's something that everyone stands to gain from. It's been practiced for thousands of years, with origins in eastern philosophy, and over the past 40 years it has taken root in western societies.

Normally people practice meditation and yoga to increase their mindfulness in everyday life. But it has also been incorporated into other therapies such as: Mindfulness Based Cognitive Therapy, Life Coaching, NLP, many healing methods, as well in the TJS Evolutionary Method.

You can build mindfulness using a lot of different strategies of the ALARM method you have been learning. It will have a good impact on your physical and mental health. As you learn and practice daily, you create an inner peace, you acknowledge the love you have, you start to achieve the results you want to have in your life, and creating everyday miracles comes naturally to you.

When you're mindful, you get to experience living life in the moment. There are a lot of different strategies you can use to build how mindful you are.

Exercise for you

**Make a list of the things that stop you
from being mindful, for instance:**

- I have trouble focusing
- I spend time worrying about the past or the future
- I want to relax
- I am anxious
- I am depressed
- I can't manage my anger
- I have bad memory
- I am emotional
- I don't sleep well
- I don't cope with pain

Continue and add your own examples to the list above.

There are a lot of different things you can do to help yourself be more mindful. Some of these things are easy and you can incorporate them into everyday life; others require a bit more time and some training.

Here you will learn two types of mindfulness meditation you can do to help you in your journey in living mindfully.

Concentrative meditation

Put yourself in a comfortable position and start to focus your attention on breathing, an image, or a sound, so that you can calm your mind and minimize thoughts. Start with five minutes a day, and increase it once you become fully present.

Mindfulness meditation

This type of meditation involves trying to make you aware of sensations, feelings, thoughts and images that you experience from moment to moment. It also tries to reduce how much you judge these moment-to-moment experiences – the point is to "notice, and let it be."

So take a moment, close your eyes, and start to take deep breaths; as you do so, bring your attention to your toes, ankles, legs, your stomach, your organs there, your heart, throat, face, scalp, and maintain the focus in each area for at least a minute so you can feel and sense each body part.

In the above mindfulness meditations you learn to remain aware of what is happening and what you're feeling in that moment, whether you like it, dislike it, or are confused about it. You increase your tolerance for seeing the unpleasant – neither identifying with it, nor running from it.

As you become more and more familiar with the usual patterns in your mind, mindfulness allows you to choose what your mind focuses on by interrupting its habits (e.g. to put yourself down).

For more information on meditation, check out EvoCalm app in the Apps and Tools section which helps you work on meditation techniques, as well as many useful tips and resources from **www.tonyselimi.com**

Here are seven ways to build mindfulness:

1. **Mindful Breathing.**
    Take a couple of minutes to focus on your breathing. When you're mindful of your breathing you need to pay attention to what breathing feels like, what happens to different parts of your body, and the sound of your breath. If your mind wanders off, it's not something to worry about. Just bring your attention back to your breathing when you can.

2. **Mental Photography.**
    Try taking mental photos of interesting things you find as you are out and about. To take a mindful photo, think about what details you'd like to capture in a shot.

3. **A Whole New World.**
    If like me you love Aladdin, then I invite you to listen to my favorite song in that movie *A Whole New World*. Look at the world through a new lens. Imagine you are seeing everything for the first time and pay attention to little things that wouldn't normally get noticed.

4. Savoring.

   Take time to enjoy and appreciate an activity you are doing. It could be any experience – food, conversation, checking out a good view. The point of it is to pay really close attention to the details – be aware of smells, tastes, sights, sounds, and things you can feel.

5. Retrain your Brain.

   Becoming more mindful involves retraining your brain, so it's something that does take a bit of time. It can be quite difficult to focus for long without your thoughts wandering off somewhere else, and it's also difficult not to get frustrated when that happens.

6. Be Consistent.

   The key here is really determination. The more you practice mindfulness, the better you will become. Don't worry if it is difficult initially, most people really struggle at first. When you're building how mindful you are using a particular strategy, get into the habit of practicing every day – even if it's just for a few minutes. Eventually, you should start to improve.

7. Change your Strategy.

   If you're really struggling with a particular strategy, try a different one. Everyone's different, and some strategies may be easier for you than others – the point is to try a few out and find one that works for you.

Now let's look at the third component of the fifth pillar of this powerful method – Meditation – why it is so important to meditate daily and incorporate it into this process and into your day-to-day life.

MEDITATION

Meditation has been practiced for thousands of years. Meditation was originally meant to help deepen understanding of the sacred and mystical forces of life.

These days, meditation is commonly used for relaxation and stress reduction.

Meditation is considered a type of mind-body complementary medicine. Meditation produces a deep state of relaxation and a tranquil mind. During meditation, you focus your attention and eliminate the stream of jumbled thoughts that may be crowding your mind and causing stress. This process results in enhanced physical and emotional well-being.

Meditation can give you a sense of calm, peace and balance that benefits both your emotional well-being and your overall health. And these benefits don't end when your meditation session ends. Meditation can help carry you more calmly through your day and can even improve certain medical conditions.

It's a piece of advice various eastern spiritual healers, Buddha, and yogis have given for thousands of years: take a deep breath and relax. Watch the tension melt from your muscles and all your niggling worries vanish. Somehow we all know that relaxation is good for us, yet many ignore to incorporate this into their day-to-day living.

So many of my clients get excited about it, then for whatever reason they stop, and when I ask them about it, they talk to me as if meditation is a chore they must do and not an activity that feels loving, calming, and one that brings inner peace.

Now the hard science has caught up: a comprehensive scientific study has been published showing that deep relaxation changes our bodies on a genetic level.

What researchers at Harvard Medical School discovered is that, in long-term practitioners of relaxation methods such as yoga and meditation, far more "disease-fighting genes" were active, compared to those who practiced no form of relaxation.

In particular, they found genes that protect from disorders such as pain, infertility, high blood pressure and even rheumatoid arthritis were switched on.

The changes, say the researchers, were induced by what they call "the relaxation effect", a phenomenon that could be just as powerful as any medical drug but without the side effects. "We found a range of disease-fighting genes were active in the relaxation practitioners that were not active in the control group," says Dr. Herbert Benson, associate professor of medicine at Harvard Medical School, who led the research.

The good news for the control group with the less healthy genes is that the research didn't stop there.

The experiment, which showed just how responsive genes are to behavior, mood and environment, revealed that genes can switch on just as easily as they switch off. "Harvard researchers asked the control group to start practicing relaxation methods every day. After two months, their bodies began to change: the genes that help fight inflammation, kill diseased cells and protect the body from cancer all began to switch on."

Pretty amazing, don't you think? More encouraging still, the benefits of the relaxation effect were found to increase with regular practice: the more people practiced relaxation methods such as meditation or deep breathing, the greater their chances of remaining free of arthritis and joint pain with stronger immunity, healthier hormone levels and lower blood pressure.

Having spent 20 years practicing healing meditations and healing many of my physical and emotional problems, I believe that the research is pivotal because it shows how a person's state of mind affects the body on a physical and genetic level.

Being a scientist, and at that time when my journey started a non-believer in any of the techniques I practice now, it helped me understand why relaxation induced by meditation or repetitive mantras is considered to be a powerful remedy in traditions such as Ayurveda in India or Tibetan medicine.

But just how can relaxation have such wide-ranging and powerful effects? Research has described the negative effects of stress on the body. Linked to the release of the stress hormones adrenalin and cortisol, stress raises the heart rate and blood pressure, weakens immunity and lowers fertility.

By contrast, the state of relaxation is linked to higher levels of feel-good chemicals such as serotonin and to the growth hormone which repairs cells and tissue. Indeed, studies show that relaxation has virtually the opposite effect, lowering heart rate, boosting immunity and enabling the body to thrive.

On a biological level, stress is linked to fight-flight and danger; when you operate in survival mode, heart rate rises and blood pressure shoots up. Meanwhile, muscles, preparing for danger, contract and tighten. And non-essential functions such as immunity and digestion go by the wayside.

Relaxation, on the other hand, is a state of rest, enjoyment and physical renewal. Free of danger, muscles can relax and food can be digested. The heart can slow and blood circulation flows freely to the body's tissues, feeding it with nutrients and oxygen. This restful state is good for fertility, as the body is able to conserve the resources it needs to generate new life.

While relaxation techniques can be very different, their biological effects are essentially similar. When you relax, the parasympathetic nervous system switches on. That is linked to better digestion, memory and immunity, among other things.

Until I learned to relax and breathe deeply, I was not seeing the rewards. I started to reap the rewards years after I started my first meditation.

Deep relaxation isn't the sort of switching off you do relaxing with a cup of tea or lounging on the sofa. What you're looking for is a state of deep relaxation where tension is released from the body on a physical level and your mind completely switches off.

The effect won't be achieved by lounging around in an everyday way, nor can you force yourself to relax. You can only really achieve it by learning a specific technique such as self-hypnosis, guided imagery or meditation, or the simple mindfulness meditation I shared above.

Research also shows that the relaxation effect, however, may not be as pronounced on everyone. Some people are more susceptible to relaxation methods than others. Through relaxation and guided meditation I have taken many of my clients, I find some people experience a little improvement, others a lot. And there are a few whose lives turn around totally.

The next time you tune out and switch off and let yourself melt, remind yourself of all the good work the relaxation effect is doing on your body. These are just some of the scientifically proven benefits: increased immunity; it helps you create emotional balance; it helps your sexual life and it helps promotes fertility; it relieves irritable bowel syndrome (one that used to keep me awake and in pain for many years until I healed it); it lowers your blood pressure; it is anti-inflammatory; and most of all it keeps you calm.

How can you use relaxation's healing powers? Harvard researchers found that yoga, meditation and even repetitive prayer and mantras all induced the relaxation effect: "The more regularly these techniques are practiced, the more deeply rooted the benefits will be."

When you meditate, you clear away the information overload that builds up every day and contributes to your stress.

Some of the emotional benefits of meditation include:

✓ Gaining a new perspective on stressful situations
✓ Building skills to manage your stress
✓ Increasing self-awareness
✓ Focusing on the present
✓ Reducing negative emotions

Meditation might also be useful if you have a medical condition, especially one that may be worsened by stress. While a growing body of scientific research supports the health benefits of meditation, some researchers believe it's not yet possible to draw conclusions about the possible benefits of meditation.

With that in mind, some research suggests that meditation may help such conditions as:

- Allergies
- Anxiety disorders
- Asthma
- Binge eating
- Cancer
- Depression
- Fatigue
- Heart disease
- High blood pressure
- Pain
- Sleep problems
- Substance abuse

Be sure to talk to your health care provider about the pros and cons of using meditation if you have any of these conditions or other health problems. In some cases, meditation can worsen symptoms associated with certain mental health conditions. Meditation isn't a replacement for traditional medical treatment but it may be a useful addition to your other treatment.

Meditation is an umbrella term for the many ways to a relaxed state of being. There are many types of meditation and relaxation techniques that have meditation components. All share the same goal of achieving inner peace.

Exercise for you

Let me share with you different ways you can meditate; start with one or more of these techniques for 15 minutes once or twice a day and in time increase it to whatever works for you.

- Guided meditation.

  Sometimes called guided imagery or visualization, with this method of meditation you form mental images of places or situations you find relaxing. You try to use as many senses as possible, such as smells, sights, sounds and textures. You may be led through this process by a guide or teacher.

- Body scan.

  Starting with your head and working down to your arms and feet, notice how you feel in your body. Taking in your head and neck, simply notice if you feel tense, relaxed, calm or anxious. See how much you can spread any sensations of softness and relaxation to areas of your body that feel tense. Once you reach your feet, work back up your body.

- Breath focus.

  Sit comfortably. Tune into your breath, follow the sensation of inhaling from your nose to abdomen and out again. Let tension go with each exhalation. When you notice your mind wandering, return to your breath.

A PATH to WISDOM

- Qi gong.

  This practice generally combines meditation, relaxation, physical movement and breathing exercises to restore and maintain balance. Qi gong (CHEE-gung) is part of traditional Chinese medicine.

- Mantra repetition.

  In this type of meditation, you silently repeat a calming word, thought or phrase to prevent distracting thoughts. The relaxation response can be evoked by sitting quietly with eyes closed for 15 minutes twice a day, and mentally repeating a simple word or sound such as "Om."

- Guided imagery.

  Imagine a wonderfully relaxing light or a soothing waterfall washing away tension from your body and mind. Make your image vivid, imagining texture, color and any fragrance as the image washes over you.

- Mindfulness meditation.

  This type of meditation is based on being mindful, or having an increased awareness and acceptance of living in the present moment. You broaden your conscious awareness. You focus on what you experience during meditation, such as the flow of your breath. You can observe your thoughts and emotions but let them pass without judgment.

- Tai chi.

  This is a form of gentle Chinese martial arts. In tai chi (TIE-chee), you perform a self-paced series of postures or movements in a slow, graceful manner while practicing deep breathing.

- Transcendental meditation.

  You use a mantra, such as a word, sound or phrase repeated silently, to narrow your conscious awareness and eliminate all thoughts from your mind. You focus exclusively on your mantra to achieve a state of perfect stillness and consciousness.

● Yoga.

You perform a series of postures and controlled breathing exercises to promote a more flexible body and a calm mind. As you move through poses that require balance and concentration, you're encouraged to focus less on your busy day and more on the moment.

All the different types of meditation above include different features to help you meditate. These may vary depending on whose guidance you follow or who's teaching a class. Some of the most common features in meditation include:

● A quiet setting.

If you're a beginner, practicing meditation may be easier if you're in a quiet spot with few distractions – no television, radio or cell phone. As you get more skilled at meditation, you may be able to do it anywhere, especially in high-stress situations where you benefit the most from meditation, such as a traffic jam, a stressful work meeting or a long line at the grocery store.

● A comfortable position.

You can practice meditation whether you're sitting, lying down, walking or in other positions or activities. Just try to be comfortable so you can get the most out of your meditation.

● Focused attention.

Focusing your attention is generally one of the most important elements of meditation. Focusing your attention is what helps free your mind from the many distractions that cause stress and worry. You can focus your attention on such things as a specific object, an image, a mantra, or even your breathing.

● Relaxed breathing.

This technique involves deep, even-paced breathing using the diaphragm muscle to expand your lungs. The purpose is to slow your breathing, take in more oxygen, and reduce the use of shoulder, neck and upper chest muscles while breathing so that you breathe more efficiently.

Don't let the thought of meditating the "right" way add to your stress. Sure, you can attend special meditation centers or group classes led by trained instructors. But you also can practice meditation easily on your own.

And you can make meditation as formal or informal as you like – whatever suits your lifestyle and situation. Some people build meditation into their daily routine. For example, they may start and end each day with an hour of meditation. But all you really need is a few minutes of quality time for meditation.

In my one-to-one coaching or healing meditation classes, I help clients build meditation skills step by step, they learn to relax and let go of the expectation and judging their meditation skills as this only increases stress levels. Meditation takes practice; you can use this method to help you practice.

Keep in mind, for instance, that it's common for your mind to wander during meditation, no matter how long you've been practicing meditation. If you're meditating to calm your mind and your attention wanders, slowly return to the object, sensation or movement you're focusing on.

Finally, experiment, and you'll likely find out what types of meditation work best for you and what you enjoy doing. Adapt meditation to your needs at the moment. Remember, there's no right way or wrong way to meditate. What matters is that meditation helps you with stress reduction and feeling better overall.

MINDSET

If you are interested in enhancing your own life and shaping your future, then for sure you will need to incorporate in this process the fourth component of the fifth pillar of this method: have the right Mindset.

To unlock more potential for yourself, as a parent, grandparent, or coach, in business or in family relationships, it requires for you to build the right mindset.

Have you ever wondered why some people are more open to possibilities, growth and change? If you answered yes to this question, then you must work toward having the correct mindset.

When I read *The New Psychology of Success* by Dr. Carol S. Dweck from Stanford University, it helped me understand why it's not just our abilities and talent that bring us success but whether we approach our goals with a fixed or growth mindset.

She explains that with the right mindset we can motivate our children and help them improve in school, as well as reach our own goals – personal and professional.

Your mindset is the foundation on which miracles are built and the very way in which you begin to create something out of nothing.

If you think about it, mindset is like a thermostat: your mind too is set, like a thermostat, by you. The setting holds the "temperature" – temperament as in mindset – in place. Mindset settings have two basic ingredients: thoughts and feelings. A belief is formed from emotionalized thought that has an "assigned" meaning.

Brain research shows that we are assigning the meaning to what happens to us – it is not "objective" in general. Your perception of life is different from mine.

Don't be fooled, mindset is not about the "intellect" alone. In fact, it is emotion/feelings that act as the glue that seals in a "belief."

Recently, I had a series of coaching sessions and I heard others talk about the heart and the importance of the role of the heart in guiding our choices.

On a few of these occasions I heard: "The heart is always right, so I should/you should listen to your heart and how you feel."

Of course, I've also heard: "Ignore your feelings, leave them at home – logic and the rational mind is all that matters"... as in forget the "touchy feely" stuff. Both are extremes – let me explain.

Well, I've been thinking about this over the years and as I've become more aware of how to consciously engage my "Neo-cortex", feelings, intuition and my "still small voice" – the source of the wise heart – more, and at the same time retrain my brain's perception about old cellular feelings, I've come to experience the difference between the "(wise) heart" and "feelings."

In a recent coaching session with Paul, a successful fitness professional, we talked about exactly this. He did find it hard to differentiate the two. In our conversation he understood that the difference is subtle but very important.

After hundreds of times of reacting to my "feelings" that said to do something and finding the choice to be less than stellar later, I slowed down enough to pay attention to something very important. There is a difference between "heart" (that is intuitive and comes from a place of clarity, spirit and "knowing") and "feelings."

To be clear: I'm making a distinction here between "heart" and "feelings."

True, for some this "knowing" comes via feelings, for some it's a "thought" and for some it's a mental image. The trick is to distinguish old subconscious feelings that cause you to stay stuck in a pattern, and the deeper "heart" of your inner self.

If you don't deal with old emotion and feelings from the past that come up to be changed and perceptually rewired, you can keep finding yourself repeating self-sabotaging patterns.

If you only go by "feelings" without waiting on the wisdom, the "knowing" of the heart, you can rush blindly into old stuck relationship patterns, money and poor health patterns.

You simply use logical justification to rationalize it – and sometimes this rationale is that you are "following your heart" – and you continue to repeat old behaviors that no longer serve your highest potential. You become run only by your feelings.

For example, once I was coaching a client I now know very well who was part of a threesome who were planning to be roommates. During the apartment-hunting adventure, it became clear that his chosen companions were inclined to drama – poor communication, controlling behavior, and lack of honesty. Yet, this man told me he "felt" he should be loyal and even though the red flags were there, his "heart was feeling" that he should keep his word so he was "feeling guilty" and he asked: "Isn't the heart always right?"

Since I knew this young man very well, after listening to him I saw the pattern of the behavior of his companions to be virtually identical to several other relationships that he had in the past. They were relationships that he had discontinued because he wanted to honor his partner's value of "relationship harmony."

He had begun to have more success at healthier friendships. This was a new way of being for him. It was not yet a consistent "pattern" however. So I asked: "If you slow down, be still and listen, even right now, what does the still small voice (my description of "the heart") "know" about what you should do here?"

Long/short his response was, he knew at a deep level that he should kindly tell them that the situation was not good for him and since they could not happily agree, he was going to honor their value of living in a space of harmony.

He made up his mind there and then, followed through and, lo and behold, the very next day a situation materialized that exceeded his expectations: a long, long childhood friend called and asked him to be his roommate and this friend was already living in an apartment building that the young man desired.

The point is your feelings are sometimes reacting to old familiar subconscious behavior patterns that you don't know how to change. The "heart" is not just about "feelings"; the heart is an inner intuitive "knowing." We come to know our "heart" by making time to reflect, go within and understand our "self" better.

When you come to a place that honors your values and purpose, a place of clarity, you can use your "intellect" to bring this wise heart insight into your experience – in this case by simply speaking up and taking action.

Sometimes you need to use your intellect to just say no. You were given an intellectual and an intuitive mind – represented by the left brain hemisphere and right hemisphere, respectively – for a reason.

The right brain is representative of your heart and feelings – you just need to learn to discern the subtleties if the feeling is an old pattern that no longer serves you.

When you partner the mind/intellect and heart, you can be most effective, though admittedly, when you come from our heart "knowing", you may have to override the intellect occasionally!

If you do, just make sure you are listening to the heart and not just being sentimental or succumbing to old feelings of guilt, "shoulds", "musts" and "have tos."

If you don't learn how to make these distinctions, your mindset is likely to be stuck with the intellectual, emotional and feeling glue of old subconscious patterns.

If you integrate and implement all of the knowledge shared so far, you can create not only "miracles", good health, peace, but also great success in all eight key areas of your life.

Having a positive, open to learning and loving mindset will set you free and allow you to experience life in a whole new way – the way it was naturally intended for you to live.

My familiarity with everything I have shared so far helped me go deeper in myself, and creating the supporting mindset is directly due to the challenges I have faced in my lifetime. Let me inspire you and share with you my personal journey.

Although every human life comes with its fair share of challenges, I have had four major ones that have significantly shaped my life because they required a "miracle" in order for me to overcome them.

The first major challenge occurred when I was nine and hospitalized for almost two years.

The second challenge 10 years later when the civil war in the former Yugoslav Republic broke out. I was forced to join the army and over 18 months in the army witnessed many atrocities that left me emotionally handicapped.

My third challenge came straight after the civil war when I flew the country to find refuge in England. I had no home, no money, lost friends, family and my sense of identity and was in a new country I knew nothing about.

And the last major challenge I experienced in 2009 when, after 12 years of building skills and a successful career in IT, I faced redundancy and the many challenges that came as a result. My life once again destabilized, and I felt as if I was dropping into the abyss.

Nonetheless, now I'm sitting in my comfortable home, writing this book, having my own successful business and feeling full of life.

Each of these challenges required me to learn something new about life, how it truly operated and how we as human beings actually create it around us.

And one of the most important things that I learned was that anything is possible when you have the right mindset, education, nurturing, and teacher to guide you and help you in your journey.

Overcoming situations believed to be "impossible" led me to truly understand that I never have reason to close my mind off to any possibility. This was the first mindset I created.

In my personal journey I came across the work of Carol Dweck, a world-renowned Stanford University psychologist, who talks about the power of mindset or our beliefs (especially around change). She explains that either you can have a Fixed Mindset where you let failure (or even success) define who you are, or a Growth Mindset where you see setbacks as opportunities to grow and improve yourself.

Just like how you learned how to walk, there are many stumbles along the way, but to reach your potential and live the life you desire, it takes practice and perseverance.

As you read in one of the earlier chapters, you always have a choice about which view to adopt about yourself, and it is never too late to change it either.

Here is a table you can use to help you determine your personal mindset and help you know the difference, as only then can you change.

	Fixed Mindset Belief that my intelligence, personality and character are carved in stone. A person's potential is determined at birth	Growth Mindset Belief that my intelligence, personality and character can be developed. A person's true potential is unknown (unknowable)
Desire	Look smart in every situation and prove myself over and over again	Stretch myself, take risks, and learn. Bring on the challenges
Evolution of situations	Will I succeed or fail? Will I look smart or dumb?	Will this allow me to grow? Will this help me overcome my challenges?
Dealing with setbacks	I am a failure (identity) I am an idiot	I failed, what can I do? (action) I learned and will try harder next time
Challenges	Avoid challenges, get defensive, or give up easily	Embrace challenges, persist in the face of setbacks
Effort	Why bother? It is not going to change anything	Growth and learning require effort
Criticism	Ignore constructive criticism	Learn from criticism, self-reflect. How can I improve?
Success of others	Feel threatened by success of others; if you succeed, I fail mindset	Finds lessons and inspirations of other people's successes
Result	Plateau early, achieve less than my full potential	Reach ever higher levels of achievements

I was glad to learn what a Growth Mindset was and how it is maintained, and I was also glad to learn about having a "wild mind", which was the next point.

A wild mind is full of thought patterns that hinder rather than serve, and are often unconscious, autopilot reactions. Personalization is one side effect of a wild mind that 10 years ago I was especially guilty of. With personalization, I used to think every little event and conversation was a reflection of my worth.

For example, I might have a tense conversation with my mum and think afterwards that the whole conversation happened because she hates me, even though it's clear we're both just having a really rotten day and taking it out on each other.

Common sense and our fun times together should make it obvious it's not because she hates me, but that's what the wild mind will do: impede common sense through personalization, catastrophizing (making small obstacles into huge disasters), mind-reading (assuming how people feel) or other illogical thought processes of the mind.

But knowing when you indulge in the harmful effects of a wild mind is the key to, yup, self-reflection, which will help minimize any wild mind moments in the future.

Another important facet of self-reflection is to understand how you think, feel, and act or react. What drives you? Do your thoughts, for example, snowball into certain feelings and behaviors? Do you react to external circumstances or deliberately choose how you will respond to a given situation? Knowing the answers to these questions can only increase your skills of self-reflection, I learned.

I came across The Four Rivers, a term coined by cultural anthropologist, author, and educator Angeles Arrien. It's an amazing concept where she describes four rivers in each of our experiences: the River of Inspiration, the River of Surprise, the River of Challenge, and the River of Love.

1. The River of Inspiration centers on creative fire, knowing what motivates us purposefully.

2. The River of Surprise centers on flexibility throughout the day's surprises, recognizing if our happiness has become dependent on routine.

3. The River of Challenge centers on embracing the invitation challenges bring, which is an invitation to further develop our sources of strength and tolerance of chaos.

4. Finally, the River of Love (my favorite) examines what gives our lives great meaning, helping to strengthen a daily sense of gratitude and connection with others.

And the time has come to look at the final component of the ALARM's fifth pillar: how to create miracles in your everyday life.

MIRACLES

"There are two ways to live: You can live as if nothing is a miracle; you can live as if everything is a miracle."

Albert Einstein

Now that you have learned the importance of meaning, living mindfully, adopting meditations your daily practice and how having the right mindset helps you create the miracles you want, let's look at where you fall along what I call "Einstein's Miracle Spectrum."

Do you wish you could live as if everything that happens in your life truly is a miracle? If so, I think paying attention to your inner voice gives you the perfect place to start.

By nurturing your inner voice (or what some call a "gut feeling"), you are strengthening your intuition – your best guide to creating a life you love.

When you honor your intuition, you will see all kinds of incredible events unfold that will create a life you love. You will be aware of an astonishing number of so-called coincidences and you will experience life as a constantly unfolding miracle.

Let me share with you in more detail my personal story about the career breakdown that led to my breakthrough experience.

When I lost my job in 2009 I felt so lost, I was in an unhappy relationship, and everything around me started to collapse again. I felt like all these bad things were happening and I couldn't understand why, there was one thing after the other.

I realized that my entire life was at the mercy of a pay check, what my family expected of me, and I was a victim of the financial crisis.

One night I woke up in a panic and I asked God, the universe, whoever would listen: "Why is this happening? Please give me some sort of sign, show me which way to go. Tell me what to do."

The very clear answer I got was: "You're not supposed to be here. You are meant to achieve bigger and greater things, you are meant to be free to express who you are."

I knew the voice didn't mean "here" as in my bed. I knew it meant something much bigger and deeper. At that time I did not know exactly what, though I trusted this deep voice that came from the depth of my heart.

Frankly, looking back the answer was there all along, though the other voices were too loud for me to even listen to my heart's desires.

As I calmed my mind, I knew that I invested a lot in my professional career as well as in my personal development, I knew I was a healer, and that I have a tremendous amount of skills to teach to the world. I had many talents, healing gifts, I had helped and coached so many people already and I knew how much love I have to give and share.

I knew I wanted to be free, travel the world, and create abundance by doing what I love: inspiring, empowering and helping people heal. I started to access part of me that had been long forgotten or even had no awareness that existed.

Before I get into that more, let me back up a little further. Shortly after having this conversation with God, I received an email from old friend who owns a boutique hotel in Florida asking me for healing and if I would consider going there.

Having written thousands of applications to find another job, I knew the universe had different plans for me, and as soon as I read this I knew the time had come to embrace my gifts and create the miracles I always wanted to have in life.

I flew next day, six weeks turned into a few months, and I not only helped her overcome the many physical, emotional and health issues, I also ended up helping with grieving as she had just lost both of her parents and her cat.

When I got back to the UK I decided to start my coaching and healing business as a side thing. I still loved IT and I continued to work until I was making enough money from coaching to cover my basic living costs.

I loved IT more than anything and at the time I couldn't imagine giving up that job. I loved technology, teamwork, and all the benefits the work provided for me, my partner and my family.

And while I still love technology and IT, I never really enjoyed all the bureaucratic aspects of my job.

As I "became my own boss" in my business, I bristled more and more with the expectations my employer had of me as an employee in the various jobs I had.

Couple that with a downturn in the economy and severe cutbacks, and about this time four years ago I knew that my days at my job were numbered.

But I had many commitments that at the time I felt stopped me from fully listening to my heart and simply doing what I love doing. The steady income and the health insurance are things I always provided for my family. Many times I wondered how we would be able to survive without my monthly pay check, and the benefits that I was receiving working in a full-time position.

I knew that I didn't want to stay and live in fear any more, but I believed that my family needed the "security" that my job provided.

I thought my coaching business and healing career could support us, but I had no guarantees... which led me back to wondering why I couldn't just find another IT job as I knew I loved the buzz that technology, new gadgets, and infrastructure improvement gave me.

I was an engineer by trade, and loved finding solutions to the problems. Those stressful thoughts are what led to experience breakdown and suicidal thoughts.

Despite all of my education, I could not find a job and I couldn't believe I was in such a bad place – overwhelmed by doomsday scenarios and too scared to think straight.

In 2009, that's when I learned that a breakdown is almost always followed by a breakthrough. It's always darkest before the dawn, you know?

So here's what happened. Along with all the dark fears, I'd also get a moment of clarity when I knew I should embrace my healing gifts and focus on my coaching business.

But then the moment would pass and my heart would start racing again and I would be in tears thinking that I couldn't possibly leave 20 years of investing in my IT career.

And then I would get another flash of insight. It was like I was walking on a dark road and every once in a while a car would go by and its headlights would illuminate the path and show some sign, like a guidepost, and I would know again that I was on the right track.

But the insights and the clarity always seemed so fleeting. I would get them and almost immediately I'd be back in the fear and despair.

I remember when I got back from Florida in 2010 I sat down and had another conversation with myself and asked the question: What Do I Really, Really Want?

I couldn't believe that I was in such an undesirable, untenable position. I couldn't believe that I had been brought this far to fail. All I kept thinking was about the redundancy, and the manner in which it was done; I was being a victim.

Having had so many healing, coaching, and therapy sessions, as well as being trained in so many disciplines, I knew I had to go east to seek the answers to my questions.

I meditated every day, and at some point in the depths of that despair, I heard a small voice inside that said: "What do you want?"

My answer was: "I want to be free, to love, to travel and teach around the world, and to do work that's completely aligned with my life purpose. I want to do work I love, and be paid handsomely for it. I want to be free of corporate environment and meetings that go on forever, free of everything negative that I was experiencing as a knock-on effect on relying on a pay check to be happy, and free from an environment that is not helping me fulfil my soul purpose."

I did not know what the future held, but deep down that little voice told me to trust my abilities and that I knew I could figure this out.

Once I got clear about what I did want, I started to get all these ideas about how I could make it happen and I now act with unwavering faith that I can have everything I want.

Sometimes when you are in the midst of it all, seeing the magical "whole" is difficult. Life will always have its challenges, but they really are there to help you focus on what you do want.

When you resist the challenges and judge them as "bad", you effectively close the door on learning. Instead, you can face challenges with openness and light. You can read the messages and learn from your inner guidance and grow.

When you learn from your challenges and live your life with an appreciation of coincidences and their meaning, you are creating synchronicity – you are making a magical "whole" that is so much more than the sum of its parts.

Many of my clients ask me: "How do you meet the challenges with openness for what they have to teach you about your life and manifest the miracles you most want?"

My answer is always with love, empathy and acceptance; it is entirely up to you if you choose to accept everything about you and your life.

Right now you might be asking yourself: Are there really miracles?

Yes, of course there are. All of us have heard of miracles in the form of physical healings that cannot be explained by medical science. There are also miracles when the perfect solution presents itself at just the right time.

There are miracles when some action taken by a person puts him or her in just the right place and results in a greater good than ever seemed possible. There are miracles in finding the perfect job, the perfect mate, and/or money when it's most needed.

All I know and trust is that miracles happen through natural and normal circumstances, and the "new science" of quantum physics is proving that we are – every one of us – already wired for miracles.

The reality is that every one of us can consciously take control and work to create a miracle or miracles in our lives. The truth is you are not a victim of a random existence in a confusing and possibly hostile world. Life is for you, not against you.

Not only is it possible to experience a dramatic healing or find the perfect solution to your problems, but it's also possible to express the dream or desire that you haven't dared pursue up to now and learn how to bring such wonderful experiences into your life more often.

To help get you started on the path of creating your own miracle, here are 12 simple steps to guide you in the process.

1. Know your ALARM

   This sophisticated built-in technology you have been learning so far is there to help you grow, heal, and achieve the life you want. Once you learn how to navigate through your inner turmoil, and listen to the feedback that your body is telling you, you start gaining control of your life.

2. Be Very Clear

   You need to be very clear about the miracle you desire – about the good you want in your world. As you clearly visualize or imagine your miracle, focus only on the end result of what you want, not the means by which it comes about. Let the "how" be up to the Infinite Intelligence that's working for you in response to your thinking.

3. Expect the Best

   We tend to attract that which we love, fear, or steadily expect. So expect the best, even when negative circumstances appear – in fact, especially when they appear.

   When we expect less than what we want, we get less than what we want. Remind yourself that you do deserve the good you desire. You deserve it by the right of your very existence. Consciously and consistently expect that everything is working to your greatest and highest good.

4. Make your Fear your best Friend

   Fear is simply short for False Evidence Papering Real, it is you having faith in something negative. Be watchful about your thinking. Your thoughts magnetically attract others like themselves. When you think negatively, your mind will go on a stream-of-consciousness journey into all sorts of related realms of negativity until you consciously stop yourself.

   All of this will block your miracle. Of course, you can't eliminate every single negative thought for the rest of your life. But all you need is 51% faith and your life will begin to turn in the right direction. When you realize this truth, you will begin to feel empowered, and your faith will become more and more self-generating.

5. **Be Open to all possibilities and outcomes**

When you open to a greater flow of Universal Power and Intelligence in your world, you also need to let go of the way you want it. Let go of your expectations, control, and one way of receiving mindset.

Although miracles always unfold in a very natural manner, they often come through unexpected channels. Whenever we hold tight, mentally or physically, to having things unfold "our way", we run the risk of delaying our good, diminishing it or even blocking it all together. "What" is up to you. "How" is up to Spirit.

6. **See yourself as you want to be**

If you desire health, you need to see yourself healthy and filled with energy and enthusiasm for life. If you desire abundance, you need to see yourself enjoying an abundant lifestyle. And so forth.

This does not mean living in a state of denial. On the contrary, you are clear about the facts of your present situation and handle what needs to be handled. But while you are doing all of this, your thinking about where you are headed is focused on what you want, not on what you don't want or where you are today.

7. **Keep the power**

Don't talk about it until you are clear and have manifested it. Keep your miracle secret. To share it prematurely is to dissipate some of the power of your idea.

Further, a negative or envious person will contribute a certain amount of negative energy, either spoken or unspoken, around your idea. The integrity of the relationship between you and Spirit with respect to the enfoldment of your miracle must not be violated. Wait until it is absolutely necessary to share your idea in order for it to continue unfolding. Even then, share as little as possible with as few people as possible, and share it with people who support your vision.

8. **Do what needs to be done by you**

   Through the Law of Attraction, many good things move into our lives, apparently unbidden. But almost always, there are things you need to do and choices you need to make. When you are very clear about what it is you want or need, your mind becomes calm and focused. This, in turn, provides a clear channel for the guidance and direction you need in making your choices and decisions about what to do – whether it's choosing the right doctor or taking the right job.

9. **Pray often, it works**

   Prayer is effective whether you're praying for yourselves, praying for others, or being prayed for by others. You don't have to be religious for your prayers to be effective.

   A few suggestions: Pray at a time and in a quiet place where you won't be disturbed. Allow yourself to feel empathy, love, and compassion for yourself or for whomever you are praying. Pray with a complete expectation that your prayer is being answered and that the desired result is right now in the process of manifestation.

   After you pray, "let go and let God." At that point, your job in the creative process is complete. Your continuing work is to guard your thinking. Creatively praying several times a day is a major key to success in obtaining your desires.

10. **You become the man you think you are**

    Everything means exactly what it says. There are no exceptions to this rule in the universe. In order to create miracles in your life and to allow amazing shifts to occur, you must have a mind that is open and believes that everything is possible.

    The truth is that none of us knows enough about anything to be pessimistic. In fact, in the total scheme of things, we don't truly know much at all in comparison to what there really is to know.

    Imagine what the people of 300 years ago would think about the world we live in today. Many of our accomplishments in technology, our social and cultural dynamics, even our physical achievements would "blow their minds" because most of what we take for granted as our daily necessities were once thought of as "impossible" and completely unfathomable.

It was only 50 years ago that the science community said it was physically impossible and totally improbable that a human being could run the 100m Dash in under 10 seconds. They ran all the tests and gathered all the data and concluded it absolute truth until Jim Hines did it in 1968. Now, it's common practice in track and field to run under 10 seconds – as a matter of fact you can't be an Olympic hopeful unless you can.

11. Adopt new Beliefs

Open-mindedness is the fertile soil for progress, creativity and growth. Without an open mind, miracles are not possible, and you will continue to experience stagnation, limitations and frustration. So start now, do it now, change the way you think and the person you are.

You live in an unlimited universe but the only way you get to experience its true power is if you believe in your own unlimited potential.

One of the quickest ways to manifest a miracle is to let go of what you've previously believed and open your mind to all the possibilities that exist.

Whether you believe something is possible or impossible, you're right because reality is based upon the beliefs and perceptions you hold.

If you want to experience a different reality from the one you're currently living, it is going to require that you shift your beliefs about what's real and what's possible for you.

Quantum physics has found that at any given moment there are 400 million bits of information available to the human mind. However, the mind only processes 2,000 bits from that pool. These 2,000 bits determine what you get to see in your reality and are determined by your perceptions about life and your belief systems.

A PATH to WISDOM

Every possibility exists in any present moment. However, you'll only see what can pass through the openness of your mind.

If you believe that making money is hard, healing is impossible, you don't deserve a relationship, you don't have what it takes to be famous, then that must be your reality. You have effectively collapsed the 400 million bits into your specific 2,000, and life will make it so every time.

The reason I was able to "miraculously" heal my body is because I believed it was possible for me. I opened my mind to another reality other than the one the doctors were offering me, the one that my family and culture taught me, and I never allowed it to close down again.

Anything is possible, even miracles, but only when you start to do what you are saying you are going to do with an open mind. The power is all yours and it lies in your decision to do so.

12. Develop your Intuition

Your intuition has a lot to do with what I am talking about; as you go through your life experiences, your intuition develops too; you can also consciously choose to strengthen your intuitive abilities.

Take five minutes at the end of the day (and every night from now on) and find a comfortable quiet place to sit and think. During this time think about what happened in the day that challenged you the most and ask: "What was that supposed to teach me? Can I find what was good and necessary about it?"

Then let go and let your intuition, your quiet inner voice, offer the answers. Then when the five minutes is up, write those answers down.

Keep doing this exercise. Sometimes it will be a challenge to get it done – but then you can ask yourself what that is supposed to teach you. And I guarantee that as you get better at reflecting on life's lessons in calm moments, you'll become better and better at seeing them more quickly as they confront you during the day.

You'll become more adept at plugging into your intuition and trusting it to help you learn what you were supposed to learn. You may even find yourself enjoying challenges as they arise, knowing that whatever happens, that challenge will connect you more deeply with your dreams and the miracles you wish to create.

So, you have come almost to the end of your journey of learning the TJS Evolutionary Method, its five main pillars that take you through a journey to acknowledge the wisdom that is you, to Love Your Life, Achieve the Results you wish to have and empower you to create Miracles. So, give yourself a big reward now – you may choose from one of the rewards that I have already shared with you in the methodology or choose one that brings you most joy.

Conclusion

This book and TJS Evolutionary Method: The ALARM is all about going within so you can start to acknowledge the body wisdom that is there to help you in your spiritual, mental and emotional journey. It empowers you to uncover the layers that prevent you from seeing your true power. It supports you in doing your highest work. You will feel connected from within, listen to your true authentic voice, and start living a heart-centered approach to life. It becomes effortless to then do what you love, and love what you do!

I talk to you as someone who has been through many body, mind, emotional, and spiritual challenges and learned to live from a place of acceptance, trust and higher levels of awareness.

You will reap your rewards as you learn to adopt daily the principles of this powerful method. They help you return to your natural healthy state of being.

To a space that is quiet, from which you can then question and unclutter your body, mind and feelings, so you can listen to your intuition that empowers you to see your inner light, transform, and create your own Miracles.

Now you know that you are a powerful creation that has the ability to program yourself in whatever way you may choose. The journey I have taken you so far in is to help you truly embrace the intelligence that is YOU, to bring you to levels of awareness that you consciously choose what you think, feel, behave, and what outcomes you wish to create in your life.

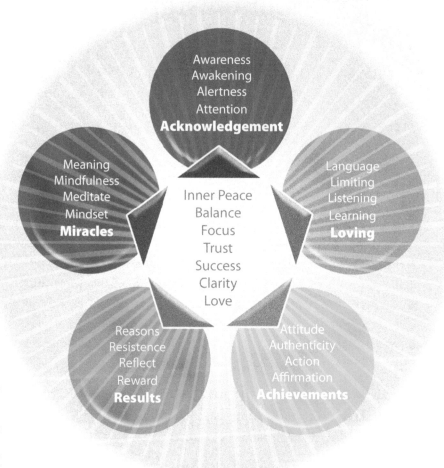

Awareness
Awakening
Alertness
Attention
Acknowledgement

Meaning
Mindfulness
Meditate
Mindset
Miracles

Inner Peace
Balance
Focus
Trust
Success
Clarity
Love

Language
Limiting
Listening
Learning
Loving

Reasons
Resistence
Reflect
Reward
Results

Attitude
Authenticity
Action
Affirmation
Achievements

Now you realize how powerful you can be, it's time for you to harness this and literally create the life of your dreams faster than you ever thought possible.

From the very beginning of going through this process, you opened yourself to a whole new world, a world in which you start living in a state of bliss, trust, happiness, joy, abundance, balance, and success.

A PATH to WISDOM

By curiously gazing in your inner universe, you learn to navigate through a space that will always have unfamiliar territories you have never visited. It will always present you with obstacles that get created with the power of one thought, and it will always have new challenges. You open up to infinite possibilities to live your life according to your own design.

Now you have a powerful tool to change your current blueprint that determines if you have the ability to create things like wealth, success, solutions to your problems, obstacles, and barriers that prevent you from living a balanced, peaceful, healthy, purposeful and inspiring life.

You have learned how to identify, know, and use your own body's ALARM intrusion detection system to overcome the obstacles in the key areas of your life that keep pushing you to live your life on snooze.

You have learned that everything you perceive negative about you is as powerful teacher to you as anything you perceive to be good about you. You rebalance the skewed perceptions you may have about you, so that you can free up time, unleash your potential, and live an inspiring life.

In this space you also operate from a self-reflection, everything that pushes your buttons you turn inwardly and start to make the changes from within.

You too can now use this powerful method to create the trust, the belief, and the clarity you need to have so that you live a balanced, successful, and purposeful life.

Once you apply all of the pillars that are embedded in the acronym ALARM in each of the eight key areas of your life, you will learn things about you through each and every step you make.

Each layer you uncover, there is something more you can question; you will learn how to navigate through this sophisticated intrusion, detection and prevention built-in system. You can reach higher levels of consciousness, balance your energy center, align your life to your existential program, and inspire others to do the same.

10 CONCLUSION

As you then apply this method consistently, it restores and strengthens your connection to yourself and your divine inner wisdom. You will experience inner transformations that emanate through your entire being.

Being empathetic becomes natural to you, you consciously choose to "walk in another's shoes" without egotistically needing to "fix", teach, tell, one-up, advise, sympathize, interrogate, explain or "set them straight."

You let go of different illusions, ideas, habits and attitudes, empathy becomes a heartfelt choice to engage intimately with others, on a deep level by "be-ing" with another – providing a safe environment for another to be vulnerable in your presence, feeling safe, secure, valued and heard.

Thus changes in your consciousness are then manifested in your physical body. You create the evolution that gives unlimited access to levels of ancient inspirational knowledge, stability and endurance.

This will open up echelons of energy that were previously unattainable to you.

The TJS Evolutionary Method is particularly effective in stimulating the body's inherent healing and repair system and in reaching and then releasing deep-seated and core emotional issues, thus treating the harmful effects of disease and then offering an ongoing tool for health and vitality. The expansion gives you and your energy body unlimited possibilities and a redeveloped healing potential that is significant, functional, enlightening and constructive.

All of these advancements and re-awakenings open the bridge to higher awareness, giving you the opportunity to "re-form, re-member and re-structure" and to offer a healing structure that is effective.

Unfettered by energetic baggage masquerading as fear, pain and self-hatred, your consciousness is once again free to grow. If you find the thought of clearing your energy fields disconcerting, simply think of it as cleansing the energy that surrounds you and releasing any stagnancy.

You may not be able to see the results of your efforts, but you will experience a lightness of being and clarity of mind.

The journey for sure will have its ups and downs, though you come to an understanding that higher consciousness allows you to enter into communication and harmony with others from a place of a "universal mind" where you relate to others as "one."

You become congruent with self and others, you are true to yourself without worrying, and have real empathy. You become authentic. The energy of love and warmth fill the space between two people, not the coldness, resistance or resentment of a "me vs. you" ego-perspective.

As you bring your eight areas of your life to balance, you will experience how empathy allows equality between and among all individuals.

Following this process you truly learn, know and see that higher consciousness, not cognition, is the "secret sauce" of cooperation, collaboration, compassion and connection with others.

You come to realize that higher consciousness is a heart-based state that allows you to "feel my pain." In this state of awareness, with each person you meet, as you gaze into their eyes you can see yourself.

You can apply this method now, or in the next 30 days, 60 days, or for the rest of your life, to change your blueprint. It is there as a key that you use to wind up your clock and it keeps you on time.

As you go through this method, I recommend you set aside at least half a day, a day, or more, where you won't be interrupted, switch off any cell phones, have some water and some snacks available, and make the final investment you need to do for you. It is the time for you to create all that you have read so far and much more. Let nothing stop you, let us begin, and you will be grateful you did.

Lastly, as you complete this process, you experience a shift and you know it is not your cognition that did it, it is the shift in your consciousness that puts a microscope on your emotional, psychological and spiritual orientation to the planet and the peoples inhabiting it.

Everything I have shared in this book helped me in my journey to create the life that I have now, and in writing this book I wish to help you bring your life back into balance.

10 CONCLUSION

As you start practicing daily the method you have learned, your life becomes your paradise.

The way you see, think, do, and feel is through the lens of a heart-centered approach to living. Each decision you take is conscious, it reconnects you to your body, mind, spirit, emotions, and your heart.

Thank you for allowing me to share my heart's wisdom with you on this journey. May your heart be filled with love, our paths cross one day in the future, and may this book bring that day closer to you.

It is my mission to help you heal, to grow to new levels of awareness, and to trust the infinite wisdom that is you. I love nothing more than helping you see, feel, and breathe love. May this book help you know yourself and what is true for you, may it help you live an inspired life.

I believe that you are all that is required to begin, trust, and walk the path that leads you to living an inspired and purposeful life. Knowing you is the key to unlock the inner wisdom that is required for you to live a healthy, balanced, and meaningful life.

Where there is love, there is peace, and when you listen to the voice of your heart, you learn to navigate through your life's challenges with ease to create your purpose.

Your heart has great wisdom, when you listen to it you align yourself to the divine universal energy that leads you toward living a healthy, happy, successful and peaceful life.

How long will it take for you to accept that each one of us is a being of light, each one of us is a spark of that light that created us all, and each one of us at the core has an infinite power, we have the wisdom of the creator built in our DNA?

It is not our job to control others, but to learn how to control ourselves to remain switched on to the light, the love, and Godly energy that lives in our hearts.

It is at times when your ego takes control of your light switch, the switch that puts you in the dark, and the one that keeps you in your own prison that you need to trust and have faith.

Recognition, love and acceptance of your ego creates the breathing space that the heart needs to remain in the flow, to remain open to the infinite wisdom of love, to love unconditionally through the wisdom of the spirit, God, and not through the perception of your mind or your five senses.

Only when you truly embrace that the good and the bad come in equal measures are you truly in peace with self and others. As you accept self, you let go of judgment of self and others. Only then can you fully unlock and maximize your true potential.

From this resourceful state you can then always remain the light, without you having the need to control who sits in its presence, who needs to see it, who needs to come to it, or what intensity you need to shine. Your job is to give yourself permission to shine.

You are here to create your life, live purposefully, and to uncover your magnificent life. You too can make an extraordinary difference in the world and leave behind an immortal legacy that serves the evolution of mankind.

You exist because you are a call for love, as you embody love in every inch of your being you start to illuminate and become the light beacon that other souls can use to find their way back home, back to their inner light, back to the source that created us all – LOVE.

Helping you become healthy, abundant and wise.

Tony Jeton Selimi
Elite Life Coach & Mentor
Healer, Author, Speaker and Teacher of Inner Wisdom
www.tonyselimi.com
Twitter: @tonyjselimi
Linked In: tonyselimi

What Next?

After reading this book you might want to learn more about TJS Evolutionary Method and how to maximize your prime asset, "you", and all you now have to do is take action, keep in touch and meet other evolutionary individuals on a similar journey.

Tony regularly hosts workshops, events, webinars, and retreats. To see what's coming up visit **www.tonyselimi.com**

Additional benefit:

If you would like to review this book, you will get rewarded for taking time to do so. Here's how:

1. *Write a review of this book.*

2. *Post it on eBay, Amazon, iTunes Bookstore, your website, blog, Facebook page, or get it published in another publication.*

3. *Send a link or screenshot to* reviews@apathtowisdom.com

4. *You will receive a free mp3 meditation, or be sent a special discount code you can use to purchase any of Tony's products and services.*

5. *Automatically be entered to a prize draw for the chance to win a one hour Elite Life Coaching Consultation with Tony.*

Good luck, you now know that you have access to your own wisdom to help you evolve, transform and live your best life.

About the Author

Tony J Selimi is an internationally renowned Elite Life Coach, speaker, healer and author. Born in 1969 in the town of Gostivar, Macedonia, he moved to London in 1990 at the age of 20 to find a safe haven from the atrocities of a civil war and build a new life.

Having obtained an engineering degree from UCL, Tony spent 15 years building a successful IT career, managing and delivering multi-million pound IT programs. He worked with a diverse range of individuals and businesses, from entrepreneurial start-ups and family-owned companies to large corporations in London, Europe and the US.

In parallel to his professional career, his true passion was learning how to maximize awareness and human potential, so that he could be a better leader and overcome many of his physical and emotional challenges.

He studied psychology, NLP, CBT, and life coaching, as well as many eastern disciplines of natural healing of the body which helped him bring his life into balance and develop the knowledge to help others do the same.

In 2009, having been made redundant, he took the time to reflect and re-evaluate his life, and started his entrepreneurial journey by turning his passion into a successful business.

His successful track record in IT, working in senior high-pressure roles in a wide range of sectors, including transport, retail, government and recruitment, gave him a unique insight into the lives of the people he now helps and the challenges they face on a daily basis.

Tony now specializes in working with a variety of individuals who experience profound emptiness and feel their life lacks clarity, vision and purpose.

Through one-to-one coaching, healing, workshops and retreats he has helped thousands of people release doubts and fears, resolve inner conflicts, and achieve balance and greater performance in all areas of their life, so they can move forward purposefully.

His clients include celebrities, actors, MPs, coaches, PTs, therapists, doctors, leaders, entrepreneurs and senior executives of companies such as Microsoft, Bank of America, Santander and Mishcon de Reya to single mothers, students, young adults, graduates, and the unemployed.

Tony is renowned for his ability to get to the core of the issues that prevent his clients from having greater inner control of their emotions, mind, and heart.

He has over 250 testimonials, has appeared on radio as Mr Motivator, and been featured in a number of magazines.

He is a qualified coach recognized by a number of reputable institutions including ICF, ILM, CThA, and Martin Brofman's Foundation of Advanced Healers.

Combining the teachings of western psychology and eastern methodologies of natural healing of the body, he developed TJS Evolutionary Method: The ALARM.

Using this method he helps clients go on an inner journey and discover the body's wisdom that is there to support them in their journey to higher states of awareness and excel beyond their dreams. They start experiencing a sense of relief, increased energy, increased performance, feel grounded, and have a greater focus.

TJS Evolutionary Method is a new empowerment framework that can be used by individuals, therapists, professional coaches, psychologists, entrepreneurs, educational institutions and can be applied in your business.

Tony is known for creating amazing transformation and leaving his clients feeling inspired, empowered, peaceful, and reconnected to the infinite wisdom of love.

He is living his dream: he heals, coaches, teaches, speaks, inspires, and contributes toward unleashing human potential.

Testimonials

'Working with Tony is a journey that will impact your life and who you are. Tony's focus is to identify your real goals and what are the real blockers. His approach enables you to resolve these to allow you to move forward healthily.

Tony has been a very Positive Supportive and incredibly focused coach and mentor to me. He is always looking for the good of his clients. I have learnt a lot from working with Tony, I choose to work with Tony as he was not the normal coach whom I had met who believe its just a simple process to identify goals and charge through, Carpet over cracks of your life.

Tony takes time and puts all he has into his work with clients he engages on many levels with you.

His book "A Path to Wisdom: How to live a healthy, balanced and peaceful life" and TJS Evolutionary methodology is exceptionally powerful and brings together the best of many western and eastern practices. Throughout the book Tony will challenge and push you to reach for your star.

Thank you for being extremely patient with me, for being my Life Coach, Healer, Mentor and personal friend. You are a shining star who's light has the ability to reach the darkest parts of everyone you touch and work with.'

Michael Bell, Global Alliance Manager

"If you are searching for that one book that will help you lead a more fulfilling life then this is the book for you. Packed with insights and tools from Tony's own personal and professional experience, this book will help you map out your own route for living the life that you were always meant to live!"

Viv Grant, former Head Teacher and Director, Integrity Coaching Ltd.

"Tony brings together a wealth of experience and insight in this book about spirituality and healing. Well worth exploring to know yourself in a deeper way."

Avni Trivedi, Osteopath and Doula

20 minutes with Tony will change your world. His wisdom, insights and ability to help you fine tune your own life purpose is a powerful ability that he has as a coach and mentor, bringing out your own inner wisdom and help you live your best life.

Tony has spent the past year mentoring and coaching me and has helped in removing some of the controlling actions I had put in place to protect myself from deep routed fears, fears that had prevented me from living the life I was meant to lead. This massive shift has enabled me to embrace a new way of loving life, both personally and professionally.

Tony's unique methodology - TJS Evolutionary Coaching Method - provides tools, methods and principles that will help you live a balanced and happy life, the best life possible.

Tony's book 'A Path to Wisdom' is a must read for anyone who wishes to embrace life fully, excel in love, business and happiness. On a personal level Tony is an amazing person. He touches the souls of all he meets, and leaves lasting impressions in the sand that no water will ever wash away. I often describe him as a bright shining light, a light that gets brighter ever time I meet with him.

Amanda Kennedy, Entrepreneur and Founder of Clients In Abundance

"Tony's coaching methods, tools and style lead you quickly to fine-tuning your values, mission purpose and goals. Rather than coaching through a scripted or pre-programmed path, Tony's wisdom directs you toward a practice of self reflection and purposeful action.
A personal journey like this is no easy ride. Be prepared to be confronted and challenged, be prepared to delve deeply into how you live, how you lead others and to answer questions other people in your life may never ask. In a time where "authentic leadership" has emerged as a corporate imperative or personal mantra, the time invested in reading or experiencing Tony's wisdom will yield significant returns personally, spiritually and professionally. "

Denis Taylor, Managing Director within Financial Services

"Tony is an inspired teacher, mentor and a coach who will definitely awaken you to your greatness through being a mirror from which you can see the light within you. He challenged my core beliefs and helped me draw the line and realign my life to my true values. His love, wisdom and energy will open up your heart, switch on your inner light and empower you to live a healthy, balanced and meaningful life. "

Jellmaz Dervishi , TV presenter & Journalist , Alsat Tv Macedonia

"Tony's coaching work has helped me to ground deeper and fly higher. His integration of love, craft, sensitivity and clarity is incredible. His healing work is deeply enlivening and laser like in its focus and impact."

Stephen Morallee - Artist and Creator of Deetell

A PATH to WISDOM

"I have had the pleasure to work with Tony on a one to one basis. Having exhausted what I thought to be every avenue in personal development I went to him out of desperation to succeed in business and in my career as a whole. What came out of it was far beyond my wildest expectations. Tony is so much more than a business coach. He is an incredible spiritual life coach. He has taken me on the most remarkable journey in my life and as a result I have been able to destroy my limiting beliefs and start tuning into my intuition to discover where my true passion lies.

It is because of the trusting and open space that Tony creates in our sessions that I have been able to create my amazing business. I honestly do not know where I would be if I had not met Tony. One thing is for sure, I would not be where I am now.

Having Tony as my personal coach is by far the best investment I have ever made. He has enabled me to create so much balance in my life and has increased my happiness, self belief and confidence exponentially. He has taught me so much about the spiritual world.

Tony is on the most amazing mission to create so much good in this world. I am privileged to have experienced his work. Thank you Tony!"

Paul Miller, Entrepreneur & Founder of Move Play Explore

"Tony is a powerful coach and healer. He is the person I go to whenever I need healing. Not only does he heal, he gets quickly to the psychological and spiritual cause of physical ailments.
He makes the miraculous seem ordinary."

Daniel Browne - Performance coach and Best Selling Author of "The Energy Equation: how to be a top performer without burning yourself out"

"In my sessions with Tony it soon became obvious that I was not speaking with another "individual" as such. I felt no influencing ego or personal agenda around what I should and shouldn't do. I got massive clarity, but it felt almost like I was speaking to a higher version of "myself". He would reflect back to me exactly what I needed to hear and at the perfect time for me to both understand and utilise it.

This allowed me to own the changes and power within me, from a place of being asked and not being told. Now I live through my potential, making a massive impact on thousands of lives around me as a fellow coach and healer.

Without meeting Tony I suspect another 20 years or more would pass by for me to reach this place. Tony is a true magical being of light and the only person thus far that I have met and that I can acknowledge and call "a true teacher".

Adam Frewer - Inspired Life Coach & Heale

Tony has that unique combination of grounding and energy that empowers you to question and to act. Those words resonate with me.

Previously, I spent a lot of time in my head overthinking, whether it be as a scientist, worrying about money or wandering about past or future relationships. I'd lost the joy of the present moment and my own self worth. I'd succumb to my inner fear of being alone.

With Tony, he guided me to look within, to question my mind beliefs and open myself up to seeing my self worth. I'm still learning, but with his help I am working to a grander vision.

I've created a buisness for future space tourists providing preflight body development training, started towards a PhD on spaceflight countermeasures and begun to realise how amazing the world is when you stop thinking and start living.
Thank you my dear friend Tony.

Phil Carvil, Space Physiologist and Fitness Professional

"Tony is an amazing coach, mentor and healer. He is not only the most-loving human being, but also incredibly challenging, intense, sharp and to the point. You leave his coaching sessions feeling blessed, empowered, enormously motivated and blissfully happy."

Sandra Wick, Germany

A PATH to WISDOM